The
MGM
Girls

Louis B. Mayer himself, in a somewhat characteristic pose (1943).

The MGM Girls:

Behind the Velvet Curtain

Peter Harry Brown and Pamela Ann Brown

St. Martin's Press/New York

Library of Congress Cataloging in Publication Data

Brown, Peter H.
  The MGM girls.

  1. Moving-picture actors and actresses—United States
Biography. 2. Metro-Goldwyn-Mayer, inc. I. Brown, Pamela
Ann. II. Title. III. Title. The M.G.M. girls.
PN1998.A2B6868 1983   791.43′028′0922 [B]   83-9599
ISBN 0-312-50161-7

Editor: Toni Lopopolo
Assistant Editor: Karen Johnsen
Design by Manuela Paul
Production Editor: Mitchell Nauffts
Copyeditor: Eva Salmieri

First Edition

10 9 8 7 6 5 4 3 2 1

All photographs are reproduced courtesy of the MGM Archives.

This book is for Irene Scott Strain

CONTENTS

PREFACE AND ACKNOWLEDGMENTS

Metro-Goldwyn-Mayer's sprawling studio in Culver City, California, is fashioned of brick and mortar, glass and steel—not that different from any other large corporation. But other companies sell insurance, build cars, or manufacture women's ready-to-wear. MGM produces dreams as insubstantial as a firefly in a glass jar. It's hard to build fantasies and preserve the truth at the same time—perhaps impossible. So any history of MGM, or a part of it, is told by men and women who believe in magic. They might be lighting technicians who turned Greta Garbo's hair into a spun-gold halo. Perhaps they were seamstresses, assembling a ball gown that transformed Norma Shearer into "Marie Antoinette."

On the lot the line between fantasy and reality is a tightrope made of piano wire. So when the personalities of MGM's Golden Age tell their stories they occasionally cross that boundary and venture into a twilight zone made of celluloid. This makes the history of MGM so burdened with gossip, innuendo, speculation, and, at times, outright lies that any book focusing on the studio's past must follow obscure trails.

The vast pageant of the world's most fantastic film factory has also become a bubbling cauldron of what Norman Mailer calls "factoids." And these are nothing but folk legends rooted in a foundation of truth but gilded and transformed by the hopes, fears, and delusions of the people involved. Since this book is a psychological, economic, and social portrait of the MGM Girls and makes no attempt to pass itself off as a film history, these "factoids" are less troublesome than they might have been. On the other hand, the major characters, being high in the ranks of the rich and the famous, have softly wrapped themselves in their own cushions against reality. Recreating their lives and the world in which they existed was fraught with land mines. Any margin of success this book may achieve could not have been possible without the cooperation of hundreds of stars, journalists, researchers, and a few candidly inclined former MGM executives.

Interviewing for this book began in the fall of 1978 with a wide-ranging session with one of the earliest MGM Girls, Lillian Gish. Interviews followed with Debbie Reynolds, Eleanor Powell, Ann Miller, Cyd Charisse, the late Dore Schary (the former MGM production chief, who submitted to eight hours of interviews), Jane Powell, George Cukor, silent film expert and author Kevin Brownlow, Kathryn Grayson, MGM archivist Dore Freeman, Henry Rogers (founder and head of the large Rogers and Cowan public relations network), John Springer (former publicist for Elizabeth Taylor and Joan Crawford), former MGM publicist Esme Chandlee, Harriet Parsons (daughter of Hollywood's foremost gossip columnist, Louella Parsons), columnists Dorothy Manners and Dorothy Treloar, Vincent Minnelli, Connie Francis, and Lana Turner. Of particular help were the interviews conducted by *Los Angeles Times* arts editor Charles Champlin as part of his cable show, "Charles Champlin On the Film Scene."

Full access to the notes, scrapbooks, and files of both Hedda Hopper and Louella Parsons proved to be a boon. Particular thanks go to the late Terry Roach, director of the Margaret Herrick Memorial Library of the Academy of Motion Picture Arts and Sciences. Her assistant, Carol Epstein, produced still photos and clips believed to have been missing. Additional help was provided by the UCLA Film and Theater Library and the special film collection at the University of Southern California. Another particularly enlightening source was the massive, thirteen-hour TV documentary "Hollywood, the Pioneers," written and produced by Kevin Brownlow. Special historic photos came from Larry Edmunds Bookstore in Hollywood and Eddie Brandt's Movie Matinee. We thank Irv Letofsky, editor, *Sunday Calendar Magazine* of the *Los Angeles Times*, from whom the idea for this book originated—as the article "The MGM Girls."

Finally, we thank our editor, Toni Lopopolo, for her invaluable guidance and advice.

It stood there on a silver-plated dress rack surrounded by balsa wood furniture and faded brocade drapes. From a certain angle and the proper distance you could get flashes of the allure that had made moviegoers gasp thirty-four years earlier.

But as the curious moved up to touch it—to brush against the ball gown Greta Garbo had worn in *Camille*— the illusion shriveled as dramatically as the Wicked Witch of the West in *The Wizard of Oz*.

It was fashioned out of row upon row and flounce upon flounce of dime-store netting with nineteenth-century sleeves that had wilted forlornly. The dazzling shower of diamonds so incandescent on movie screens around the world was made of paper-and-glitter stars whose points had curled up from the dampness of the Metro-Goldwyn-Mayer sound stage in which it sat.

Without the amber lights, the soft focus of kindly camera lenses, and the expert tugging and fluffing of a wardrobe mistress, one of the most famous gowns in the history of the movies was a promise betrayed. Its shredding hems allowed glimpses of the insubstantial reality upon which cinema dreams rest.

It was much the same all over the crumbling studio that hot, smoggy April of 1970 when MGM unashamedly sold off the physical trappings of its special magic. Even the fans who trooped through to finger the two million artifacts (including almost five hundred thousand costumes) seemed to sense it as a betrayal exposing secrets that should have been hidden forever from all those wonderful people out there in the dark.

As the tawdry parade proceeded through the endless sound stages, the men of MGM's past fared better than the women. Clark Gable's trench coat, worn in twenty films, remained virile with its thick, well-used belt. Andy Hardy's roadster might have just driven back from the malt shop, and Stewart Granger's swords from *Scaramouche* had retained enough flexibility and strength to dispatch the most intrepid of villains.

But the men dealt in virility and forcefulness unenhanced by the wizardry of the artisans' workshops. Gable's off-kilter smile needed no help. James Stewart's ambling style would have worked fine on an empty set. And Mario Lanza's voice overpowered, whether he was dressed as a truck driver or as "the Great Caruso."

So it was the MGM Girls whose facade was crumbling. Judy Garland's ruby slippers were little more than well-worn pumps with tarnished red sequins stitched unevenly across the toes. Jean Harlow's shadowy boudoir negligees drooped shapelessly on bent coat hangers; the clinging curves so sensational onscreen had merely been painted onto the plain shifts by members of the art department. Esther Williams' fabulous swimming pool was full of trash. Moss grew up the side, and the underwater grottoes so identified with her spectacular ballets had been smashed with jack hammers.

"I sat in tears on the big sound stage watching all the properties of the golden years being sold at a public auction," remembered Ann Miller. "Elizabeth Taylor's wedding dress for *Father of the Bride* went for six hundred and twenty-five dollars. Ava Gardner's dresses from *Show Boat* went for a song. They were even bidding loudly for Lana Turner's bra and panties."

Both the physical and spiritual walls that had sequestered the MGM Girls while they were nurtured on style, dusted with sex appeal, and polished until they had a luminous aura were being torn down forever. "I realized right then that our kind would never be produced again," said Ann Miller. "More than anything else, Hollywood's shifting economics ended our era forever."

The few actresses who summoned the courage to revisit the crumbling debris that had been their guarded, creative cocoon wandered about as if shell-shocked.

One of the last MGM Girls, Shirley MacLaine, drifted through the ghostly rooms echoing of the vibrant past.

"I walked across an alleyway to Makeup and Hairdressing. The door was standing open," she said. " 'Hello, can I come in?' I asked. 'Is anyone there?' "

Shirley could hear the old air blower still whirring.

"I walked into the empty makeup rooms. The makeup lights surrounding the mirrors had been removed, and more hair dryers were discarded in the center of the room."

She hesitated a minute and then edged into the hairdressing department. "Ornate brass-bound work lights stared down at empty worktables beneath them. And this is the room in which it had all happened. The room that was more magical from six to nine every weekday morning than the dressing room of the Wizard of Oz himself."

Shirley remembered Greer Garson swathed in a brilliant blue robe that set off her Technicolor red hair; Elizabeth Taylor flopping into a chair with a Danish in her hand; and Debbie Reynolds bubbling into the early stillness and lighting up the morning with bawdy jokes.

Silence and memories finally drove her out of this ghost town of glamour.

The surviving MGM Girls like Shirley, Ann Miller, Lana Turner, and Debbie Reynolds hadn't come to look back or to say good-bye. They came, it seemed, to reinforce the knowledge that now even the reminders were being erased.

The entire breed of MGM Girls, which stretched all the way back to 1918, had become extinct fifteen years before the auction. They had become dinosaurs with the advent of New Wave movies, television, and the concurrent collapse of the studio system. And although it had nothing to do with the survival of the fittest, MGM's male stars weathered the revolution, becoming their own producers, negotiating picture-by-picture deals, and coasting into the new era on a wave of chauvinism.

This adaptability was denied the MGM Girls. They'd always been treated condescendingly, as daughters who, supposedly, made it through their films by stepping over the chivalric cloaks thrown down by their ersatz fathers, uncles, and big brothers in the front office.

It had been that way since the beginning, when Louis B. Mayer climbed onto the frail shoulders of the first MGM Girl, Anita Stewart, and hoisted himself out of the lower ranks of film distribution to the heights of full-scale production. Almost forgotten today, Anita Stewart was eased into Mayer's suffocating arms by a strategy he would use on all Anita's successors—"Promise them anything but give them only what you have to."

Louis B. Mayer had made a minor fortune in the East by acquiring the distribution rights to D. W. Griffith's masterpiece, *The Birth of a Nation*. And he was doing splendidly, feeling the first tugs of the obsession with power that would eventually land him on top and then topple him from the hill decades later.

Distributors were functionaries, he decided. Producers were king-makers. But how to break in?

Born Eliezer Mayer at Minsk, Russia, in 1885, he had emigrated to America and become a successful junk dealer by 1904. Several years later he took over a defunct chain of small theaters.

But he was stopped in his tracks. Clans and families had already established nepotistic control over film production. Mayer was frozen out. There was only one solution: He had to steal a star. Not just any star, but a performer with such proven box office power that he or she could launch a company.

A deformed, dwarf news vendor whom Mayer patronized daily knew of his plight and decided that his favorite star, Miss Stewart (under a tight contract with Vitagraph Pictures), was the only answer to his friend's problem.

"I can set it up," said the vendor.

"Just name the day," Mayer answered.

Within several weeks Louis B. Mayer, having invested in a new, more mogul-like suit of clothes, called at Anita Stewart's hotel suite in Atlantic City to begin negotiations.

Anita Stewart is neither well-remembered nor interesting enough to warrant much comment. Mayer, finding out that her Achilles' heel was her superbly handsome, meagerly talented husband, Rudy Cameron, put together a deal that not only gave Anita her own production company but provided a job for her husband on the board of directors. Although Mayer had to wage a vicious court battle with Vitagraph, which wanted its star back, they managed to reach a financial settlement.

The first MGM Girl was on the set of Mayer's first film, *Virtuous Wives*, the same year (1918). While casting supporting members, he picked up the second MGM Girl, Hedda Hopper, who in time became a mixed blessing. Soon Mayer, his wife, and Hedda Hopper, dragging along the wary Anita and husband, were on a train to Hollywood.

Mayer loved the wide-open spaces. Hedda gloried in a regular pay-check. And Anita Stewart sat on the steps of the Hollywood Hotel and cried.

It didn't take too much intelligence for Anita to figure out that

Mayer was flying by the seat of *her* pants. She arrived in the middle of an unprecedented Southern California monsoon that didn't let up for ten days. When the sun did shine, Anita discovered that Mayer had purchased a half-studio/half-zoo near downtown Los Angeles in which to film his distinguished and growing list of productions.

After forcing Anita into several inferior films (in spite of having guaranteed her script approval), Mayer went after bigger game. He wanted a publicity stunt to let the movie establishment know he was a mover and a shaker. Since he couldn't get Charlie Chaplin, he settled for the next best thing: the comedian's new teenage wife, Mildred Harris Chaplin. She couldn't act, concentrate, or even walk very well. But the publicity was fabulous.

Marcus Loew, fast becoming the most important film distributor in the world, purchased Metro (the company Mayer had been associated with briefly), bought out Mayer and his zooside studio, and by 1924 had appropriated Goldwyn Pictures. Loew merged all three companies, and Mayer was named vice-president and general manager of Metro-Goldwyn-Mayer. He would retain that control with an iron hand until 1951, drawing $15,000,000 in salary alone—a figure vastly swelled by percentages and stock options. By 1938 he was the highest-paid man in America with an annual income of $1,400,000.

By the early twenties Hedda Hopper was the only original MGM Girl left. Anita had jumped ship because Mayer reneged on all his promises, and Mildred had bolted because she was laughed off the screen.

Mayer's next move was probably the most important. He used hefty financial ammunition and considerable pressure to woo Irving Thalberg, Hollywood's boy genius. Thalberg gave in, and Mayer made him second-in-command of the West Coast studio.

There were a few harrowing months at the old Selig Zoo site before Mayer convinced Loew that they needed to build a full-sized film factory, (with a backlot the size of many small towns), on the flatlands of Culver City.

That nerve-wracking time at the zoo did result in one masterful publicity gimmick that still endures. Naturally, Hedda, who seemed to be everywhere at MGM, was involved:

"Norma Shearer and I worked until midnight one night and then started for our dressing rooms at the other end of the Selig Zoo."

Hedda, whose chiffon gown was trailing behind her, was already in her dressing bungalow when she saw a lion crouched near the door.

"I let out a screech you could have heard in Pomona. Norma dropped both her purse and her makeup kit as she ran through the thick African brush planted in the area."

Huddling in the dark, Hedda heard members of the security patrol dissolving in laughter. "Just what, I'd like to know, is so damn funny?" she asked.

"He wouldn't hurt you, missy."

Hedda assumed her frostiest manner. "He's a lion, isn't he? Lions bite, don't they?"

"He ain't got no teeth, missy."

"But he's got claws."

"Nope, they're clipped."

The very lion who called on Hedda was to become the first of the symbols to roar out at the audience to announce an MGM picture.

The stage was now set for the emergence of the MGM Girls, the most physically pampered and psychologically bullied coterie of stars in Hollywood history.

In its first great publicity campaign, MGM made it clear that an expensive sorority of actresses would be the heart and soul of the studio, setting a glossy style that no other studio could imitate. During that public splash a complete roster of MGM stars was announced in full-page newspaper ads throughout America and much of Europe. Seventy percent of the list were women, including Marion Davies, Norma Shearer, Mae Murray, Eleanor Boardman, Viola Dana, Renee Adoree, Greta Garbo, Joan Crawford, Pauline Stark, and Mae Busch.

The humor, pathos, tragedy, and victimization of many of these actresses is the subject of this book. There will be no attempt to present the material in statistical or chronological order. Nor are the portraits here meant to be full biographies. They simply place these obsessively famous and patently original actresses in the epoch known as the Golden Age of Film.

BOOK ONE

Daddy's Little Girls

Mayer with one of his favorite MGM girls, Greer Garson, on the set
of *Blossoms in the Dust* (1941).

Father Knows Best

LOUIS B. MAYER

It must have seemed easier to approach the great Kublai Kahn than to be admitted into the presence of Louis B. Mayer, emperor of all he surveyed and the most feared man in Hollywood.

His office was less a place to work than to worship. Carved from two floors of the MGM executive office building, it was a silver-gilded tower reflecting a muted and regal light down onto his desk—Louis XIV would not have seemed out of place there. His desk was an ingenious creation of the MGM art department, like the crystal globes and outsized mirrors that turned the insignificant Wizard of Oz into an authoritarian but entirely fraudulent bully. It was a prop the size of three large bankers' tables—and behind it Louie came to experience ultimate power. Artisans in France had specially woven a rug of silver thread that had a white fur runner—the path leading to the presence. The thick carpet had a purpose far more important than decoration. It cleverly masked a platform that provided Mayer with the height nature had denied him.

The men of MGM—rough-and-tumble executives and he-men stars like Clark Gable and Spencer Tracy—paid little mind to the decadent temple. They saw through it, having played poker with Mayer and rubbed shoulders with him at the men's clubs that so typified the early Hollywood. In any case, men ruled the town of tinsel. It was a chauvinistic land where men who were once junk dealers, rag pickers, and olive oil mer-

Sincerely Yours
Anita Stewart

Anita Stewart, the star Mayer stole from Vitagraph to start his own production company. She was the first MGM girl.

chants spent the money, ruled the careers of the ladies of the films, and encouraged them to dwell on finery, gossip, and a foolish social order that kept them harmlessly occupied. Some of the studios were less chauvinistic. Some of the moguls would, here and there, allow a Bette Davis or a Mary Pickford to think that they ruled their own destinies

At MGM, however, chauvinism was the religion. Louis B. Mayer was its pope. And the MGM Girls were medieval chattel. This was a necessity, for Mayer had founded his studio and its success on the delicate backs of star actresses. He had grasped early the secret that drew the fantasy-starved hordes into the dark and lush movie palaces. Heroes were the bread and butter of the MGM product. But heroines brought the magic and emitted a glow luminous enough to propel millions of Americans into a dream far removed from the dusty streets, the dime store counters, and the nine-to-five grind that dominated their lives.

The problem was, Mayer was still a five-and-dimer himself. Over at Paramount, Gloria Swanson was offered up to the public in cascades of sable, dresses covered with a million seed pearls, and ostrich plumes reaching to the floor; the furniture on her sets had been made in Paris; and the lighting technician alone earned more money than most of MGM's stars. Douglas Fairbanks, Sr., built a medieval castle for *Robin Hood* that cost more to construct than the entire MGM establishment slowly taking shape in Culver City. One of Mary Pickford's directors was, every now and then, paid a sum roughly equal to the budget of a Louis B. Mayer production.

Having achieved his dream of heading a studio, and having got there so fast, Mayer had to bring in the bacon to keep Metro-Goldwyn-Mayer afloat in the rough competitive waters of Hollywood—where moguls were made with one good film. He had already started the process by lying to Anita Stewart, whom he advertised far and wide as Louie's Prize Lily. (In one silly ad, scores of Anita facsimiles peered from the leaves and petals of a slightly wilted bouquet.) Anita did *not* get script approval, but was stalled again and again until Mayer could get some dreadful, low-budget work out of her. Worse, he provided no job for Rudy Cameron, leaving Anita's husband free to roam through the groves of starlets as the whim struck him.

Stars like Mae Murray and Claire Windsor—inherited from Goldwyn—and Mae Busch—furnished by Metro—looked mighty good in ads, but financing was really a producer's best friend.

Walking up and down Hollywood Boulevard with his wife, Margaret,

Mayer slowly devised the battle plan to which he would adhere through four decades. Since he couldn't hire Pickford or Swanson, he would create his own stars—stars who came from the faceless millions that sought escape in the dark of a movie theater. He would mold them like fine mousse, give them new names, and gradually turn them into stars who owed their very existence to him. If things went wrong, they would be sent right back to Olathe, Kansas, or Rantoul, Illinois. "There are girls out there every bit as pretty as Gloria Swanson and maybe a great deal smarter," he told his wife. "It shouldn't be too hard to find them."

He wasn't worried about finding handsome men to support the birds of paradise he planned to import. After all, it was less than a decade since the end of World War I. Dashing pilots, cavalry officers, and stalwart ex-lieutenants crowded around the studio gates to get extra work—with the golden promise then, as now, that their faces would flash on the screen and draw a thousand sighs from the girls in the audience.

Nope, men weren't the problem. Louis B. Mayer needed a stable of girls so alluring, so exciting, so beautifully dressed that they could be the foundation for a billion-dollar harem to entrance the world.

And since it was he, Louis B. Mayer, who would dress them, pamper them, and then hand them the opiate of fame and power, they would be his family—Daddy's little girls.

They had to be low enough on the social ladder, or hungry enough, or so lacking in identity that MGM in general, and Mayer in particular, would become their salvation. For the gifts lavished on them, no sacrifice would be too great a repayment. They weren't hard to find—these girls who would drink from Mayer's goblet of temptation.

From France came Renee Adoree, a sickly, melancholy circus performer. And from Missouri, Billie Cassin, or Lucille LeSueur—soon to be rechristened Joan Crawford—who'd been tossed out to earn her way in a community kitchen, eventually clawing her way into the chorus of a tinny little musical. Even a girl with such a patrician background as Norma Shearer's grasped at a $150-a-week contract after serving humiliating time advertising tires as "Miss Lotta Miles" (her family's Canadian assets having vanished long before). They arrived in the sun-drenched exotica of Los Angeles where some minor MGM functionary handed them enough cash to keep them for a week, and ordered them to report to MGM's talent office, a grimy, impersonal suite of rooms where they were handed some papers to fill out before being sent on to Wardrobe. Later that day, clad in some castoff dress, the back of their heads or a distant view of their profiles would be immortalized onscreen.

Risk to MGM was small. Joan Crawford, for instance, was given six months at $75 per week to prove herself or else be summarily sent home to Missouri. Most of them weren't allowed to keep their own names— much less their identities. Lucille LeSueur was grandly informed that her name would be chosen by the public in a lengthy and degrading contest that finally produced the decidedly unmelodic "Joan Crawford."

"It sounds like 'crawfish,' " Joan complained to her new friend, actor William Haines.

"Just be happy it wasn't 'cranberry,' " he said, not entirely in jest.

While Mayer was building his stable of daughters, some of the grande dames inherited from the Metro and Goldwyn stables had to be reduced to the subservience for which MGM was to become famous. Some, like Eleanor Boardman, were allowed to languish in roles that became increasingly mundane. It took her four years to give up.

Anita Stewart, upon whom Mayer had based his entire empire, was given such dreary scripts that she was about to buy back her own contract when Marion Davies, the lover-companion of millionaire publisher William Randolph Hearst, insisted that Anita become a part of the Davies clique at the studio. (Ironically, Anita Stewart worked quite successfully for ten more years as part of Hearst's Cosmopolitan Pictures.)

Hedda Hopper, the second MGM Girl and later the all-powerful gossip columnist, had come West with Anita Stewart after decorating Mayer's first personal production, *Virtuous Wives.*

"He never got away with anything when it came to me," said Hedda. "He knew better. Not only was I already established, but he needed me for character parts.

"But all the new girls, and I mean hundreds of them over the years, were called into his office and told, as sincerely as the old goat could muster, that they were to think of him as a father. 'You can come to me with anything,' he told them. But actually, they couldn't go to him with anything."

Mayer was quite willing to bait the trap. When Joan Crawford was noticed in a Constance Bennett picture, *Sally, Irene and Mary,* Mayer immediately ordered a new contract drawn up for her at $250 a week. "She was thrilled," said Hollywood author Bob Thomas. "For the first time in her life she had enough money to do anything she wanted. She bought a Ford roadster and drove it proudly through the studio gate every day."

Almost a year later, when Joan realized she needed a house of her own to escape her freeloading family, she found a lovely house on Roxbury Drive in Beverly Hills. But the $18,000 price scared her.

She timidly went to Mayer for advice—and there was very little he liked better than this ritual of the girls coming to Papa. "You have a very promising future at MGM, Joan," he said. "Buy that house, Joan. The studio will lend you the money for the down payment."

It seemed so easy, as easy as getting quick cash from a loan shark. For years, as long as Joan did as Mayer wished, her own road was paved with the yellow bricks Judy Garland would sing about later. Then, when the good roles began going to other actresses, Mayer humiliated her by reminding her how often MGM had come to her rescue.

Even big stars, some of them with immortal names, were subject to this form of creative blackmail.

Nobody knew this better than Lillian Gish, who had been greeted at MGM with a glorious reception after she finally bowed to Mayer's entreaties and signed a term contract with the studio. She was probably the most respected screen actress in the world at the time. Having been film pioneer D. W. Griffith's favorite actress, Lillian's face was known on sight after her starring roles in *The Birth of a Nation, Intolerance, Way Down East, Orphans of the Storm,* and a dozen others.

When she arrived at MGM, she found that the greater suburban neighborhood around the MGM lot had been converted into one huge celebration of her arrival. Banners stretched between buildings, portraits of Lillian in her most famous roles were plastered on the side of buildings, and a wagon full of roses awaited her at the studio gates.

But Lillian felt a slight chill as the welcome became even more hysterical. "Looking at it all, I said a silent prayer that they would be equally warm in farewell." Her premonitions weren't unfounded.

While she was making *La Bohème,* a series of sinister threats were made against the actress, although they were kept hidden from her.

"I was vaguely aware of a strange behavior of almost everyone in the house," Lillian said later. "The Irish chauffeur disappeared overnight and a new man took his place." (Though she didn't know it, he was a policeman.)

The affair had started with a threat over the telephone that was intercepted by Lillian's secretary. The secretary took a taxi to MGM and tried to get in to see Mayer.

"Sorry," said Mayer's receptionist.

"Look," said Lillian's secretary. "This concerns the safety of Miss Gish, and, since you're paying money to her, I should think Mr. Mayer would be interested."

Even after she was admitted to the great one's office, it took her half an hour to interest him. "Then it seemed to dawn on him that there was

Joan Crawford, on the set of *Rose-Marie* (1928), posing to publicize a
new form of projection light. The man with her is unidentified. *Below:*
Lars Hanson, a star from Sweden, grasps Lillian Gish in an attempt to
wring some romance out of her in a scene from *The Scarlet Letter.*
While watching the daily rushes from the picture Mayer said, "If she
keeps this up they're going to think the 'scarlet letter' stands for abstinence."

This is as close as Norman Kerry ever got to his screen lover, Lillian Gish, in *Annie Laurie,* a film so void of romance that Mayer threw his hat on the floor and stomped on it at a preview. "One kiss? Is that too much to ask?" demanded Mayer. "Yes," said Gish.

considerable money wrapped up in the picture. *Then* he called the police."

About halfway through her contract with MGM, Mayer decided
that Lillian should star in a million-dollar film based on Leo Tolstoy's
Anna Karenina.

Lillian was on the set of another film when a page ran up to her and
said, "Mr. Mayer wants you right now!"

"But I'm not through here," Lillian protested.

"He said right now!"

Mayer barely greeted the actress. Then he shoved a sheaf of papers
across the desk at her. "Sign these. We need it done right now."

Lillian pointed out that her attorney had always refused to allow her
to sign anything until he'd had a chance to study it.

Mayer's face turned red. "I want to take you off salary until we have
a property for you," he yelled

Lillian remained calm. "Look, Mr. Mayer, you've had plenty of time
to find a film for me to do, and, I must repeat, I can't sign anything until
my attorney studies it."

The MGM chief leaped to his feet, screaming, "If you don't do as
I say, I can *ruin* you!"

Lillian slowly put on her gloves, grasped her handbag, and stood
face-to-face with Hollywood's most powerful mogul. "This is the second
time you've said that to me, Mr. Mayer. I'm sure you can ruin me. But
I will *not* sign anything without the advice of my attorney."

Through mutual agreement, Lillian's contract was not renewed.

The defenders of Mayer, and there have been many, claim that
his imperious ways developed only after years of corrupting, absolute
power.

But there is evidence to the contrary. After having made only one
film, *Virtuous Wives*, Mayer sought out screenwriter Frances Marion.

Hedda Hopper, a close friend of Frances Marion's and a co-star of
Meyer's *Virtuous Wives*, arranged a dinner meeting to discuss the upcoming project. Frances pestered Hedda for days about Mayer—an almost unknown commodity in films at that early date. "I had no particular
intention of rejecting his offer," said Marion. "But he'd made only the
one picture so I was naturally curious."

"First he was a junk dealer," Hedda told her. "Then he bought a
nickelodeon and finally parlayed it all into a producing company."

"Ah, rags, bottles, sex," said the screenwriter.

"You might sell his rags and bottles in your story," snapped Hedda, "but Louis B. is more puritanical about sex than any of my Quaker relatives."

Frances learned the truth of that only too well during a turgid family dinner.

"I worship good women, honorable men, and saintly mothers," Mayer bragged at one point.

Mayer and Frances agreed on a price, which Mayer let it be known he thought was "stupidly high."

"That's Hollywood inflation, Mr. Mayer," she answered.

Several weeks after Frances Marion turned in her screenplay, she received the royal summons. Mayer, dressed in the height of Hollywood fashion, strode around the room praising the script.

"It hit me here," he said, pounding his heart. Tears spilled down his already flabby cheeks. "If a story makes me cry, I know it's good," he said. He hemmed. He circled. He tried to draw the writer into further conversation.

"Mr. Mayer, I'll tell you what I'm interested in," Frances said. "How about a check for my script?"

Mayer's face fell in mock sadness. "Now, Miss Marion, we shook hands like two gentlemen. I not only paid you what we agreed on, but I threw in a little bonus. You will find them at your house when you get home."

Then Mayer reached out and gave her a healthy pinch on the ass.

Ahhh!, thought the writer, I'm finally getting a taste of what the others all talk about. Frances Marion told him if he did that again she would see that he ended face down in a bowl of his favorite chicken soup.

And the bonus? When she opened her front door she saw it immediately. It was a huge photograph of Mayer in a Napoleonic pose. "To a clever young writer," it was inscribed. "From her friend Louis B. Mayer."

By the time Mayer pinched his most attractive writer, he might have seemed all-powerful. Within two years of his takeover of the merged leadership, MGM had registered a profit of $6,388,200—a quarter of a million dollars more than that earned by any other studio at the time.

But that suggestive pinch was a sign of things to come—a lustful, petty, egomaniacal streak that was to grow through the years until he was infamous for those qualities (rightly or wrongly).

Bosley Crowther of *The New York Times*—Mayer's major biographer—said there was little doubt of the veracity of his amorous proclivities. "In his more delicate personal relations with both established and aspiring actresses he was naturally careful and decorous," said Crowther. "But that did not mean he was any less vigorous in pursuit of the women he lusted after."

Luise Rainer, an actress Mayer imported from Austria as a potential successor to Greta Garbo, believes that part of her sudden and permanent downfall resulted from her refusal to play lust in the office.

Luise took Hollywood by storm in a nineteen-minute appearance in *The Great Ziegfeld* and became the first performer to win back-to-back Academy Awards—first for *The Great Ziegfeld* and then for *The Good Earth*. She was then shoved into one terrible part after another until she was washed up. And although she admitted that Mayer was persistent about getting her onto his lap, she said little else about it.

But Joan Crawford, who watched the developing tension, told friends there was "no doubt that Mayer washed his hands of Luise when she gave him the cold shoulder. She'd won those Oscars but hadn't created waves at the box office. He could sacrifice her and get away with it." Which is precisely what happened.

Bosley Crowther believes Mayer laid siege to both Myrna Loy and Jeanette MacDonald "by rewarding them with richer roles and disciplining them with poor assignments. Both Myrna and Jeanette suffered the experience of being indulged and then disfavored by him."

During one particularly oppressive period, Myrna (who developed into one of MGM's top twenty all-time box office champions) went on strike. On leaving for Europe she claimed, "MGM has pushed me through twenty pictures without rest. It's a violation of contract." Crowther said he believed "it was a major protest against some machinations."

The slowly creeping rumors about Mayer and Jeanette MacDonald were taken more seriously, finally becoming a sort of folk legend. The legend has grown through the year like a fungus on Jeanette's reputation, eroding her luminous career and tarnishing the stature of her talent. And it has done no small amount of damage to Mayer's, having been used as proof of his closet lechery.

James Robert Parrish, who spent two years researching his biography of the singing star, believes that Mayer indeed may have made frequent if not Victorian approaches to Jeanette. But had the soprano made the slightest hint of capitulation, Parrish believes, Mayer's loveliest fantasies would have crumbled apart.

Still, the rumors flourish. In 1978 a lurid-colored book with the obscure title *Farewell to Dreams,* appeared on the bookshelves of Holly-

Gable—the charismatic figure who created MGM stars by merely appearing with them. *Below:* Jeannette MacDonald finally won the crown Mayer wished to win for her; she was his favorite pristine symbol of the ideal star. Being crowned as monarch with her was Tyrone Power.

Jeannette MacDonald and Clark Gable in the love scene from *San Francisco.* The movie made a whopping six million dollars for MGM in the late thirties.

wood purporting to prove that Jeanette had slept her way into starring roles by keeping herself forever at Mayer's beck and call. The authors, Sharon Rich and Diane Goodrich, (listing as an address the Jeanette MacDonald–Nelson Eddy Friendship Club), recreate a scene where Mayer's messenger to Jeanette yells to her: "He says to meet him in the same place."

The book further claims that Nelson Eddy and Jeanette had a running affair over the years and that her marriage to Gene Raymond (considered one of the most glorious in the annals of Tinseltown romance) was only a cover.

Interviews with more than twenty people who were at MGM during those years resulted only in denials of the peculiar claims in the book. All attempts to find Rich, Goodrich, or the Jeanette MacDonald–Nelson Eddy Friendship Club failed.

Truthfully, Jeanette was being wooed by Warner Brothers, Twentieth Century-Fox, and Universal Pictures when Mayer finally found her in Europe and signed her to a seven-year contract. Ironically, Thalberg, whose production company was competing with Mayer's on the MGM lot, missed signing her by thirty hours.

Mayer spent $300,000 preparing for a production of *Naughty Marietta* to begin as soon as the last of her appearances in Europe was concluded. Back in Hollywood, however, she backed off. "I failed in this type of thing at Paramount, Mr. Mayer," she said. "What makes you think it will work here?"

"It will work. It will," Mayer said. "But you've put yourself up on the high pedestal of grand opera. Climb down off of it. Now. Climb off of it now."

Mayer's secretary, Ida Koverman, who had been in the office to update Jeanette's contract, saw Mayer get down on his knees in front of Jeanette and sing an old Jewish lament, "Eli, Eli."

The singer had tears in her eyes as Mayer finished. She was sold.

Howard Strickling, publicity director at MGM for more than forty years, said Jeanette dated Nelson Eddy, James Stewart, and Henry Fonda —"but it was all for publicity's sake. It was already a strong thing between her and Gene Raymond. It was one of the most unaffected love stories I ever came across. I remember that Gene threw her a *Rose Marie* birthday party in 1936 with the men coming as Royal Canadian Mounted Police and the women as 'Rose Maries.' "

When they married a year later, Mayer threw the entire resources of the studio behind it, and the guest list was so extensive that the five

Two-time Oscar winner Luise Rainer (shown here with Melvyn Douglas in a scene from *The Toy Wife*) saw her career disappear—many believe the cause was her refusal to play footsie with Louis B. Mayer. Her career ended soon after winning her second Academy Award, giving rise to the legend that winning an Oscar was a jinx.

largest party tents in Los Angeles County were needed to hold the crowd. And Nelson sang "I Love You Truly," hardly the act of a secretive, jealous lover.

This happy interlude hardly means that Mayer was a harmless figure in the lives of the MGM Girls. He badgered them. He took advantage whenever he could. And he was truly outmaneuvered by three of the ladies on the most select superstar list in Hollywood.

First to get him was Katharine Hepburn, who had deserted Hollywood in 1938 after being labeled "box office poison." Having bought out her RKO contract, she returned to Broadway to star in the Philip Barrie play *The Philadelphia Story.* But before she agreed to do the play on the road as well as on Broadway, she purchased the film rights—sitting quietly on them like an egret on her eggs.

One night, after a particularly vibrant New York performance, Louis B. Mayer and Norma Shearer appeared backstage with three dozen gardenias and a card: "We'd like to congratulate you. . . . Louis and Norma."

Her heart sank for a millisecond. He must be here, she thought, to buy the rights for Norma. But the visit was purely social, ending with a promise by Mayer to get back to her.

In the intervening weeks, he discovered that Kate owned the screen rights. So be it, he told Ida Koverman. "Why shouldn't she do it?" Not only did she do it, but a term MGM contract was offered at the same time. There was only one hitch. She wanted Gable. Mayer said it was impossible.

"But I will give you a hundred and fifty thousand dollars. Hire any leading man you wish."

The result, of course, was the combination of James Stewart, Kate, and Cary Grant (her $150,000 purchase). He'd been bested and knew it —and respected it.

The next MGM Girl to get him—and get him good and wet—was Esther Williams, who had been seen in an aquacade by Louella Parsons. "You better hire her before somebody else does," Louella told Mayer.

"Louella, how are we going to build movies around a swimming pool?" he asked.

"The same way Sonja Henie built a career around an ice rink."

Mayer was on the phone that afternoon.

Esther Williams not only named her own terms at MGM, she made some demands concerning co-stars and scripts that nobody else could have made. She never, however, got a truly fine dramatic role.

"You know," she told Rona Barrett some years back, "I was in the water for only twenty minutes of the two hours. What did they think? Did they think I blew bubbles for the rest of the time?"

The third to get Mayer's number was a natural. He first saw Margaret O'Brien when she stood barely higher than his knees. Vincent Minnelli was directing tests for a child's part when Margaret toddled in wearing kilts. She clasped her hands together and got down on one knee, saying, "Don't send my father to the chair . . . don't let him fry!"

Minnelli interrupted the audition session and ran across the lot to the set of *Babes on Broadway.* "You've got to put this little girl into the movie just the way she auditioned for us," said Minnelli. "The audience will go wild."

So they did.

Margaret O'Brien became the darling of the lot—the only MGM Girl who could bust in on Mayer at any time.

As Mayer passed her in the hall one Christmas Eve, he stopped to ask, "And what do you want for Christmas?"

Margaret thought about it for a minute, looked up seriously, and said, "Busher. I'd like Busher." Busher was Mayer's $750,000 racehorse.

Some of Mayer's actions, however, left him open to all the condemnation he has received in the years since his death, none more so than his treatment of his long-time secretary, Ida Koverman. While still working in her seventies, Ida was stricken with a critical illness. Hedda, convinced that MGM was providing handsomely for Ida, began hearing disturbing rumors from people on the lot. She went to see Ida immediately.

"I should have quit years back," she told Hedda. "But I couldn't. I should have provided for myself when I was younger. Then it was too late."

"But what about the MGM pension plan?" Hedda asked.

Ida dodged the question, obviously embarrassed.

"What about it, Ida?"

"Hedda," she said with tears in her eyes. "Mr. Mayer wouldn't put me on it."

Even Hedda made no progress with Mayer and the MGM establishment. But Mayer got worried when Louella Parsons joined in the fight.

Ida's bills continued to pile up. Then Mayer came up with an idea that would solve the problem, he thought, and keep Hedda off his back.

"Put her in the Motion Picture Relief Home," Mayer told MGM publicist Howard Strickling. "Sound Hedda out for me," he added.

Esther Williams with Tom and Jerry—three stars who could not be maneuvered by Louis B. Mayer. *Below:* Margaret O'Brien, just ten, sits with her pet lamb and a recently published version of her *My Diary* to celebrate Children's Book Week in 1947. Margaret, a durable child star, was one of the few who proved to be a match for Louis B. Mayer's temper.

MGM makeup man Terry Miles literally paints Esther Williams's face with oil-based paint for *Dangerous When Wet*, a sea-and-sand epic that earned almost five million dollars. Her hair was covered with a type of marine varnish, and parts of her body had to be kept free of the paint so her pores could breathe.

"You let him do that, and he will be the sorriest man ever born," Hedda yelled into the phone. Then she slammed down the receiver.

There was only one way Ida could pay her medical bills—sell the grand piano upon which she played everyday. Hedda came over just as the moving men were rolling it out the door.

"Oh, no, you don't!" said Hedda. "Put that back in the house."

Then Hedda went into Ida's bedroom and called MGM–New York.

What exactly happened, nobody knows. But Ida Koverman's bills were paid, and there were some red roses on the piano the next day.

And the card? "Hope you're feeling better. Louie."

2

Jazz Babies

MAE MURRAY AND JOAN CRAWFORD—THE TWENTIES

George Shaker dropped his sandwich on a plate and grabbed for the phone by his side in the MGM security command post. He cranked the handle and rang once. No answer. He cranked again and again. "Damn!" he said. "Wake up, Jon. Get off your ass and wake up." George was cranking the phone continuously by that time.

Finally, Jon Mardian, keeper and resident diplomat at the VIP gate, sleepily picked up the phone. "Yeah?" he said, holding back a yawn.

"Get up and put your coat on," said George, shakily. "She's comin' in."

"Jesus Christ! It's six in the morning."

"Shut up and get your coat on," ordered Shaker.

Jon pulled on his dress coat with the epaulets, tousled his thick brown hair for proper effect, and then stepped out into the morning fog and stood at attention, his Prussian officer's boots shining like glass.

Out of the mist, like an apparition, came a lemon-yellow Pierce Arrow with seal skin upholstery. The driver, in matching yellow trappings, had a rhinestone-draped poodle on the seat beside him.

As the car slowed to a stop at the gate, the vision in the backseat leaned forward and extended a patrician hand.

Jon Mardian, an aspiring actor used for decoration at the front gate, knew power when he saw it. He walked out, bent at the waist, took the hand, and kissed it between the star sapphire and the fire opal. "Good day, Your Highness," he said, making sure the lady noticed his blue eyes and white teeth.

The lady acknowledged the cardboard hussar with a slight dip of her head.

Jon kept the laughter in his chest from escaping, and drew himself back up to full height.

It was quite a sight. The Princess Mdivani, Grand Duchess of Georgia and Chatelaine of Bulgrava Barony, had draped herself in what she considered the accoutrements of her station. Her blond hair drifted upward in a cascading spill that would have delighted only Dracula. Her mouth had been painted in three colors of gloss, forming a teeny bow that pyramided almost up to her nostrils. Soaring behind her head was a flowered umbrella with blossoms trailing in the wind. The dress? It was a pleated confection of canary lace, tiny topaz buttons, and spriglets of cream-colored lace that seemed to have a life of their own. An ermine lap robe had been draped casually over the royal knees. She looked not unlike a Parisian fashion doll that had been put through a shredder.

Ending the ritualistic procession was the mandatory black maid in a second car, all starch-capped and carrying a silver coffee urn, a lace basket of croissants, and the Belgian chocolates so preferred by the princess.

The car with the purring engine finally stopped in front of an enormous glass studio where a pair of pages, also in uniform, opened the building's double doors. Almost bowing and certainly cringing, an assistant director opened the door of the carriage—for this is what it resembled. The ermine robe was tossed aside and she began her laborious journey to the set. Since the yellow-silk-flowered hem at the bottom of her dress narrowed to twelve inches, her itsy-bitsy shoes could move only inches at a time.

When they finally got her inside, the rest of the cast and crew bowed, scraped, and cursed quite prolifically under their breaths as the Princess David Mdivani, the sometime Mae Murray (the fifth biggest box office attraction of the year), descended to soil her hands in honest labor.

There were other onlookers to this pageant—not all of them amused or even entertained.

"Look at that, she's getting worse," said Louis B. Mayer, glaring down at the baroque spectacle unfolding just below his executive office. "What's the matter with her? The next thing you know she'll be wearing a crown."

Irving Thalberg, at his boss's side, laughed. "Gotcha beat. Two nights ago she wore a ruby tiara at the Coconut Grove."

Mayer yanked down the shade. "She's not an actress, she's a window display."

Thalberg, who was quickly becoming the Henry Kissinger of MGM when it came to dealing with the stars, calmed Mayer down instantly by pointing out that Mae Murray's last two films had brought the studio $2,900,000 in profits. "She's our personal 'extravagance.' There are people out there who actually believe she's a queen."

"Well, Irving, you handle her—keep her and her weepy eyes out of my office."

"You bet," Thalberg answered.

Downstairs in a dressing room, a plump, shivering starlet wolfed down a doughnut, following the sparkling vision with hunger in her eyes. Princess Mdivani thrust her pouting lips toward the sky and pointed her umbrella toward a red velvet dress being held up for her inspection. "No, too bright," said the princess as she wobbled onto the set.

The girl in the dark, Billie Cassin, was famished physically and emotionally: a girl with good cheekbones, great round eyes, and an awkwardness and naiveté painful to see. To her, Mae Murray appeared much as the exquisite Marie Antoinette must have seemed to the ill-fed, wooden-shoed fishwives of the Paris streets.

Billie had washed dishes for her schooling, danced in tawdry chorus lines in little more than underwear, and waited in a cold-water flat to be discovered. That had come eventually. Not the way Billie wanted it perhaps. But it had come. A rude, chubby man looked at her in a lineup, made her swivel so he could see her ass, and then told her, "I'll call ya later."

New Year's Day, 1925, she was on a train headed for a dusty town she'd barely heard of.

"You'll get seventy-five bucks a week, sister, and about six months to prove yourself."

The greasy man at the pay window knew Billie as Lucille LeSueur, a name she had dropped when her mother remarried for the first time. "It won't do, just won't do," said a man in the casting department. "But we can talk about that later."

Billie, to tell the truth, didn't really care. She didn't know who she was anyway. She did know what she was: a "jazz baby" who could dance the Charleston better than anybody in Missouri and who had a scorching ambition that burned in her gut and kept her up at night. She had no way of knowing that she, plain little Billie Cassin, would become the biggest star on the MGM lot within two years—bearing the immortal name Joan Crawford. Nor could she know that the dazzling Mae Murray (the stroked, the bejewled, the all-powerful) would be reduced to touring the second-rate vaudeville circuit in rented dresses.

Mink one day and a linen coat the next. Champagne out of slippers at the Beverly Hills on Christmas Eve and canned soup off a gas burner at Easter. Woolworth nail polish in May and the $200 Max Factor manicure and hand bleaching in August. Riding the bus on Monday morning and spinning home in a Stutz on Friday night—these were the vagaries of Hollywood in the twenties.

MGM and Mayer grew fat as thirty million Metro fans rushed into the darkened palaces of illusion by 1926. Fans became greedy but necessary vultures, buying more than twenty million movie magazines before the decade closed. They read about Lillian Gish and her refusal to kiss MGM idol John Gilbert. They clucked over vicious tattling about Barbara LaMarr's five lovers. But as they sat under their hair dryers, picking at chocolate caramels, and turning the pages, they prized two types of stories above all others: the long and degrading fall of an idol they'd themselves built into near royalty, and the sudden rags to riches tale of a shop girl, like themselves, who charmed her way to wealth and a fame that would live forever.

So it was thumbs down for Mae Murray—the crowd that Nathanael West called "the locusts" tore the crown of stardom from her head and hurled it at Joan Crawford.

The Princess Mdivani was nothing of the sort. Not a princess. Not an aristocrat. For that matter, not even middle class. She had been Marie Adrienne Koenig, the daughter of an immigrant Belgian welder, whose physical form thrived on the cabbage and potato soup she was given in the back room of a downtown flat.

From there it was the usual story. Unbeatable legs in the back line of a chorus. The walk-on in a transparent costume. The Ziegfeld Follies. Stardom. Hollywood. The discovery was too quick. Not a new story even in the movies' first decade. The peculiar glow caught by the silent cameras was what they would later call vulnerability, bottled love.

Not all that young when she made her first film—thirty, to be exact —she decreed that she would be, forever, the "baby vamp," cutely making love and then snapping at her gallant's machismo with her garter. The titles tell it all: *Sweet Kitty Bellairs, Princess Virtue, The Delicious Little Devil,* and *The Gilded Lily.*

Just what the audiences of the day saw in Mae defies the imagination. Her eyes narrowed and blinked as if her preshooting cocaine had been a bit too tiddly. Her breasts heaved as if she'd been speared by a hyperactive Cupid. And her dramatics consisted mainly of pulling her hair out à la the bride of Dracula. But like her they did. Mae was second only to Gloria Swanson in popularity during the early twenties and amassed a fortune of a million dollars in two years.

Then the Roaring Twenties hit, bringing bathtub gin, rolled hose, and brash, overtly sexual dolls called flappers. These babes showed their knees. They giggled and squealed at the slightest diversion. More importantly, as far as Mae was concerned, they were younger. Younger like Joan Crawford, who was becoming too much of a threat for Mae to ignore.

So she took the fastest Santa Fe Chief to New York for a session with the beauticians who serviced the Ziegfeld Follies. Since Mae had an $800,000 penthouse a stone's throw from the citadel of beauty, she was able (wrapped in thick scarves and a navy peacoat) to slip into her orchid bedroom while the transformation was occurring. Not one of the tattlers in Hollywood was ever able to uncover the details of the overhaul. But one infamous Swiss doctor was known to have docked in New York, headed for the beauty emporium, and not left until four days later.

On the train back to the harsh sunlight of Hollywood, Mae kept to her cabin as trays were slipped through partially opened doors.

In Los Angeles the train had completely emptied before the former "Orchid Girl" deigned to show herself to the world. First a maid stepped down laden with two furs and carrying a small white dog whose bark sounded not unlike Mae's own voice. Finally, the lady herself moved out of the shadows. Five hundred seed pearls gleamed on a dress cut shorter and more daring than any Tinseltown had seen since the flapper craze began. The knees they revealed were newly slim and outlined with white silk hose.

The two dainty feet, in precarious high heels, negotiated the steps as if they were the start of the Yellow Brick Road. Seconds later, Mae Murray, then thirty-nine years old, faced the sun with a white fox muff held casually in her right hand.

There were not a few gasps as the news photographers began immortalizing the latest creation of Manhattan cosmetology. The hair, the color of desert sand, was a sunburst of ruffled curls. The face was slimmer (that of a twenty-year-old). But it was the lips that were to change the entire range of lip painting in the Roaring Twenties. In four colors of red they began in a needle point of color at the edge of the mouth and soared upward like the Washington Monument.

"Looks like a bee stung her," cracked one of the photographers.

"Maybe! Maybe," said Mae.

So was born "the girl with the bee-stung lips," an epithet that was to the twenties what "platinum blonde" was to the thirties. The lady, the image, and the epithet (so perfectly designed for billboards) had suddenly become very important to Mayer, Thalberg, and their emerging Metro-Goldwyn-Mayer.

Over her protest, Mae's contract had been sold to MGM as part of the deal that ordered her to report to the Metro lot within ten days of her arrival in Los Angeles. At the unfinished studio, Mae had hardly endeared herself to the boss by placing one hand on a slim hip and snarling, "Is this it?"

Louis B. Mayer was still fuming. His egomania, pomposity, and a fair amount of heartlessness were then well hidden. So Mae was received with a spray of orchids and tea in his office. The "girl with the bee-stung lips" planted herself on a silk sofa, lifted a veil from her face, and leaned close to Mayer's badger face. Pursing her lips into a hummingbird pout, she said breathlessly, "Mr. Mayer, you'll be delighted to know that I have finally found 'the real Mae.'"

She waited for a reaction, but the fish eyes continued to stare back placidly. "No, Mr. Mayer, I mean the true Mae. I have found my soul. I intend to make only the most meaningful of pictures—films designed especially to allow 'the real Mae' to be shared with the entire world."

Mayer didn't know a hell of a lot about "the real Mae." But he sure knew the implications of Hollywood's most unhappy phrase, "meaningful pictures." Meaningful pictures, Mayer knew, meant dull pictures. And dull pictures could work like a shoehorn to ease the mogul out of his newly found power. Spare me, he must have thought.

This was a critical juncture for the MGM Girls. Mae, Barbara LaMarr, and Aileen Pringle, with their extravagant, Gothic manners, were heading for a collision course with the new breed who, watching the mistakes of the old, were moving in from the sidelines. The final "Mae Murray epoch" broke down the walls through which Joan Crawford, Norma Shearer, Greta Garbo, and Lillian Gish would storm the velvet harem so lush and so soothing to the ego.

Senseless indulgence destroyed the old school. And there was no spendthrift as adept as Mae. For one of her films, *The French Doll*, she

Mae Murray was a credible actress and a box office star before she ruined herself as the "vamp with the bee-stung lips." Here, in a wardrobe test for MGM, she has the look of Lillian Gish, then Hollywood's top star.

And it made her a star! As the vapid flapper (with Ernest Torrence),
Joan Crawford finally hit it big at MGM where she was one of Mayer's
rare favorites.

ordered a fringed costume costing $1,500 and a headdress to match costing $2,700. (She added them to her own wardrobe.) For a film called *Circe the Enchantress,* Mae recruited a fifty-four-piece Negro band, "The Mae Murray Select String Orchestra," which played her favorite songs as she moved through her silent scenes. She continued to insist upon using the band. One afternoon the cameras were still for ninety minutes while Mae tried to make up her mind whether a waltz or a romantic ballad would provide her with the proper inspiration.

Billy Haines, the All-American hero just emerging at MGM, co-starred with her in *Circe* and later assembled an accounting of her trans-gressions to show his friend Joan Crawford. "This day is over, Joan," he said. "Remember that, and you'll always be a star."

But in 1925 ego still ruled, setting the stage for one of the most perverse on-set battles in Hollywood history.

Both Mayer and Thalberg had purchased *The Merry Widow,* the Franz Lehar operetta, and earmarked it as a project for the imperious and highly gifted Erich von Stroheim, whose style they hoped would trans-form the simple musical into an epic—a genre they needed to develop in order to compete with Cecil B. DeMille's Paramount productions.

Von Stroheim was the wrong person to work with Mae Murray on any project, so there was bound to be disaster on the *Merry Widow* set. Mae, a forerunner of Jennifer Jones, Rosalind Russell, and Betty Hutton —who all took their roles too seriously—traveled to Vienna and spent days lounging around the city in order to, as she said, soak up the "true meaning" of her character. She hadn't been informed that Von Stroheim, who despised the star system, was to direct her most important film. So before the studio's two most difficult artists clashed on their own, Irving Thalberg invited them to tea and detente in his office.

No sooner had Mae gingerly nibbled the first tea cake than she laid a gloved hand on Von Stroheim's arm and said, "I know you share with me the great romantic aura in this play. It will be a temple of love."

Von Stroheim, in cavalry pants, an officer's dress jacket, and carrying a riding crop under one arm, disengaged his arm and glared into her wide-open eyes. "This, my dear Miss Murray, is a story of the brutality and decadence of the Austrian Empire. It is not a romance."

She dropped her cup. "Mr. Thalberg, my agent will call you."

Mae remained quiet for several days, wondering whether or not to buck Von Stroheim, whom everyone believed to be the descendant of a noble Prussian military family. His father, the story went, had been a captain of the Austrian Royal Hussars and his mother a lady-in-waiting to the Empress Louise. Mae, who was to marry Prince Mdivani merely because of his title, was properly awed. She needn't have bothered. The director was really Erich Oswalk Stroheim, the son of a Jewish hatter from Gleiwitz, Silesia.

Unarmed with this data, Mae showed up for the first week of shooting and bowed and scraped to the director's supposed aristocracy. She had her hands full with silent screen lover John Gilbert, anyway, and paid little attention to the realistic, oversexed backgrounds being staged to infuse pure bawd into the innocent operetta.

Jack, with the face of a Paul Newman and the body of a Robert Redford, admittedly demanded "screen lover" roles because of the lusty excitement it added to an already jaded career. He had his costumes tailor-made and paid his writer friends to give him at least one, and more often than not, two horizontal maneuvers with his leading ladies. When Mae demanded rehearsals, Jack dashed over to the home of his friend John Barrymore to impart the good news. "A hot one for sure," he said.

Mae unwisely selected an empty stage for their first encounter. She was in afternoon cocktail wear, Jack in clinging tennis clothes. The effusive Miss Murray began moving through the scene unemotionally.

Jack took off his sweater and used it as an amorous lasso to pull her face close to his. "We've been attracted to each other for a long time, Mae, you know that!"

"Nonsense," she snapped. "I haven't seen you five times since I came to MGM."

Jack hooked his thumbs in the waistband of his tennis shorts and thrust against her. "But you asked for me. You told Irving you wouldn't make it without me. We've already got the chemistry."

"Well, then let's just save it for the movie, huh?"

In the succeeding days, Jack laid siege to Mae at her home, in her dressing room, and even invaded a costume fitting to plead his case. Mae finally snapped, "Jack, let's just save it for the movie; people don't buy tickets to see a burned-out pair who've already thrown themselves at each other on an everyday basis."

It was one conquest Jack was never to make. "I'm neither romantic nor lusty," Mae told Thalberg, who enjoyed seeing his friend Gilbert strike out.

Since Mayer had already promised the nine hundred Loew's theater owners a year ahead of time that *The Merry Widow* would be the major attraction for Christmas, he assigned three executives to constantly man the foxholes on the deteriorating production. But an era was ending on the rococo sets of *The Merry Widow*, where the relaxed, friendly country-clubbish standards still prevailed. Economics far out of line with the newer, smaller-picture era could no longer be hidden. Mae Murray was taking home $10,000 a week in salary and other benefits. It's estimated that Von Stroheim received as much plus slush funds used to finance "hidden" costs such as real wine in the orgy scene and crystal goblets (not glass) that were smashed against a fireplace.

Across the lot, director Jack Conway was filming a simple college romp, *Brown of Harvard*, with young William Haines, whose salary was then only $500 a week. Conway's set ran on a day-by-day ledger and was brought in at one-fourth the cost of *The Merry Widow*. And King Vidor, who borrowed the highly disciplined Jack Gilbert from *The Merry Widow* when possible, was creating one of the silent screen's great classics, *The Big Parade*, which cost $382,000 to make and earned $3,485,000 in profits (compared to *The Merry Widow*, which cost $592,000 and earned only $758,000 in profits). The years of hiring temperamental and costly beauties from the Ziegfeld Follies—such as Mae herself—and then pampering them like a prize horse, were over.

It was into this revolutionary era that Billie Cassin–Lucille LeSueur–Joan Crawford walked, taking just the right steps.

The year before *The Merry Widow* began shooting and Mae Murray's marriage to Prince David Mdivani took place, Billie Cassin had already set her course. As a $75-a-week extra player, the future Joan Crawford was called up for small roles now and then. But mostly she was free to roam the studio. She had box lunches with the cinematographers and held gab fests with the hairdressers and makeup artists. She even cajoled several pliant directors into showing her how it looked from behind the camera.

She had a mind like a steel trap, filing away the details she would later use to create the Crawford eyebrows, the Crawford hair, the walk, the talk, the ability to look into the camera and appeal to an audience as perhaps no other star would until Marilyn Monroe several decades later.

She came to Hollywood because she needed a meal ticket. She stayed because she found a life.

After her first two days on the lot, Joan finally admitted to herself that she didn't even know what a movie star was or how they got that way. With her first paycheck in hand, she went into a small mom-and-pop drugstore on the way home to her apartment. She tore through the little store like a drunken sailor in port, and bought one of each fan magazine they had, a manicure set, hair rinse, twenty-five different items of makeup, and an alarm clock.

It took her three nights to read the fan magazines. And some of them she read twice.

Hesitantly, she took the best covers over to the mirror in her small apartment and held them up to her own, fresh-off-the-farm face. Something was missing, she said to herself, but that would have to come later.

This Joan Crawford bore no resemblance to the high-fashion media darling into which she would shape herself. This Joan Crawford wore brightly printed dresses that emphasized her broad shoulders and thick legs. She still sported flapper makeup, and she bolted about like a colt.

The fan magazines became her bible. Three nights after her first reading session the MGM guard was surprised to see her dash through the main gate at 6:15 A.M. The magazines said that Clara Bow and Gloria Swanson never arrived later than that.

Neither would she.

But they gave her no work.

Marceline Simmons, the head manicurist, told Joan she should get angry. "Who brought you out here?" she asked.

"Harry Rapf," Joan answered.

"Well, go on up there tomorrow and tell him you want to go to work."

Done. In a bitter touch of irony, Joan's first role was a one-liner. The camera focused on her back as another starlet, Norma Shearer, performed her scene. (Was this the beginning of her feud with Norma?)

About that session, Joan once said, "I was afraid I couldn't act . . . never would understand it. Then I spent so much time watching Norma Shearer and how much she was able to do with those three little expressions on her face, I realized I could sure as hell do better than that."

She was an Eliza Doolittle looking for the right Henry Higgins to mold her. Outgoing at the time, Joan found not one Henry Higgins but two!

The first was a cameraman who'd photographed her in several minor appearances. Joan got to know Johnny Arnold well enough to hitch a ride home with him and, once, they took in a movie together—a Paramount movie. They sat there watching Gloria Swanson's face on the screen. It appeared as if her eyes were enormous, her cheeks patrician and alabaster. "God, how does she do it?" Joan asked.

Arnold looked over at her and said, "Joan, I think you could be more beautiful than that . . . you could be almost hypnotic on the screen."

Joan immediately dragged him out of the theater and onto Holly-wood Boulevard. "What do you mean? What were you saying?"

"Look, Joan, your face is 'built.' "

"How?"

"It's not like the other actresses'. Your bones are perfect for the camera. But, Joan, you're too fat."

"'What's that got to do with anything?" she said defensively.

"We can't pick up the beauty of your face. You're chubby. Take some of that weight off and you'll see what I mean."

Back at her bungalow near MGM's Culver City headquarters she began a diet not unlike the protein regimens that came in during the sixties. Steak, tomatoes, and grapefruit were all she ate.

The pounds were gone in two weeks. Now when she held the picture of Gloria Swanson up to hers, she didn't feel so bad.

"You," said cameraman Arnold, "are halfway there."

The handsome Billy Haines gave her the crucial boost. A man-about-town with a much photographed face, Billy told Joan to get out of "that dumpy little apartment of yours and let Hollywood know who Joan Craw-ford is."

"What about money?"

"Sister, with that face of yours and the right clothes, if you take off twenty pounds and get a decent dress you can take this studio by storm."

Joan's salary was $100 a week by that time. But tea gowns—at least tea gowns that would attract the satiated press of Hollywood—went for as much as $65. One Monday morning she hiked over to Wardrobe for a bite of lunch with her friend Marylynn Lugo.

"Marylynn, what chance have I got to borrow a couple of those dresses every day or so?"

Marylynn laughed. "Finally catching on, are you? Borrow anything you want," she said, indicating racks of swank evening gowns and fur wraps. "Just make sure you have it all back here at dawn." (Crawford wasn't the only actress in town passing off studios costumes as her own at dances and premieres.)

If there is an exact moment when Joan Crawford stopped being a Hollywood starlet and became a Hollywood personality on her own it was at a Wednesday afternoon tea dance at the Coconut Grove. Wearing a clinging hostess gown (which Aileen Pringle had worn in a 1923 MGM film) altered with safety pins to fit her new lithe curves, and a spray of baby white orchids for her hair provided by Billy Haines, Joan had them lined up to cut in.

"I just hope the safety pins hold," she whispered to Haines.

As she was doing a Charleston Strut with a young lawyer, a Hearst photographer snapped a couple of shots that were on the street by the next morning. More followed, until Mayer himself suggested Joan for a part in the modern soap opera *Sally, Irene and Mary*. Given a brief test, the part was hers. Thus was born Joan Crawford the movie star.

"But she never gave up the social whirl," said columnist Dorothy Manners, a close Crawford friend at the time. "She was drawn to the attention, the chic atmosphere and surroundings which made her forget her own background. She was as wild and gay as anyone in town."

Sally, Irene and Mary went before the cameras at about the same time as *The Merry Widow*—the first of the new and the last gasp of the old were underway.

Sally, Irene and Mary was one of the first in a series of films the MGM brass used to break the old system of directorial omnipotence. It was budgeted to the last dollar, didn't run one hour over its weekly schedules, and was turned out with no feuds or tantrums.

Joan was frightened of her first scene. Like all actresses, she could smell a hit. An ambitious former chorus girl, she was sure she would be able to infuse some of her own experience into her part. She paced back and forth in her dressing room that first day, repeating over and over again how good she was going to be, how good she would have to be.

As the cameras rolled, her power almost short-circuited the smooth atmosphere on the set.

Veteran director Edmund Goulding took Joan aside. "You're giving too much, Joan," he said. "You can't play every scene at fever pitch."

He didn't have to say it twice.

Even before the film was wrapped up, Joan was given a raise to $150 a week. And the small-budgeted film went on to become one of the hits of the season and established Joan as a star.

Over at *The Merry Widow* set (where Mae was drawing $10,000 a week), the Stroheim–Murray War, Part Two, was gathering steam.

Mae's costumes, designed especially for her but not necessarily for the time frame of the film, made Von Stroheim laugh out loud when she appeared on the set. "How much worse can it get?" he asked. "She must be wearing every egret feather to be found in the world."

Mae soon had other grievances. Gossips told her about the lewd scenes Von Stroheim had filmed on the days she wasn't scheduled to shoot. So she waited until the master went home one night and had a few of them shown.

"I am appalled," she told Thalberg that very night—waking him at 3 A.M.

"Well, Mae, he told you this wasn't going to be a tame romance," Thalberg replied.

"Yes, Mr. Thalberg, but he didn't say it was going to be a dirty picture either."

Thalberg ordered up the rushes of the film at 7 A.M. the next day, finding some things offensive and others merely realistic. The main objection was to a scene where one of the principals thrashes around nurturing his erotic foot fetish. "That's too much," Thalberg said.

"But the man has a foot fetish," said Von Stroheim.

"Yes," answered Thalberg. "And so do you."

Filming commenced again.

There were fights over the waltz scene, disagreements over the crude handling of the wedding night, and, finally, it all disintegrated into a personal shouting match.

Mae, her egret plumes shaking, called Von Stroheim a "filthy Hun."

He told her to follow her true profession—"streetwalking."

Mayer, with no choice left, shut down the production. Twenty-four hours later the MGM chief persuaded Monte Bell to take over the shooting schedule. Bell had been on the set for less than an hour when the crew members turned off their lights, walked away from the cameras, and retreated into a corner of the sound stage.

"I give up," said Mayer.

Finally, Von Stroheim's wife volunteered to call a summit conference that same night. The picture was already overdue and had to meet release deadlines or it would cost the studio as much as it had cost to make. Mayer, Thalberg, Von Stroheim, and a number of sublieutenants for all three dashed back and forth, with Mrs. Von Stroheim acting as the mediator.

At 12:05 A.M. a settlement was reached. Mae agreed to beg humble forgiveness for calling Von Stroheim a "dirty Hun." And Von Stroheim, his lower lip trembling in anger, whispered an equal apology to his star. It was considered so important that two Los Angeles newspapers had extra editions on the street before dawn. "MAE–VON STROHEIM KISS AND MAKE UP," said one headline. "MURRAY–VON STROHEIM IN UNEASY PEACE," said another.

Mae called reporters personally before breakfast the next day, making it clear that she certainly "did not kiss Erich von Stroheim. Nor will I."

Since a Hollywood epoch isn't lived out only on the sound stages, every whisper, Coke date, and sometimes even a handshake (be it too lingering) is as significant in Tinseltown as the birth of Great Britain's royal heir. It was always that way. Louella Parsons said she would rather learn about a juicy new love affair than about all the new movies in Hollywood.

Mae Murray and Joan Crawford, thanks to their position as representatives of the MGM Girls in two decidedly different worlds, were observed minutely through all their love affairs, degradations, and misfortunes. They were smothered by success.

Mae Murray *should* have been used to attracting attention of almost any kind. Her Nordic profile filled the front cover of a New York City tabloid when she was still a teenager. "The most beautiful profile in America is on display at the Ziegfeld Theater," said the caption. After that, she was never fully out of the public's eye.

She had several undistinguished husbands (meaning: not worthy of headlines) before she found herself in the arms of what society came to call "the million-dollar stud." His name was David Mdivani, and he was from the Georgia section of Russia. He called himself the "Prince of Georgia."

Joan, still the fear-ridden Midwestern girl under her movie star clothing, found a prince of another kind—the crown prince of Hollywood. There was really no other way to describe Douglas Fairbanks, Jr., whose father and stepmother ruled film society from their hulk of a castle, Pickfair.

The greedy little minds in the MGM publicity department found both stories to have been made in heaven. Two princes, two superstars. Fan magazines could print for years without exhausting the hype.

Prince Charming had walked into Mae's path during an afternoon party given by Mae's sometime friend, silent star Pola Negri, who had been introduced to the Mdivani family in Europe. (Even she wouldn't admit what she'd heard about them.) One thousand potted mums, and orchids cascading from the ceiling, gave Pola's party the look of a flower convention that had issued the wrong dress code. Is silver lamé, after all, appropriate for afternoon drinks . . . particularly when it has a train slithering along behind?

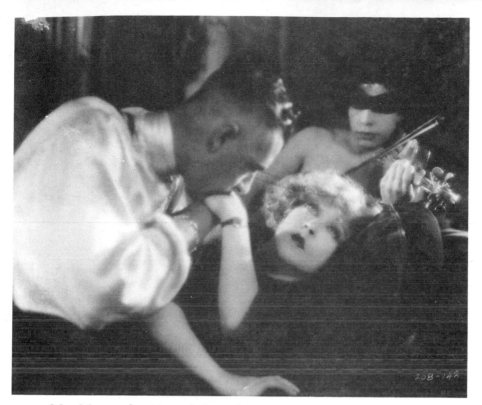

Mac Murray about to melt from the attentions of John Gilbert in *The Merry Widow*, a troubled film that almost brought down the MGM walls. *Below:* The only existing print of Mae Murray entering the MGM lot to sign a million-dollar pact—it was found in her effects at the Motion Picture Country Home.

Mae Murray, the fifth top moneymaker for MGM in the twenties, in one of her grandiose poses that passed for acting. She tore 'em up in Topeka, however.

With her "bee-stung" lips waiting, Mae Murray prepares to kiss her bridegroom, the fake Prince David Mdivani—a man who bilked her of three million dollars.

An increasingly embittered Joan Crawford eating her de rigueur diet meal. She was beset by personal troubles and fought a bitter rivalry with Norma Shearer.

Joan Crawford, her first husband, Douglas Fairbanks Jr., and actor William Haines arrive at the first Academy Awards ceremony. Joan still retained the bloom of an ingenue. *Below:* Joan Crawford and Dane Clark at the *Hollywood Canteen* (1944).

The Joan we all know: a consummate expert at public relations—down to the training of her poodles.

Finally! The recognition Joan Crawford had been waiting for all her career—the Oscar. In this photo the actress receives her Oscar and the press in bed. She was too frightened of losing to attend the ceremony (1945).

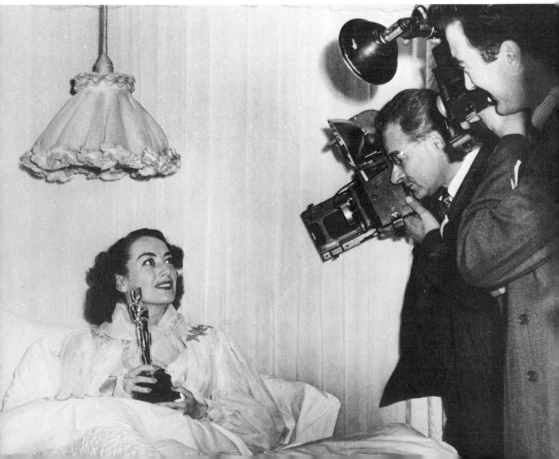

Ten years after Louis B. Mayer kicked Joan Crawford off the MGM lot, she was again the "queen of Hollywood." Here she arrives at the Academy Awards ceremony with Humphrey Bogart in 1954. *Below:* Comedy star Dick Martin kisses a somewhat exploited Joan Crawford during the taping of a "Laugh In" episode. It was Crawford's last professional appearance.

As the blue bloods of the cinema world arrived at Pola's, Mae sat impatiently down the street in her Pierce Arrow. The forty-five-minute wait was worth it in order to make her grand entrance. Finally, Mae arrived. She tiptoed up to Pola. A kiss here, a kiss there, a little talk about the hair, a little chat about the dirt, then on to the reception room.

It was a setup. While it seemed to Mae that the divine David, in his Bond Street formalwear, had been driven wild and crazy by her updated beauty, he had, in fact, been dodging the young quail and waiting for his quarry for more than an hour—not an easy task with starlets fingering your cravatte and other items of attire. But with three million dollars at stake (a conservative estimate of Mae's fortune), the "million-dollar stud" stood his ground, finally honing in on those beakish little red lips. He took her hand, pulling off her gray glove seductively, finger by finger. "I've so much wanted to meet you, Miss Murray. Prince David Mdivani at your pleasure." (Notice that he said "pleasure," not "service.")

Adela Rogers-St. Johns said David had one of the handsomest faces in the Western world. "Why else would so many women have paid so much for it?" she asked her boss, William Randolph Hearst.

"Adela," said Hearst, "I hardly think it's his face."

Part of the stud's success with Mae was his deferential approach. Having played four queens and three princesses in her films, she had become one of those stars who believed her own publicity. The crown they placed on her head may have been made of paper, but it looked as good as the real thing when Mae looked in the mirror.

"Damn broad really does think she's royal," grumbled her driver one hot afternoon. "If she'd only act like one."

There are so many versions of what transpired between the sighing couple that speculation is senseless. Pola Negri simply said that they "eased each other" onto a couch in a nook provided for just such an event.

"And he had her hooked," reported Walter Winchell several years later. "Hooked like a marlin. And he wasn't about to throw this one back."

At first, Pete Smith, head of the MGM publicity department, was ecstatic. Here the studio had a picture about an actress and a prince (*The Merry Widow*), and now they had the real actress and a handsome prince to exploit from coast to coast. There was even talk of a vaudeville tour with enough hand kissing to chap the prince's lips for many a winter to come.

"Never!" said His Highness, drawing himself up to his full six feet. "To the premiere we go. Nowhere else."

The Merry Widow opened weeks later to sensational business, catapulting Mae Murray to a position as the number-one box office attraction in the world—the first time an MGM star had ever achieved that distinction. (For years the top spot had been dominated by Mary Pickford, Douglas Fairbanks, and Rudolph Valentino.)

There was one small problem causing consternation, however, at the Mae Murray digs. How did one marry a prince? Especially if the bride to be was Marie Koenig, whose parents were not long off the boat from Europe. She wrapped herself in her marten furs and cuddled up to her old friend Pola.

"Now, Mae," said Pola, reassuring her. "Times have changed. You know many think that *we* are royalty." (And nobody thought that more than Pola and Mae themselves.)

What happened next?

Mae's version was downright comical. David, in a cavalry uniform and sword, burst through her door one afternoon. "He leaped on me. I felt faint. But I cried for him to get off. 'David, we don't do those things here.'"

He became more insistent. Mae swooned.

Lo and behold, the next thing she knew she was stretched out on a love seat in a hunter's lodge heaven-knew-where. Logs were burning in the fireplace, a dinner of tinned lobster and wine was on a perfectly set table, and David stood over her in the red tights and cadet coat of what he called "the Georgian Hussars."

"It was finally too much, too romantic," said Mae.

"I was married soon after with lovely Pola as my hostess," said David.

Mae, dressed in a sedate wedding ensemble and resembling a Grecian bath slave, appeared on the steps of the wedding site and answered questions as if she were one of the original vestal virgins. "I held out for four days," she said. "Then it was no use." It must have slipped her mind that she'd been married three times before—one of those times to the not-so-noble doorman at her Manhattan apartment. ("He did have one hell of a body," said Mae's friend Pola.)

Much, much later Pola told what she believed to be the true story. "Mae couldn't keep her hands off him at the party. Then he went home with her."

The next day he was on the phone to Pola. "She wants me to marry her." Pola said she told him he could hardly do better since Mae had $3 million salted away in a bank and property worth hundreds of thousands.

Marion Davies put it more bluntly: "She phoned him from my bungalow on the MGM lot and proposed to him right there. There were two reasons for this: one, he had the right equipment, and two, by making Mae a princess, she could make her arch rival Gloria Swanson, a mere marquise, and Pola, a mere countess. . . ."

Louis B. Mayer grudgingly approved of Mae's marriage, sending a silver tea set that had been given to him by the Duchess of Alba.

At the other end of the MGM spectrum, Joan Crawford, suddenly a triumph in *Our Dancing Daughters,* had won the respect and the attention of Mayer, who ordered the publicity department to launch the biggest buildup in the studio's history (even bigger than Norma Shearer's). He also raised her salary to $500 a week and gave her a new roadster. "I felt envy around me like a fog bank," she said.

Joan's rush to matrimony was more all-American.

Douglas Fairbanks, Jr., had grown from an awkward, plump child into one of the handsomest men in Hollywood, and so he began to take acting lessons. Doug, Sr., remained frosty.

Since he was getting no help from movie contacts, Doug, Jr., began performing in Hollywood's booming live theater—most notably in the play *Young Woodley,* which opened on October 17, 1927. Mary Pickford was there, as were Swanson and Mayer.

Joan, on the arm of Paul Bern (later Harlow's tragedy-plagued husband), told Paul that "he's the handsomest man I've ever seen. Let's go backstage."

At closer quarters, the attraction seemed less potent.

The actress sent a telegram anyway. Doug answered, and a dinner followed that had Mary horrified. "She's just the type in Hollywood I wish we could avoid," Mary told Louella Parsons over lunch.

Doug began the chase. But he made it clear that he wanted Joan Crawford the actress, not Joan Crawford the eternal flapper. He lectured her and then kissed her good-night.

She called Sally O'Neill in tears. "What can I do?"

"Tone yourself down, honey," said Sally. "How long can we remain flappers?"

The wire service reporter and author Bob Thomas, who interviewed Joan dozens of times and was a close friend, said, "She gave up gum, dressed conservatively and began reading books Doug recommended."

When the engagement was announced, Mayer rubbed his pudgy

little hands with glee. He called in the production team. "Put something together—doesn't matter what—in which we can star Joan and Doug. Can't miss." (It did miss, artistically at least. They called it *Our Modern Maidens.*)

Louis B. Mayer had told Joan from the beginning to think of him as a father. A wishful romantic, Joan took him up on it. And it was to his office she went to plan the wedding. "Let me handle it, dear. We have to be very careful."

Mayer's concept of "careful" was different from the rest of the world's. The wedding he set up for the lovers would have pleased P. T. Barnum. First there was the premiere of *Our Modern Maidens* at Grauman's Chinese Theatre. Then they put their footprints in the cement in front of the theater. Finally they were married, with Mary Pickford and Doug, Sr., conspicuously absent.

Doug, Jr., was broke and in considerable debt, so Joan bought the house and furnished it. The seeds of the first rift had been planted.

Joan was on her way to becoming one of the screen's great stars, and everyone knew it. It rubbed against Doug's fragile self-confidence. And, to quote Bob Thomas, "the differences in their bank accounts didn't help." Doug was bringing home $72,791 while Joan made $150,000 plus benefits and options.

If anything did the marriage in, though, it was the horror of trying to live in the shadow of "the big couple," Doug, Sr., and Mary.

Mary, with a firm set of her jaw, finally allowed the couple to spend every Sunday at Pickfair—an impersonal cavern of a house. These long afternoons were as ritualistic as the awakening ceremony of Louis XIV. Father and son went out for an afternoon of golf. Mary, smiling absently at Joan, drifted upstairs to nap until dinner.

Joan was alone. She often said there were echos there and that "it felt like those two were dead already." But she sat—with the sun on her face—Sunday after Sunday.

The relationship finally ended.

One Sunday afternoon, while Mary napped and the men golfed, Joan Crawford stood at the window and realized it was Lucille LeSueur or Billie Cassin who was meekly waiting for her betters to drift in and condescendingly toss her a few leftovers of love. She set her jaw, took up the hall phone, and called for her own car. As she headed down the long driveway she was Joan Crawford—now and forever. She would never look back at Lucille or Billie again.

She knew the torment this would bring and, in a Faustian gesture, traded for fame. "I wept each morning on my drive to the studio, and I wept all the way back home. I couldn't sleep at night even though I had a horror of staying awake," she wrote in a diary. "So I'd lie in bed thinking about the future. I fear it with all my heart and soul even as I fear the dark."

The Joan Crawford the world came to know was forged during these years—toughened by what she had seen happen to the fragile silent stars.

She faced the night as perhaps no star then or since. Her servants would hear the car roar out of the driveway at 2 A.M. "I would find a peace, a consolation in those wild night rides. As my car roared along, susceptible to my slightest whim, fully under my control, I felt that I was lord of all.

"I ordered my car to move faster and faster, to rush away from the terror of the night that chased me and tugged at my soul. Sometimes I could even fool myself into believing that I'd succeeded in crushing that restless urge."

But as the world now knows, the terror of the night finally caught up with her.

Mae Murray's fate was, if possible, more tragic—as so many of the MGM endings proved to be.

Not long after Prince David Mdivani carried Mae over the threshold of the house she had bought him, the news leaked out that David wasn't a prince at all, wasn't even a duke, was, in fact, probably a peasant. Oh, it's true he'd come from Georgia—an escapee from the bloody revolution. But he came as a sort of tradesman for hire. On his way to Hollywood to snag the big one, he'd stopped to work in the oil fields and haul freight. He used the money to buy the tailored clothes and trappings with which he won Mae.

He was cheating on her less than a week after the wedding, when Mae was in the middle of a new MGM opus, *Valencia.* It was a good picture, and she liked it.

But one night "the Prince," as she still called him, burst into the dining room in a rage. "I can't afford to have a wife of mine, a princess, working in trade. It must stop. You must quit."

Mae shuddered at the thought. She was torn in half. David wooed her back, coaxed her slowly over to his way of thinking. "You must come to France with me and become the mistress of my chateau," he said. "This is your new job—not that drivel at MGM."

Her trunks were packed that night, and they made it out of California on the last train.

At 10 A.M. the next day, Louis Mayer got a call informing him that there was trouble on the *Valencia* set. "Mae hasn't shown up. There's no answer at her house."

"Give her half a day," said Mayer, trusting Mae as much as he trusted any of his chattel.

Ten A.M. the next day. "She's not here, Mr. Mayer," said an assistant director. "We sent a page out to her house . . . he found it closed for the season with the furniture covered."

The search was on.

Mayer and Thalberg didn't dare issue a public statement. They couldn't even let it leak to the studio population. "Damn it, Irving, we have more bookings for this picture than *The Big Parade*."

Thalberg nodded. "Reaction has not been so hysterical since *The Merry Widow*." In all, *Valencia* was set to go into five hundred theaters in less than six months.

They put Pinkerton detectives on the trail. They cabled their offices in code, asking representatives in London, Paris, Madrid, and New York to pull out all the stops.

It was a gossip columnist who found Mae and David on a transatlantic liner, halfway to Europe.

"Come home immediately," read the shore-to-ship wire. "*Valencia* is promised and you're violating your contract. Return to MGM immediately."

His Highness intercepted the telegram, leading Mae to believe that Mayer was graciously assenting to her vacation. But the Paris office told her the score. She ran in tears to David. "I've got to go back. I can't leave them like this."

"Tell them you're with child," he ordered. "Tell them now, because you're staying."

A contrite wire was sent to Mayer from Mae but remained unanswered. "We don't believe you," said the Paris representative. "We insist you return to work."

David forbade it, and, eventually, she was bearing his child.

For almost two years they lived an idyll in Paris, with Mae as hostess to a restless, freeloading band of Russian exiles. At their marriage, David had convinced her that it was a Mdivani rule for the wife to assign power of attorney and co-ownership to the husband. And Mae had agreed.

Then a check that Mae wrote for children's furnishings in Paris was returned because of insufficient funds. She demanded the books. She was broke, exiled from Hollywood, and living with a man who had already shifted his attentions to a rich heiress.

The downward spiral assumed the proportions of a Greek tragedy, with Mae, dazed and unsure of where she was, finally found sleeping on a St. Louis park bench in the snow. Returned to Hollywood, she died at the Motion Picture Country Home. In her hand was a framed photo of herself at her loveliest—in the wedding scene of *The Merry Widow.*

"We never promised you a heart," Mayer once screamed at Judy Garland.

3

But Not on the First Date!

LOVE AND THE MGM GIRLS

"Hey!" said Mickey Rooney in a loud voice. "How would you like to hear my imitation of Cary Grant?"

With his red hair resembling a thatched hut and a suit that made him look like the oldest "Little Rascal" playing dress-up, he hardly looked like Hollywood's latest Romeo.

The beautiful brunette sitting across from him rolled her eyes upward. "Well, would you really like to impersonate Cary Grant?"

"You bet I do," answered Mickey. "I do it great."

He smoothed the sides of his hair, unsuccessfully, and sucked in his breath to gain some slight facsimile of Cary's broad shoulders. He mumbled a couple of sentences.

The lush beauty let her chin sink further into her hand and mumbled, with great ennui, "How very interesting."

The scene was Chasen's—a richly furnished chow palace and the spot at which to be seen in the early forties.

Mickey tapped the table with a bread stick, letting his mind whirl for a couple of seconds. He had to have this girl. He had to. She was his dream, a Venus so withdrawn that the macho energy of the city had yet to focus on her.

He thought, for a microsecond, of taking her hand. But no, better stick to something he was good at—comedy.

"I also do Jimmy Cagney," he said.

The girl's voice seemed a bit more perturbed. "That's so interesting," she said, searching the room for perhaps a more sophisticated man.

Mickey did Jimmy anyway. Silence.

"And you know what?" he said in a voice that was growing steadily tremulous. "How about Lionel Barrymore playing Dr. Gillespie?"

"Well, just how about it?" was her answer.

Mickey became furious. Who the hell was this Ava Gardner anyway? Pretty, sure. Sexy, sure. Ambitious, sure. Could he live without her? Absolutely not.

He angrily attacked his chocolate mousse, gulped wine like a truck driver, and then paid the considerable check. He escorted her to his red convertible, shined for the occasion, and drove through the streets eratically. His head was turned away from his companion. He was embarrassed. His macho was melting onto the sheepskin seat of the Cadillac that he described to friends as "my stud wagon."

With the car stopped in front of Ava's undistinguished apartment in Hollywood, Mickey slid an arm across her shoulder. She opened the door and was out on the sidewalk before he realized what was happening. "Listen, buster, you may be able to get away with that on others—on your precious Judy Garland. But not on me, bub."

He apologized. She mumbled a "thank you" as she let him come into the lobby of her building. There was a dim light hanging above them, swinging in the light breezes that waft across Los Angeles at midnight.

Mickey shoved his hands in the pockets of his suit. "Ava, will you marry me?"

Ava whammed her purse against the banister and moved up closer so she could look right in his eyes. "Are you crazy?" Then she was gone.

The pursuit in a red convertible was underway—he had chased after her in full view of his MGM peers, but worse than that, he'd been so incautious that Mayer was now watching his every step. But Ava was becoming the hottest sex symbol on the lot. Like Francis I, who had himself locked in his chamber to prevent his indiscretions, Mickey was obsessed, gravitating toward the forbidden fruit without looking back.

To be fair, Mickey wasn't entirely to blame. Love and, quite often, sex were the ultimate currency at Metro-Goldwyn-Mayer, which sold *amour* wrapped in the most inviting of packages. The studio was king of the Hollywood Love Parade, an affair with onscreen clinching and kissing that had started on the nickelodeon boardwalks of New York in 1909 and culminated with the million-dollar love goddesses of the twenties and thirties, when a kiss on the great Garbo neck added $1.2 million to the box office value of an MGM film.

During the years since Metro had been founded, a kiss, the meeting of two thighs, and the satin slide onto a bed had become the most enduring symbol of box office power. If the onscreen embers of affection blazed into a hot affair off the screen—so much the better. When it happened between Greta Garbo and John Gilbert in *The Flesh and the Devil,* box office receipts increased ten-fold.

If a star couldn't make it in the sack, his career frequently withered as quickly as his ego. The MGM graveyard was littered with screen lovers who got bad report cards for their private bedside manner.

And Mickey knew it. The time had come for "Andy Hardy" to date, to get caught in the clinch, and, heaven forbid, become engaged.

Until Ava, Mickey's romantic interest had been aimed solely at Judy Garland. In between takes, at the studio's Little Red Schoolhouse, Judy and Mickey had begun exchanging notes. "I love you, I'll always love you," said a note passed in a matchbook.

"Your hair, your eyes—they look beautiful this morning," wrote Mickey back to Judy.

Ma Lawlor, the teacher, preferred to ignore it—in spite of the giggles from Lana Turner, who was able to intercept the missives and make copies next to her algebra quiz.

"About that time Judy and I became lovers onscreen," said Mickey. "That took some of the fun out [of it]. The passion growing in Ma Lawlor's schoolroom was counterfeit, and we both knew it. Only our love of fun was real."

Mickey Rooney needed a powerful aura of romance. He was heading into the crisis years of his career—he had to make the public believe he was no longer just a little innocent kid with red hair.

The Ava Gardner of 1940 bore no resemblance to the grand and glorious love goddess she was to become. Just out of the fields of rural North Carolina, she had six dresses, lived with her mother, and did little more than decorate films of the *Andy Hardy* genre. She even cavorted through one film with the Bowery Boys.

"When I speak of her as a naive girl from Carolina, who made a good-night kiss the end of sex, I'm not simply romanticizing my first love. I am describing Ava then—Ava as she lived and breathed and thought before life had inflicted so many scars," said Mickey. "I am not now what I was in 1940. Nor are you. Nor is Ava."

The "Rooney–Gardner Debacle," as MGM came to call it, finally alarmed the front office and, most importantly, Louis B. Mayer.

"But he does have to grow up," Mayer's secretary, Ida Koverman, reminded him.

"But not this fast and certainly not with that girl."

"How would you like to be called 'Mr. and Mrs. Andy Hardy?'" Mayer asked Mickey at one of those dreadful summonses to the king's throne room.

"But I love her," said Mickey.

"There'll be others," Mayer said.

"Not for me," said Mickey—a hysterical statement in retrospect considering the eight times he eventually marched to the altar.

With the grudging approval of the MGM brass, Mickey and Ava were finally married at an interdenominational church in Ballard, California, on January 10, 1941. Ava was nineteen, Mickey twenty-one.

MGM couldn't have written a honeymoon script any better. They checked into a small inn where Mickey was jumpy—afraid he wouldn't live up to what Hollywood expected of their men and women. "My hands were shaking when I reached for my pajama tops and tried to step into them. The pajama arms were too short for my body but I had shoved my leg through one of the sleeves before I realized my mistake. I finally stumbled into the pants."

Ava was waiting.

Looking back on it, Mickey realized how inept he must have seemed. "But not to Ava. There was no way in which she could have measured my ineptitude. For I was the first man ever to possess Ava Gardner. I was proud."

It was a short idyll. Their differences were so great that friends of the couple knew better than to interfere. They surrounded their troubles with protective silences. They settled, unhappily, in the bridal home Mickey had bought.

"Then I was speeding out of the driveway, looking back at a brightly lighted home, my home, from which I had just been evicted by one of the most beautiful women in the world. We had lived together exactly eight months."

Mickey was back on the dating circuit within a week—with a blonde at Ciros, a brunette at the Coconut Grove, and a table full of girls at a Louella Parsons backyard reception.

But Ava, still a hothouse flower with the scent of the woods from which she had emerged, seemed to be overwhelmed by sorrow. She'd watched heartbreak all around her at the dream factory, wondering if she hadn't been better off back in New York modeling hats and gloves. She drifted into Mayer's outer office to confide in his secretary, Ida Koverman. "You know, Ida, I come here, work on movies I don't even understand, and then go back home to have dinner with my mother. I read the script, go to bed. The next day it starts all over again."

Ida chose her words carefully. She knew that Mayer had decided to build Ava Gardner into a sex symbol who would make the others pale in comparison—a sizzling beauty to light up the marquees.

"You know, Ava," Ida said, "this can all be a lot of fun if you let it. Don't take it home with you and don't believe your press releases."

In essence, Ida was telling her to take the money and run. Ava was wearing psychological track shoes the next day.

When Ava took the train to the Coast with her sister, she had decided she wanted a paycheck, not a famous name. "I knew there were plenty of ambitious girls, straining every nerve to become a star. But for me, the whole idea was a joy-ride, and an intriguing experience. I was like a girl heading for a vacation. I had no more real acting plans or ambition than a flea."

She never changed her opinion—not after she became the hottest property at MGM; not after her beauty made her an empress of love.

They gave her an acting coach. And Ava repeated her lines until they had some minor polish and she had a superficial sense of how to talk before the camera. They taught her to dance, to sing, how to wear clothes, and how to move like the predatory feline she was to depict so forcefully on the screen.

"The only thing pleasant about it for me is drawing my paycheck," she made the mistake of telling one of her producers.

The awesome summons from Mayer arrived the next day.

"Ava, come on over here," said Big Daddy, "and sit right over here on the couch." He had a nice cup of tea brought in, handled the service himself, and gossiped about the constant envy and rivalries that abounded in the harem.

He leaned his florid face close to hers and murmured in a fatherly tone, "You can consider me your father . . . we're all a big family. Any trouble? You come to me. You can always count on me . . . always. We're going to make you one of the biggest stars in the history of this studio. But you gotta help. Leave it to me."

Her halfhearted battle with fame ended that afternoon. They started peeling away the layers of the backwoods and eventually created a svelte love goddess to surpass Jean Harlow and Rita Hayworth. And it was as a love goddess that she would always be known.

The whirl of nightlife continued, spreading to the watering holes of fame. Paris, St. Moritz, Madrid, Rome, Acapulco. Sable coats trailed behind her, designer dresses were flown to her from Paris.

"I loved the Ava Gardner of that era. It was a daze of fun and excitement. It was the Ava Gardner up in lights that I didn't like," she once said.

After one too many late nights—with the exhaustion of dawn setting in—she was introduced to the stud of the music world, Artie Shaw. Their eyes met, pulses pounded—all that drivel for which Hollywood was so famous.

Either he was one of the most unphotogenic men of this century or Artie, with his wisps of hair and modeling clay face, was simply an unlikely lady killer—but his marriages to Ava, Lana, and the beautiful Evelyn Keyes proved otherwise. To one confidante, Lana described him as "simply wonderful in bed." Ava, asked about it, shrugged her shoulders. Evelyn Keyes wisely kept silent.

But Artie had something rare—almost extinct—in Hollywood: a fine mind. He read, recited Pulitzer Prize plays, and haunted art galleries. A matrimonial dictator, he demanded that his wives keep up with his intellectual passions. He positioned a chair for Ava next to a bookcase of the world's greatest books. He watched as she read. And read. And read. "But a lot of the times I just turned the pages," she said.

Ava's reluctant affair with the printed word ended about the same time as her marriage. "Didn't work," Ava said.

"No comment," said Artie.

During the late forties, Ava played the field—men from the front offices, stars between marriages, and many, many handsome unknowns. Then came Frank Sinatra, a fellow MGM star and one half of perhaps Hollywood's most beloved marriage. Nancy, his wife, traveled within the film milieu, doing as many good deeds as Marion Davies had done decades before. Both Louella Parsons and Hedda Hopper loved her, protected her, and appointed themselves as watchdogs over Frank's fidelity.

The Ava–Frankie affair knew no shame. They cavorted through not only the movie colony but the watering holes of Palm Springs and Catalina Island as well. Louis B. Mayer screamed at them; Hedda threatened ruined careers; and Nancy took to her house in the rightful guise of the wronged wife.

Then, in 1950, came "the Incident in Madrid," a crude public scandal of international proportions.

Ava, assigned to a nauseous picture, *The Flying Dutchman,* reported to Spain sans Frankie, who sat at home and imagined Ava in the arms of the Castilian men with long legs, mesmerizing eyes, and deft talent with their hands and lips. The action, hot as chili, was soon underway after Ava, bored on a Sunday, was escorted by friends to a bullfight in the smallish town of Tossa Del Mar. She was dressed in red and quaffing the harsh Spanish wine. Every eye was on her, but *her* eyes had settled on a bullfighter who was almost too handsome.

His muscular body sewn into a white suit of lights, he bowed to Ava after each bravado maneuver with the bull. An armful of roses was carried up to her in the stands by the dashing toreodor himself, Mario Cabre. Ava smelled the roses, nodded to Mario in acceptance, and vanished into the crowd.

More flowers and Mario's card were delivered on a silver tray along with the movie star's breakfast. It was the same at lunch. When Mario phoned before dinner, Ava—still bored because shooting schedules were held up—said, "Sure, why not?" It was no small coincidence that Mario Cabre ended up with quite a long vignette in *The Flying Dutchman* (over Ava's veto, by the way).

Several news items about Mario and Ava made the wire services, and Frankie phoned through the night to get his paramour on the phone. "Oh, for Christ's sake, Frank, this is a movie, a setup. Personally, the guy's a schmuck," answered Ava.

Frank seemed unconvinced, but, being in the middle of a film, he could do little about it.

Mario had huge brown eyes, wide shoulders, and half the girls of Madrid at his feet. Suddenly only Ava was real to him. Ava, used to the hangover that sometimes comes when actors begin living their parts, tried carefully and repeatedly to explain that they were not lovers.

"That was in the movie. Even when we saw each other, that was routine. Movie companies are close together."

Mario tried to hear what Ava was telling him. It seemed to him that she loved him but was afraid he didn't love her. "I, you—in love," he whispered. "Yours," he said, laying his hand over his heart.

Oh, Jesus Christ, thought Ava. This guy's getting to be a pain in the ass.

They drank more wine, causing them to stay just long enough in their Spanish cabaret for an Associated Press photographer to capture them on film. Frankie, hearing a Beverly Hills news vendor shouting "Ava, Bullfighter Seen in Hideaway," bought a ticket for Spain.

Luckily, he missed the most embarrassing spectacle of Ava's Andalusian interlude. The night the intrepid AP photographer had snapped the troublesome shot, Mario confided in hushed tones that he had been up night after night writing poetry for his "little Hollywood sparrow." With her usual sarcasm, Ava grabbed her purse, downed half a bottle of wine, and began walking away as Mario tried to read the poems. "Oh, go hire a hall if you have to do that," she snapped over her shoulder.

Which is exactly what he did.

Two days later Mario took the finest hall in town, decorated it with roses, and showered the town with flyers announcing his command performance. "My little Avita wants it," he told his banker, who desperately tried to keep from swooning as he counted out Mario's savings.

It was a blistering May 17. Mario wore a new shocking pink bullfight suit so tight that two men were needed to pull on the pants. His broad chest sparkled with rhinestones and silken stitchery. The house wasn't exactly what you would call SRO, but there were a goodly number of friends and diehard bullfight fans, enough to make it presentable. A raggedy orchestra played love songs, tunes from "Carmen," just before he marched in, painfully mounted the speakers' platform, and began leafing through the poems he'd written on rare parchment. There was a hush as the audience noticed his hands trembling violently. He started reading:

> *"Ava, Ava. My own sweet love.*
> *Your lips, your eyes, your hair of black.*
> *Your heart, your soul so like the dove."*

There were audible groans from the audience. With only two windows in the hall, the temperature was nearly ninety-eight degrees. The roses Mario had had hung from the ceiling began dropping their petals. But he continued:

> *"Full blown, a fragrant flower.*
> *Ava, Ava, a summer rose,*
> *Follow me, follow me*
> *To our little bower."*

That was too much. An Associated Press photographer laughed out loud, and a chorus of hecklers joined in.

Mario was a piteous sight. His silk suit of lights was drenched with sweat and had turned transparent. The tousled brown hair—his pride— had withered and was plastered to his head. Covering his pants with a newspaper, he dashed out the side entrance and rushed home.

A bit of wine-tasting here and there by Ava and her cardboard matador was one thing. The public humiliation of the poetry reading was too much for Frank. He walked out on the picture he was making and flew to Spain.

MGM ordered Frank to remain in America. By refusing, he forfeited his $5,000 pcr wcck salary and thc goodwill of his own studio, which was already incensed by their love affair—which was so public that gossip columnists were able to report on the type of Frank's underwear, on Ava's remarks during a private meal in her hotel room, and on what was said during Frank's telephone calls to Nancy back in Beverly Hills.

The Spanish press could see immediately that the real love affair was between Ava and Frankie, not between the actress and thc handsome but foolish Cabre. The couple strolled through the great open gardens that had once been the property of monarchs; he bought her a bundle of fifty balloons and showered her with gifts of gorgeous Spanish leather accessories.

But Sinatra wisely kept away from the location shooting, a particularly wise decision the day following his reunion with Ava. The producers had created a ceremony for the successful matador—played by Cabre— including thousands in the streets and flowers showering from the sky. But Ava wasn't in the scene. It was simply a crowd shot with Mario and hordes of extra players. Frank didn't ask about the filming; Ava didn't volunteer any information.

The gay parade had started by the time Ava could shake free of Frank. She ran through the streets to the set, arriving just as Mario's triumphal carriage rolled by. She was wearing her matador's favorite color —green—and her hair was flowing in the wind. She shoved and elbowed her way through the extras to get a front-row view. One of the directors saw her and leaped off his camera crane. "Ava's here," he told the producer. "Jesus Christ!" he said. "Get her out of here."

While a phalanx of security guards pushed through the throngs, Ava was able to move within feet of Mario's carriage. She threw him a flower. "Mario mio, Mario mio," she called as she blew kisses through the air.

Transatlantic telephone calls almost jammed the switchboards at the hotel as Hedda Hopper, Louella Parsons, Walter Winchell, and Earl Wilson got access to the lovers and extracted interviews.

"Ava, do you realize how bad this looks here?" Hedda asked. "You've both got some patching up to do."

Finally the filming had to come to an end, with Ava heading back to a furious MGM. As she sprawled on a couch at home, an MGM flunkie told her to be in Mayer's office at 9 A.M. the next day. "But, I'm just ba—"

"Nine A.M.—sharp," the aide ordered.

Mayer began screaming as soon as she was in the office. "Are you absolutely immoral?" he asked. "I can't think of anything else that would account for this behavior. Your career is badly in need of repair. And we'll do it—this one last time."

Ava was crestfallen. After all, here was Mayer, the man who called himself her "Pop." What could she say? She chanced it. "But Mr. Mayer, Frank and I are really in love."

"It's an itch. Get it out of your system and go back to work."

She never felt the same way about Mayer (or MGM) again.

The love between Frank and Ava must have been unusually strong for Hollywood. They braved Mayer's wrath, continued to date, and let their alliance be publicly examined under the harsh California sun. Marriage followed. Then divorce—twenty-three months later.

"See?" said Mayer to Ava. "Didn't amount to a hill of beans."

The ultimate glamour girl shrugged—much as Garbo had done whenever Mayer sat behind the desk that made him into a sort of creative Saint Peter deciding who got blessed and who didn't.

Love and passion, onscreen and off, were the overriding concerns in the front offices at MGM. Since the studio was carefully fashioned by Mayer around a corps of romantic actresses, box office depended on what might have been called a "love quotient." When Lana kissed Clark was she believable or merely rubbing lips? Was Joan Crawford too hard, too much the brash shopgirl to deal in true romance?

To control the sexual outbursts of the stars' offscreen romances, Mayer established a lovers' lane undercover network to end illicit affairs before careers were ruined and profits lost. And sometimes that "kiss patrol" could be counted upon to ease stars *into* offscreen romance, however phony, to excite the audiences.

It was no surprise, then, when Mayer summoned Mickey Rooney to his office and, with tears in his eyes, asked him how he thought America would accept "a married Andy Hardy."

Mayer had absolutely no qualms about crushing a love affair if he felt it would hurt the studio in any way. He had cleverly written special clauses into the stars' contracts that legally allowed him to even stop single stars from dating each other. They weren't just moral clauses, they were puritanical statutes. Visions of orgies enjoyed by movieland bachelors danced in his head—complete with garter belts from Frederick's of Hollywood and bizarre love machines manufactured by Amorous Alfredo, who operated in a back room not all that far from MGM itself.

Mayer rolled around voycuristically as he ferreted out the most salacious gossip. And he believed what he heard: about the director who allegedly surprised Tyrone Power kissing Rita Hayworth's bare breasts on the set of *Blood and Sand;* about Evelyn Keyes's description of the suave manner used by Frederic March to convince her to caress his thighs through the thin material of his tight pants in *The Buccaneer;* and about the behind-set harem supposedly hosted by singer John Boles in the dark reaches of Warner Brothers. It maddened him, maddened him to the extent that he told his assistant Eddie Mannix that the sexual side of the business operated under a "gray flannel suit" chauvinism. "The actors get all they want," Mayer snapped at Eddie. "We don't dare."

Mayer was like a diabetic in the Hershey candy factory. Therefore his battle against even innocent dalliances resembled the Salem witch trials. Catching a glimpse of Jean Harlow lightly running her fingers over Robert Taylor's lips, he flew into a trembling rage. Blatantly sexual, he thought to himself. And brazen. Disrespectful. He was about to call Jean out on the carpet when his secretary, Ida Koverman, called the set and found out that Jean was applying a particularly thick form of makeup required by Bob's director. She told Mayer, who shrugged and went back to his desk full of papers.

Mayer was also frightened of the sensual power lurking just below the surface of the studio's everyday life. His own greed, his knowledge that just the mere appearance of sex sold tickets, made the prude inside him recoil. Gorgeous still photographs taken to promote the studio's product sent blatant messages to the millions who read the country's daily movie pages and fan magazines. Quite often the MGM still artists created sensual tableaux that far exceeded the titillation onscreen. In one still from *The Flesh and the Devil*, Greta Garbo was draped over John Gilbert's stalwart frame, her eyes rotating in passion. One shoulder of her dress had slid down until one breast was exposed. Another photo from the same session had Greta's hands fingering the rear of John's hussar pants —which fit like a second skin. One Garbo fingernail appeared to be easing the cavalry pants down slowly.

Mayer the Victorian had approved them for release.

If he let his guard down at the wrong time, his studio was open for censorship and terrible government regulation. Thankfully, his secretary was a second pair of eyes.

One afternoon in the forties Mayer was viewing some special effects in his small screening room when Ida burst in and knelt at his side. "I was just looking at some of the rushes [daily film snippets printed to monitor the quality of the production]," Ida whispered to Mayer. "I think you ought to go over there and look at them yourself," she said.

"Nonsense!" said Mayer. "We can look at it later."

Ida grew insistent. She looked around the dark room, saw some other key executives, and lowered her voice even more. "Look," she hissed. "What I saw on that screen will make your skin crawl. And you do have to see it today because they are planning to film more of it tomorrow. If the press gets hold of this the whole studio's going to be in trouble." Mayer lurched out of his seat, practically dragging Ida across the lot to the sound stage used for musicals.

Lighting technicians had been checking a production number from a Judy Garland–Gene Kelly film, *The Pirate*, when they noticed the tasteless eroticism dominating the scene. Ida had been summoned and watched silently in a stunned state. Judy's staunchest friend on the lot, she had hidden the memos pouring onto the *Meet Me in St. Louis* set after Judy began arriving later and later each day. And it was Ida who, dawn after dawn, used the phone to coax the actress out of bed and into her limousine. The fiery number that had unfolded before her eyes, however, could neither be ignored nor covered up. Since *The Pirate* was being directed by Judy's husband, Vincent Minnelli, only Mayer could halt the disaster.

She had to listen to his whining protests during the long walk to the screening room. "Ida, this is a Cole Porter musical. When have we ever had censorship troubles with a musical?"

"Now!" Ida yelled, finally losing patience.

When Mayer had grumblingly settled into his seat, Ida gave the signal for the film to roll. It started simply enough: Gene, in a heroic pirate's uniform, dashed across the sound stage as part of a fantasy segment. (Judy was supposedly dreaming of her perfect lover.)

The lights suddenly changed from cool to torrid, and Gene's thighs seemed to burst from his pants. Then voodoo drums sounded in the background. Judy Garland, everybody's kid sister, unleashed her hair, her eyes wild and piercing. A slow tribal dance began. Gene, his legs spread far apart (bursting the seams of his tights), moved closer and closer to the gyrating Garland. The drums pounded faster, more erratic. They finally leaped into each other's arms, breast-to-breast, thigh-to-thigh. Just before the film ran out, Kelly was dancing against Judy in a manner that today would be called "humping."

It made the studio head, for one rare time, speechless. "Ida," he finally said. "Get every inch of this film and have it burned. I don't want the merest trace of a frame to remain."

Word was discreetly passed to Gene and Vincent Minnelli, and a more palatable number substituted. In the long run, even this substitute was scrapped. Judy seemed to be kissing, to quote Mayer, with a bit too much joy showing on her face. "People don't seem to realize that this girl, married to her director, is burning her ass over her co-star with her husband looking on," Mayer explained later.

If onscreen dalliance made Mayer tipsy with anger, offscreen love between his serfs—he actually used the term at times—sent him into orbit. Mayer, either for real or for effect, had developed a technique over the years that guaranteed the imposition of his will. "Louie's swoons," some called them. "Freudian faints" was the label preferred by others. The mogul's gutsier assistant, Eddie Mannix, would often wisecrack, "Little Miss Louie has the vapors." Ida Koverman, however, believed them to be real. And it was she, after all, who had to pick him up off his oriental carpet time and time again.

He had just such a carefully orchestrated fall—he never seemed to crumple his suits or scuff his shoes—when an old friend called him from Topanga Canyon one evening at dusk.

"Mr. Mayer," said the lady, the keeper of a small inn often favored by the Mayer family on weekends, "I feel I have to tell you something. Gosh, I feel like a rat doing it, but we're friends, and you gotta know."

Mayer expected a report about still another John Barrymore drinking bout or, at the worst, some intelligence about an MGM star dealing with a rival producer in the relative obscurity of Topanga Canyon, which was barely developed at that time.

"Clark Gable's still married, isn't he?" the tipster asked.

"Sure and happily," Mayer answered, referring to Ria Gable, a mainline socialite who had defected to Hollywood.

"What about Crawford? She and Doug still married?"

"Of course," snapped Mayer, tiring of the cat-and-mouse fishing expedition. "Joan and Doug are one of the happiest couples I know. What the hell are you getting at?"

"You don't have to believe me if you don't want," she said. "But Joan and Clark have been coming up here every week—sometimes two, three times a week. And they ain't up here fishing."

"I don't believe it," he said.

"Well, come on up here and ask the guys who live around the lake. Don't just take my word for it. I only sell 'em lunch."

He was thunderstruck. Considering the entire MGM star stable to be his children, he liked to think he knew each of their secrets, no matter how dark or perverse (in much the same way as a mother knows about the *Playboy* magazines secreted away in her son's sweatsocks). The tipster could almost smell the fear through the phone.

"Thanks," he stuttered. "Thanks. I won't forget you."

Not since he had learned that Jean Harlow and Paul Bern were headed toward the altar without his permission had he been caught so off guard. The consequences to the studio could be devastating. Both Clark and Joan were among the top-ten box office draws. Both had publicized their idyllic and happy marriages, and both were intimate favorites of Louella Parsons, queen of gossip columnists, and of the press in general. Public knowledge of, as Mayer described it, "this sordid, sneaky little romp in the hay," would anger the fans and betray Louella and the rest of the Hollywood journalistic establishment.

In the outer office Ida heard the thump signifying Louie's elegant slide into the twilight zone. With soda water, a moist towel, and some ammonia, she coaxed him back into the real world—if MGM could, in any way, resemble the real world. "What is it?" she asked.

He held up his hand, nodded his head. That meant "buzz off" in the Mayer sign language. He wasn't ready to talk about it and wouldn't be for weeks. He felt the deepest of betrayals. Had it been any other pair on the lot his reaction would have been milder.

But Clark was almost a buddy. The most popular actor in the world would often saunter into the office of that most monarchical of producers, fall into a chair, sling one leg over the priceless velvet arm, and flick paper clips at Mayer. Marks of even higher esteem were the frequent invitations Clark received to dine with the big man alone. (The only other given that commissary privilege was Irving Thalberg.) There had been few secrets between Mayer and his most valuable star. Until now!

As for Joan, she was Daddy's best little girl. When he told her to wear a baby doll dress and sing a toneless song in *The Hollywood Revue*, there was no complaint. When she appeared in a chic Parisian slacks outfit at a command performance to greet French exhibitors, Mayer pulled her out

in the hall. "Where do you think you're at—a labor union picnic? You're
Joan Crawford. You go home and don't come back until you look like
her." She was back in less than an hour in black velvet, cascades of dark
mink, and an egret feather hairpiece. "Lovely, Joan darling," Mayer said.
When she had told him of her plan to marry Doug, Jr., tears formed in
Mayer's cold eyes. Now this!

His wrath extended to his staff, his directors, his closest lieutenants.
"You don't fall in love before a thousand people and keep it a secret,"
Mayer raved.

True enough. As soon as Joan and Clark reported to film *Possessed*,
the director, Clarence Brown, noticed a rapport that, at first, seemed like
a brotherly–sisterly sort of thing. "He got her coffee, stuff like that,"
Brown later said. As the script drew them together, Brown realized it was
not a family affair and that Joan was nobody's tomboy. "I guess it's
appropriate to mention now that I noticed the attachment growing into
a slow burn," he said. "It showed. By saying the right things or positioning
the stars in a certain way, I was able to make use of a raw material. I knew
the audiences would see it also."

Dozens of movie love gods and goddesses have droned on through
the years about the impossibility of approaching love scenes cold and
keeping them that way. "Hell," said Jean Harlow. "If they had dumped
a barrel of dry ice on us after I fell into Clark's arms during that steamy
afternoon in *Red Dust*, we would have still broken a thermometer."

Lana Turner, another aficionado of the clinch, says the warm glow
of any love scene starts with the script. "I remember sitting at home
reading the shooting pages for *Somewhere I'll Find You* and beginning
to think of Clark as that character [he co-starred]. Tears were rolling down
my cheeks, and I hadn't even practiced the dialogue.

"But, hell, that doesn't mean that you fall madly and passionately
in love with the actor you cling to on the set. And it doesn't even mean
there's anything overpoweringly physical. It only means that a pattern of
communication emerges. Both of you suddenly know what it would be like
if you were those two people. But, honey, that is all."

Lana's analysis isn't inappropriate to the developments between
Clark and Joan during the shooting of *Possessed*. They brought an inten-
sity for each other to the set—a sort of predestination. Joan had become
enthralled with the raw power Gable showed when he slapped the elegant
Norma Shearer nice and hard during an earlier film. Here was a new
screen lover, unafraid to take on a bit of the caveman.

Their lackluster marriages also served to set them up for a meaningful

Mickey Rooney and Ava Gardner at a brunch following their wedding. Appearances aside, many at Metro felt this to be the ideal storybook romance. But Ava hadn't yet become a femme fatale, and Mickey wasn't the ladies' man he was to become in the years following their breakup. The marriage lasted only a few months.

Ava Gardner at the height of her beauty and between her marriages to
Frank Sinatra and Mickey Rooney.

The infamous love scene between Kathryn Grayson and Mario Lanza in *The Toast of New Orleans*. Grayson, dismayed at Lanza's attempts to french kiss and his lewd pawing, finally had brass knuckles sewn into her costume and used them to belt him the next time he tried. *Below:* As love scenes went, Kathryn Grayson didn't like Frank Sinatra much better than Mario Lanza. "He was like kissing a monkey," she said.

Joan Crawford and Clark Gable in a shot taken at the height of their love affair. Mayer vetoed the photo, knowing of their dalliance.

encounter. Ria Gable, a motherly figure who had taught Gable to dress, to dance at a ball, and to converse with the best of the phonies, was organized, predictable, and mannered. Ever the "jazz baby," Joan roared through the café society of Hollywood and New York like quicksilver— once walking out of the Coconut Grove in mid-dance and driving to the Pacific, where she swam out to the Malibu rocks still wearing her Chanel dress. Her husband, Douglas Fairbanks, Jr., one of the handsomest men in Hollywood history, had been brought up in England, the East, and Paris. He wore a tuxedo like nobody else in California, but he lacked the bravado needed to humble Hollywood. He was a crown prince reticent to use his sword. So it was a setup.

A mad dash through the romantic and hidden bowers of Southern California began and lasted, according to Joan (who truthfully talked about it only before she died), "Many, many, many months longer than most people thought."

It was on one such dash that Mayer's tipster first saw them. A coincidence, she thought the first time. Fishing maybe, she thought the next time. But when Joan in fox furs and Gable in dinner clothes drove up the canyon the jig was up.

Besides the director, Clarence Brown, only Jean Harlow, perhaps Clark's best friend, knew the full force of the love affair. "And oh he wanted to marry her," Jean told her friend, columnist Dorothy Manners. "I think he always knew it would never happen. But he was more romantic about Joan than anyone until he met Carole Lombard."

Joan, always enigmatic, never disclosed the depth of her feelings for Clark. When journalist Adela Rogers-St. Johns found out about their secret meetings and conduct on the set, she sailed into Joan's house one morning, catching the actress still at breakfast. She knew that Doug, Jr., was away filming, so she came right to the point. "Are you ready to go through the indignities of a divorce?"

"I don't know," Joan answered in the cold voice she sported off the set.

"Well, honey, you better think about it. That would mean walking out on an obviously faithful husband to steal another woman's man."

Joan listened, admitting the risk. Forty years later a sick Joan said of the affair: "Sure Clark and I had an affair, a glorious affair, and it went on a lot longer than anybody knows . . . much longer."

Both superstars were risking all they had worked for in a town where almost nobody—from the office boy to Louis B. Mayer—endangered his career and wealth because of something as innocent as love.

"Love!" That was a word for the theater marquees. But they were soul mates, according to Joan, and this made them toss caution into the Malibu breakers as they tore through the night, careening about both physically and spiritually.

"Clark and I were both from the Midwest," Joan told Roy Newquist. "We were both peasants by nature, not too well educated and insecure. We felt sort of safe and home again when we could get together. We both had a built-in bullshit alarm system. But the only times we could really talk about it, and laugh at what went on, was when we were together."

This wild careening through their own terrified souls was soon to end in an Armageddon forced by Mayer, who had finally controlled his anger enough to confront them.

Shortly before this confrontation, however, while Joan and Clark were sitting on a deserted beach, she had suggested the unthinkable. "Why don't we both get divorces so we can marry?" Clark nodded.

Most of Joan Crawford's friends believe this backward proposal was made because of an interlude that had lasted longer than any in her life. She felt comfortable. For a few minutes, with Clark, she was able to slip out from under the monster-like Joan Crawford she'd so carefully constructed. Her determination was never to be tested.

Mayer knew he couldn't very well confront them both without making their affair a bigger issue than it already was. Besides, Joan, perhaps the stronger of the two, might tell him to go to hell and drag Clark off with her—perhaps even to another studio. Yep, Clark was definitely the weaker, the easier to conquer.

So a summons was issued. "Do you have a death wish?" Mayer asked the star. "Because if you don't, you're headed for sure self-destruction."

Looking back at the incident through the legends that grew up around Gable, it's hard to imagine Rhett Butler slinking out of Mayer's office with a bow and a scrape, promising to give up his shopgirl Scarlett O'Hara. But then, the legend was still small compared to what it would become. The year was 1931. MGM had just talked its way out of the silents, and Clark Gable had been a star for only four years—most of those in the shadow of silent star holdovers John Gilbert and Ramon Novarro. MGM Publicity hadn't even found an image for him yet—other than advising Makeup to "please" tape his ears closer to his head. ("This isn't a zoo," publicity chief Pete Smith had replied.)

Clark Gable was not an outdoorsman when he made his rawboned way into Hollywood. He didn't stride about in riding breeches, drift down to the deserts of Baja California to rough it with cactus and snakes, nor was he the beloved "man's man" who tore up the streams and let the booze flow up in Montana. In 1931, when Joan was batting her eyes and suggesting marriage, Clark was still going to an acting coach.

The best stone face he could muster helped Mayer convince Clark that he meant business. This wasn't friendship. This was money. No joking here. "Been having a lot of fun with Joan, huh?" challenged the boss.

Gable gave the office rug far more attention than was necessary. "What could I say?" he later told Louella Parsons. "The least important curtain hanger knew about us. Some people even looked the other way."

Mayer reached in his desk drawer and pulled out the latest still of Joan Crawford. "See this face?" he said. "Well, forget it." Clark nodded.

"I was such a new star that he could have ended my career within fifteen minutes after I walked out of that office," he later said. "I had no interest in being a waiter."

The studio chief's powers of retribution kept most MGM stars trembling for the better part of forty years. When the silent film star Francis X. Bushman failed to accept a dinner invitation with Mayer in Rome during the late twenties, Mayer didn't even wait until his return to Hollywood. That night he dictated a twenty-five-page telegram to studio executives, stating that the actor's contract would not be renewed and that he wanted him blackballed throughout the industry.

It had all been a mistake. Bushman's valet, a new servant, had taken it upon himself with misguided zeal to trash the Mayer message and refuse for his boss. Mayer was on the boat for America before Bushman could determine what had happened. He cabled immediate apologies. No answer. Back in America, he wrote a series of letters to Mayer at both the studio and his home. No answer. Finally, in desperation, he called the studio. There was a wait of about five minutes before Mayer told his secretary (in a voice that carried over the telephone), "Tell that bastard I'll never talk to him again." Bushman, one of the five most famous screen names of the movies' first decade, was dead as far as mainstream Hollywood was concerned.

Mayer did the same to Mae Murray and dozens of others.

Clark Gable turned heel and went back to work.

Joan found out in less than an hour, realizing that their relationship was reduced to polite telephone conversations and whatever silent rapport they could achieve on the set.

A stylish, romantic script, *Letty Lynton,* had been fashioned for Joan with Clark Gable in mind as the co-star. "Get over to this office, and get over here right now," ordered Mayer, finding Joan undergoing fittings in the costume department.

In a white, ruffled, trailing chiffon, she ran the half mile to the throne room. "I'm not going to tell you what I think about 'your problem with Clark,'" he said. "But you and Gable will not be together on this picture. The romance will stop. Or you know what will happen."

Joan Crawford walked onto the set of *Letty Lynton* in her billowing white dress five days later and worked with the Clark Gable substitute as if he was her ideal leading man. But ten minutes after shooting ended on the first day, Clarence Brown saw her crying, her head on the dressing table.

Gable, of course, went on to marry Carole Lombard, culminating perhaps the greatest love story in Hollywood history—a story that ended in abject despair when Carole's plane crashed into a mountainside.

Clark found that the tender, heartfelt connection he'd made with Joan hadn't diminished over the years. Joan heard the news while shooting stills for a war bond promotion (how ironic that Carole Lombard had died on a bond tour). She ran out of the studio while the camera was still clicking.

"Give me one of my little blue notes," she told her maid. "The personal ones—down in the bottom." She scrawled a quick message and sent it to Gable, on another stage. "I'll be home tonight, if you need to talk. Joan," it said.

Joan went home immediately, cleared the house of servants, put on a quiet blue dress, and waited—the lights burning into the night. Time drifted by. Joan couldn't read or even loosen up with a drink. She just sat —immobile and waiting. There was a quiet knock. "Come in," she said with a tremulous voice.

Clark stood just inside the door with his shoulders sagging and his eyes dead. Joan was equally still—whatever passed between them needed no words. Then the door shut. Clark came over to the couch, fell into Joan's arms, and shuddered. The lights in the big Crawford living room burned until dawn when Clark drove through the streets to the house he'd shared with Carole.

Kisses and their aftermath weren't all so deadly serious as long as they remained inside the make-believe fortress in Culver City. But they were important. It was axiomatic then—and now—that audiences found it hard to sympathize with heroines and their heros if they didn't make a pretense of contact, however fleeting.

During MGM's first half-century a great deal of time, diplomacy, and hard work went into fashioning trademark kisses for the MGM Girls. It was no problem for some, of course. Lana, Ava, Harlow, Garbo, and Hedy Lamarr took to their co-stars' lips as if they were magnetically attracted. But some of the others—starting way back at the beginning— proved to be as coy as an adolescent Memphis debutante.

The problem started with Lillian Gish, the star of stars in the monumental silent pictures of D. W. Griffith. She had been hired through a process that offered her MGM's first million-dollar contract. Unfortunately, it guaranteed her approval of everything from the lace on her underwear to the use of her lips.

When she arrived at the Culver City lot she found a banner soaring above MGM and across two streets. LILLIAN GISH IS NOW AN MGM STAR, said the banner under which paraded bands, a cart of roses, and lines of executives to greet her.

Since it was her choice, she selected the tragic *La Bohème* for her first production, with the studio's top-line director King Vidor to guide her. Lillian, pampered and convinced of her invincibility by D. W. Griffith, introduced a few bizarre practices to the lot—including full rehearsal. There were some grumbles until Vidor told Mayer that Lillian's system was helping them bring in the picture under budget and ahead of schedule.

Then "the affair of the kiss" began, almost bringing the picture down with it. As the lover of the doomed heroine, Mimi, MGM had of course provided the dashing John Gilbert, a man whose reputation was based on a sexy walk, a perfect body, languid eyes, and an ability to kiss equaled only by Valentino.

Vidor was leisurely plotting an outdoor scene one afternoon when Lillian walked up with her script. "Look at this, Mr. Vidor, there's a kiss and an embrace planned during these scenes. Now that is simply not right. Rudolphe [Gilbert] will demonstrate the powerful love he bears for Mimi if he doesn't embrace her at all—and he certainly shouldn't kiss her."

Known as "the great lover of the silent screen," John Gilbert was incensed and ran to Mayer's office. "This is a love story . . . a love story! Does she realize that?"

"What are you talking about?" Mayer asked.

"Lillian refuses to kiss me."

"What?" Mayer yelled.

"You heard me. She says the audience will believe our love more poignantly if we don't even touch," Gilbert said.

"Leave it to me," said Mayer.

Through a series of negotiations that would have strained a secretary of state, Mayer convinced Lillian that John Gilbert's career might truly be hurt if he simply mooned around making eyes at Mimi. And after three days of love scenes, Vidor managed to coax the actress closer and closer to John's embraces. He was achieving about one usable kiss every eight hours.

On the way home, Lillian complained to her chauffeur: "Oh, dear, I've got to go through another day of kissing John Gilbert." Protestations aside, Lillian must have been doing something right: John Gilbert proposed to her twice before they wrapped up filming.

Lillian Gish never truly became a major box office star for Metro, but she added greatly to its prestige. And there was one more all-out battle for a Gish kiss. This time she was filming the American classic *The Scarlet Letter*, which gave her the type of long-suffering scenes she did best.

Of course the film had to graphically show how Gish, as Hester, became pregnant and was forever forced to wear the adulteress' A. She pleaded, she trekked to Mayer's office three times, she offered her own versions of the script, and, grasping at straws, suggested that it be explained in the titles that ran before the scenes in the still silent movies.

"No, absolutely not," Mayer told Thalberg, who was now overseeing the Gish vehicles. "Irving, the way Lillian is working her way through these love scenes, the audience is going to think that the 'scarlet letter A' stands for abstinence."

Lillian never really threw her lips into those MGM pictures, but she did given them a sensuality that has endured long after the great wet kisses of Mae Murray, Pola Negri, and Gloria Swanson—the busiest lips of the twenties.

Screen kissing, MGM style, finally came into its own after World War II broke out. It was almost unpatriotic not to kiss the boys fighting for America. Andy Hardy kissed. Lassie kissed (giving Liz Taylor her very first). So did Jerry, the cartoon mouse—who did it underwater with Esther Williams. By the fifties the problem was not how to get them to kiss but how to make them stop.

The pure, somewhat pristine soprano Kathryn Grayson, chosen to receive *That Midnight Kiss*, from tenor Mario Lanza, finally ended up running from the set in hysterics on one occasion.

Kathryn, almost as beautiful a singer as Jeanette MacDonald, was no stranger to romance, having been hounded for years by the kissing millionaire Howard Hughes, and thought of herself as a singer first, an actress second, and a sex symbol (which some thought she was) third.

Mario didn't agree with her evaluation. He called Kathryn the "top tamata," to whom he would prove impossible to resist. Since the kisses combined music as well, the smooching went into overtime.

It was well into the second week when Kathryn ran screaming from the lips that framed Lanza's golden voice. "First," she told Mayer, "he purposely eats garlic before our scenes to make it all the more unpleasant. Then, when we have to hold the scene, he keeps ramming his tongue down my throat. It's the crudest thing I've ever been exposed to."

Mayer lent a sympathetic ear. "But, Kathryn, we do have to get the kiss. The movie is called *That Midnight Kiss.*"

Costume designer Helen Rose finally devised a cure. She borrowed a handful of brass knuckles from the prop department and stitched them inside Kathryn's costumes.

Sure enough, there was a love scene set for the next day. Mario, garlicked up as usual, moved in and applied the tongue power.

Kathryn, a slight, dainty lady, grabbed the brass in her silken sleeves and let her fist fly—right into the Lanza privates. "He never, never did that again," said Kathryn.

What kissing scene could top that? MGM found out soon enough.

Getting ready to make *Because You're Mine,* Lanza was in particularly bad shape. His weight could range from 185 pounds to almost 300. It was so unpredictable that the wardrobe department made seven versions of each costume he would have to wear in a film.

"Often he reeled onto the set drunk, causing us to close it down before the word got out to the gossip columnists," said the late Dore Schary, who had taken over control of the studio from Louis B. Mayer. The set was sealed around the clock since Lanza's scenes couldn't be done until he sobered up—a process that frequently took four hours.

The cast, crew, and some fellow actors had become used to his crudities, but his shy co-star in this film was devastated. Doretta Morrow was a lovely soprano who had been the toast of Broadway the year before in *Kismet,* and had been personally requested by Lanza, allegedly to head off another attempt to star him with Kathryn Grayson.

In some scenes he reeled against her, overpowering the soprano with his body odor and generally unkempt condition. She shuddered at the thought of the love scenes, telling her costumer, "I don't know why I came out here anyway. This is a nightmare."

Everyone was tense as Lanza and Doretta were "walked through" the scene by an assistant director who noticed Doretta's discomfort. "It'll be okay," he said. "Remember, everybody's with you." The first shots turned out fine, although Lanza repeatedly tried to force his tongue down his co-star's throat.

A recess was called so that additional makeup could be applied. During the recess Lanza disappeared behind a scene and pulled raw garlic out of a pocket, chewing it as if it were gum.

"That's a strange thing to do," said Lanza's makeup technician.

"It's not so strange. I'm gonna get that bitch good." (He was referring to her gentle complaints to management.)

During the closeups, Lanza lurched against Doretta as if she were a rape victim. Then he turned to the cast and crew, saying with a sneer, "And she calls that a kiss." The language deteriorated from there; there wasn't a single entry in the dictionary of sexual slang that he didn't use. He implied that Doretta was hot for his body and that she was simply a tease. Doretta began sobbing so violently that it took two costumers to get her back to her dressing room.

A limousine with Doretta's agent picked her up at a side door half an hour later. "I'm not coming back," she said.

Dore Schary and five of MGM's top executives held a summit conference with Doretta that resulted in her agreement to finish the film. (But all of her future scenes with Lanza took place with two big security guards at their side.)

The next morning at 6 A.M. Lanza rolled out of semiconsciousness to hear the shrill voice and insistent knocking of Hedda Hopper. "Mario Lanza, you open this door and you open it right now."

Lanza pulled the covers up over his face and rolled over.

"I mean it!" yelled Hedda. "Do you want the 'Doretta Morrow incident' spread all over this afternoon's paper?"

He reluctantly obliged. Pouring coffee down him (he was already late), The Hopper—as so many called her—began her lecture. "My, my, my," she said. "So the great lover of the musical screen has to bully a sweet little girl just to get a kiss. Look, buster, I don't care if you ruin your voice. I don't care if you kill yourself by drinking all day. But you're not going to get away with hurting anyone else." She turned on her heel and left.

Mario never slobbed up a love scene again. In at least one of his pictures, *For the First Time,* he was finally awed by one of the MGM Girls, Zsa Zsa Gabor. "Goddamned, she's the most beautiful woman I've ever seen," he said.

"Yeah," said Lanza's valet. "And I bet you don't french kiss this one."

Not all the love scenes during the thirties and forties were controlled, or even initiated, by men. Katharine Hepburn, Norma Shearer, Jean Harlow, and Joan Crawford (especially Joan Crawford) had to literally shove their co-stars into the clinch. "Sometimes I had to do it," said Crawford. "Especially if an actor was new and frightened by kissing a supposed sex symbol, I'd have to jump at him. And, brother, he learned pretty quick that all that 'sex goddess' bunk was stuff for the fan magazines. I had one guy tell me he'd been kissed better by a blind date in high school."

Even the great Garbo sometimes had to build a fire under a young co-star—especially Robert Taylor in *Camille*.

Taylor, admittedly scared out of his wits, fidgeted and pulled further and further inside himself when it came time for him to sweep "Camille" off her feet. It might have been easier for him if the lovely lady next to him had been the real Marguerite Gautier. He was shaking so badly at one point that a cameraman whispered to him, "Your face is going to look like the San Francisco earthquake if you don't settle down."

The love scene came after Camille had one of her grand faints—a touch of the vapors as they used to call it. She had to leave a party and collapsed onto a couch in a conveniently private room. Taylor, already smitten, followed her and knelt down beside her on the small couch. His hands still had made no move to caress the Garbo shoulders, and the director was getting impatient. That was a rare occurrence for George Cukor, Greta's favorite director and a man known for the artistry of his love scenes. Greta could sense Cukor's slow burn from behind the camera and the growing fear inside Taylor.

With the camera running, Greta moved closer without touching, letting one hand drift near his chin. Then she began kissing him lightly all over his face. Her eyes were lowered and Robert Taylor's breath was quite obviously taken away. Greta kissed him slightly less than a hundred times, fashioning each one differently from the other.

"It was pure eroticism," said Cukor. "It provided the uncensored thought flashed by Greta to the audience. She could let them know what she was thinking and that she was thinking them uncensored. She never touched him but it didn't matter. Greta was cool but seething underneath."

MGM love scenes, obviously, sometimes continued into the limousine, through the streets of Beverly Hills, and into one of the mansions lost up there in the fog. There is no proof that Greta deftly led Robert Taylor, called the handsomest man in Hollywood, into bed. But he did go home with her, being asked for dinner at the end of the day's shooting. And he was there all night.

Whatever happened during those hours will never be known. Bob refused to discuss it—even with his good friends Gable and Ronald Reagan. Greta had recruited still another protector of her glorious privacy.

Roz Russell had a somewhat similar (if less exalted) problem on her hands while trying to capture Ronald Colman's physical attentions in an Arab-and-sand epic, *Under Two Flags*. It was to have been one of the standard love scenes, successful without fail since the days of Rudolph Valentino. Roz's svelte figure was draped in cloth that the desert wind obligingly melded to her curves, the horse was flying, and Ronald, in his officer's uniform, was standing by stalwartly.

Simplicity itself, the director had said. Roz and Ron would slide torridly together when her horse stopped in front of their rendezvous. Ronald, an Academy Award winner and the perfect British gentleman, offered his gloved hand, and disengaged Roz from her horse as if she'd arrived for tea with the Queen of Rumania.

Such a bellow was emitted from director Frank Lloyd that the company doctor rushed to the set. "No, no, no, no, no," he said to Ronald. "Slide her down your body. This is a love scene, and Roz isn't your secretary."

They got that scene in one take, leaving time for a full British tea on the set.

Then came the action. With hair blowing and Colman striding to her like the ladies' man he was supposed to be, the two met for the clinch.

After the debacle with the horse, Roz had gone all out. Arpege perfume had been sprayed on her by the pintful. She'd used mouthwash, made up her face until it glowed with that romantic look only Max Factor could create, and opened her lips wide in a manner halfway between the style of Marlene Dietrich and that of Judy Canova.

Their lips met, brushed against each other, and the camera kept running. Still, Ronald wouldn't kiss her on the mouth. And Roz burned. She may have been no Harlow but she was one hell of a good-looking dame. And damn it, he was going to kiss her manly and forcefully if she had to grab his jaw with her hands. She let her lips form into a pout. No luck. She stretched them in that fine line for which Joan Crawford was famous. No good. She even tried the "bee-stung" look that had worked so well for Mae Murray.

Frank Lloyd, having lasted through twenty-five kisses, called it a night and walked disgustedly off the set.

Later, over coffee, Roz asked her makeup man why "Ronnie won't kiss me."

The makeup artist dissolved in laughter. "Roz it wasn't Ronnie; it was you. You kept trying to drag him into one of those lurid kisses we used to have in the silents. A kiss like that just photographs lewd. Ronnie was doing it right—from the side."

"I must admit, Ronnie handled it very well," said Roz. "Here he was trying to play out the kiss outlined in the script, and there was I desperately clutching him with fevered lips."

Roz survived with her lip versatility intact. "But I never became one of those whom everyone wanted to do a love scene with," she said. Trouble was, she wanted to kiss like Mae West but came off like a late-model Norma Shearer—thus, no hot-blooded kisses for her.

Added to the problems of creating believable love scenes were the rules of censorship, which might have seemed a bit conservative to the Puritans. A scene was cut from a Joan Crawford picture, for instance, because her sigh was just "too erotic." And there was a long, bitter battle over love scenes in the Lana Turner–John Garfield classic, *The Postman Always Rings Twice*. The same censors who had passed the scenes when they first saw the script, called for spirits of ammonia when they saw the finished version.

What was the matter? asked Mayer. Was it because they were wearing bathing suits? Nope, came the critics' reply. Is it because they roll in the sand in a slightly frenzied manner? No, indeed, said the prim guardians of American movie kisses.

Finally, Mayer gave up. "What the hell is wrong?"

"Well," said one particularly timid man. "It's Lana Turner's hair."

"I don't get it," said Mayer.

"Well, can't you see? It's platinum," said the man with the moral scissors.

"So what?"

"It makes it cheap; it's an affront to Lana's character. She must be turned into a honey blonde."

Mayer appealed this decision to the full censorship board, finally winning approval for Lana's platinum look, "provided, of course, that it doesn't go flying around in great abandon."

"We'll put hair spray on it," said the disgusted Mayer as he left the offices.

MGM had similar trouble with the moralists in the runaway hit *The Thin Man* with Myrna Loy, William Powell, and Asta. Since the Dashiel Hammett mystery almost always centered on the bedroom of Nick and Nora Charles (Powell and Loy), censors flocked to the set like homing pigeons.

The Charleses' satin-covered twin beds were prim and proper, though luxurious, and had just enough room for Nick and Nora to develop their theories about the murder case they were working on.

All of the *Thin Man* movies relied on a very subtle romance between Loy and Powell. In their very first romantic interlude, filming had just begun when a dictatorial little censor stopped the show and pointed out that both Powell and Loy had to have one leg on the floor during the whole scene.

"You should have seen it," said Myrna many years later. "With one leg each on the floor we could barely get our lips together. We had to use our necks like turtles—stretching and stretching until we finally got in a little love peck."

Then Asta, the wire-haired terrier who was always with Nick and Nora, was tossed onto the bed for his scene, which consisted of leaping and bumping about with his masters.

"I suppose he's gotta have one leg on the floor?" asked Powell. "Well, I'll tell you what. I've talked to him and it isn't in his contract."

Perhaps the most celebrated screen kiss—the device that turned Liz Taylor from a little girl into a developing beauty—was so well publicized that some magazines described in detail how Liz would carry herself during every one of the twenty-five seconds the kiss would last.

The film was *Cynthia* and the actor selected to break in the lips that would become the most famous in movies was Jimmy Lydon, who escorted her to a prom under the watchful and worrying eyes of Liz's screen parents, George Murphy and Mary Astor.

Liz was ready for that kiss: for weeks she had been practicing on a satin pillow and watching herself in the mirror. First she let her hands tug at the top of the pillow, then let them drift down the satin sides. She gave the pillow a peck. Then a french kiss. Then a lengthy nuzzle à la Garbo.

Few actresses preparing for Lady Macbeth put as much time and agony into rehearsal. And when the time came, she froze on the set, let Jimmy kiss her, and went dashing off to the ice cream wagon. The future "Cleopatra" had been just another girl in pigtails.

BOOK TWO

Crowned Heads

Ah, the passion and luxury of the twenties! Greta Garbo before she was ordered to hide away and create a legend of loneliness.

4

Fool's Gold

THE GREAT GARBO HOAX

The lights in the small house in a Beverly Hills canyon were still burning at 3 A.M. The curtainless windows were open to the night air, but privacy was ensured by thick eucalyptus trees planted specifically for that purpose.

In the bedroom, furnished with an inexpensive bed and a rickety makeup table, a tall, angular woman lay surrounded by newspapers, magazines, and Sunday supplements in calculated disarray. Her dirty blonde hair was kept out of her eyes by a dime store barette. Languidly she picked up one clipping after the other, reading for a few seconds and then reaching into the mountain of journalistic claptrap for another morsel. As she read she seemed to gather sustenance, and a narcissistic confidence showed itself in the glow of her eyes and the slight upturn of her mouth —a Mona Lisa expression, they call it.

It was a scene not lacking in loveliness. The amber light etched the lines of her perfect body, and the sheet draped around her might have been arranged by an artful designer. Manet or Delacroix might have painted the tableau—so rich was it in texture. But had anyone in Hollywood or, indeed, the world, been told the name of the lady he almost certainly would not have believed the report.

For the solitary woman was the great Greta Garbo. And the clippings, slick magazines, and gossip columns were stories about her. Garbo carried out this careful ritual to reaffirm who she was and what she had become.

The Great Garbo, so publicly disdainful of her fame and glory, secretly drank the elixer of her own renown in a manner that would have made an adolescent girl blush. Of particular interest to her were the fan magazines, those pastel confections written for matrons under hair dryers and slavish fans with nothing better to do. Each week, Greta's faithful house servants, whom she had imported from Sweden, were dispatched to gather the magazines, newspapers, and rotogravure sections. So carefully did she read them that her houseman was sent back to the newsstand with any duplicates to collect a refund. It was the same when the magazines were found to contain nothing about her—she would pout and send them back.

"She always locked herself away from everyone whenever she received the large bundles of foreign newspapers and magazines that her brother and mother sent every few weeks," said her houseman. "After Garbo had read all the American magazines she would have me wrap them up in heavy brown paper and mail them to her mother, underlining the articles about her which she particularly liked. It became an obsession with her."

The Great Garbo was a groupie to her own image—a hypocritical star unique in film history. But so strong was her legend that no one penetrated her celluloid shell to find the shallowness and chilly soul lurking just beneath.

Greta and the solitude she built up around her blended into a hoax that was so commercially successful that MGM stuck its corporate thumb in the dike every time it started to leak. But underneath they knew, as did Greta, that it was all a mistake to begin with—all of it: the stardom, the image as a love goddess, and even the reputation as the screen's greatest actress.

Perhaps Mayer and Thalberg were protective and guarded her because they refused to admit that they were wrong about her from the beginning; that they had been ready to send her back home until a screen test was forced down their throats.

It was Mayer who made the first mistake. After seeing a fairly obscure Swedish film in the mid-twenties, Mayer decided that he must woo the film's director to America, not necessarily because the director was so good but because MGM had to find its own version of the foreign masters then being imported by Paramount and Fox.

So it was off to Europe for Mayer with a contract in his pocket for the Scandinavian Mauritz Stiller. Stiller, whose word was law in Swedish film circles, arrogantly showed up with a rather untidy, plump actress who sprawled into a chair and followed Stiller's every move with her eyes.

"I will come," said Stiller. "But she goes with me," he said, gesturing toward Garbo.

"Okay," said Mayer, offering her about $250 a week. He turned back as he left the room. "And tell her that in America, we don't like fat women."

Now Greta didn't speak English, but she knew a nasty tone of voice when she heard it. And she never thereafter thought of Mayer as anything but a "gross pig," as she told MGM art director Cedric Gibbons.

They arrived by transatlantic liner in New York. There was a solitary reporter from *The New York Times* to interview Stiller and a phalanx of photographers who walked past Greta as if she were a lady's domestic arriving on a green card. In truth, she looked the part. Her shapeless dress, frazzled hair, and puffy face hardly identified her as America's next superstar.

Two MGM publicity functionaries had received a memo from Mayer the day before that said, in so many words, "We're stuck with her so try to make the best of it." One of them finally gave a ten-dollar bill to each of four photographers to shoot Greta as she leaned against the docking ramp holding a wilted bouquet of roses (borrowed quickly from a departed passenger).

"Where on earth did they get this one?" society columnist Maury Paul quipped to one of the studio flacks.

The man leaned over and confided, "It was a package deal. We couldn't get Stiller without her."

"Ah," said Maury, "she'll be back in Sweden within a year."

The Swedes were then put aboard the Santa Fe train for the Coast. And while MGM put out no brass bands, when they arrived in Pasadena there were at least a handful of reporters, including Louella Parsons, to buzz around Greta. After half an hour of trying to pull an interview from the star, Louella finally called the *Los Angeles Herald* and reported that there was no story—unless, of course, they wanted to print an interview that consisted mostly of "Yah" and "Nooo."

It was assumed by Stiller and Greta that Mayer was a man of his word. After all, he'd been so congenial in Sweden, promising the moon. A script was rushed out, *The Torrent,* an elegant soap opera that made Greta cry when it was translated for her. Unfortunately, when she cried she began to eat, and the cheekbones would disappear again. "Oh shit," said Mayer. "We better work on her fast."

A screen test was ordered and completed in three days. Poorly lit,

Greta was just off the boat when MGM publicist Pete Smith talked her into this silly picture in an ermine-lined coat. *Below:* This MGM publicity shot was killed by Mayer when he saw how plump and dowdy she appeared. "Tell her we don't like fat women in America," he told her director, Mauritz Stiller.

dreadfully costumed, and crudely printed, it convinced Thalberg and Mayer to postpone *The Torrent* and try Greta in some cheapie productions first. Stiller told Greta to go home to the Santa Monica hotel suite they shared together and wait for his call. He had the test run for him several times, spotting the problems instantly. Without MGM's blessing, he decorated a small corner of a sound stage with oriental touches, draped a panel of black velvet around Greta Grecian-style, and shot her in a Rembrandtish light.

While running the new test through the movieola, editors stammered, "Jesus Christ, what a beautiful woman." The gossip spread quickly, leaving Mayer and Thalberg no choice but to cover their collective asses. They agreed behind closed doors to wipe out all traces of the early test, informing the New York office that Stiller's version was the only version, adding that it had been ordered by them.

Meanwhile, the overanxious publicity department roped Greta into a series of publicity stunts that would have shamed P. T. Barnum. They made her don track attire (which revealed her ungainly shoulders) and had her run with the UCLA track team. She was snapped strumming a mandolin outside the Miramar Hotel, depicted cuddling a quite dirty pet monkey, and shown candidly kissing the MGM lion, which sported a better coiffeur than Greta.

Far more detrimental were the interviews conducted one after the other in routine studio fashion. By this time, she had learned a little English. "How do you like Hollywood?" she was asked by Louella. "The climate, I like it," she answered. What about her relationship with Stiller? "He's a great director, and we live together," she responded. Her favorite form of relaxation? "To swim in the nude," she snapped. "In the nude?" asked Adela Rogers-St. Johns. "What's wrong with that," Garbo retorted. "Have you ever known of a fish to wear a swimsuit?"

"We've got to find a way to shut her up," Mayer told MGM's head publicist, Pete Smith. "When she opens her mouth—shit comes out."

In spite of the odd press, Greta's first film, *The Torrent*, pleased the public. Audiences forgot about Ricardo Cortez, Metro's answer to Rudolph Valentino, whenever Greta appeared onscreen. Looking at the film today, it's difficult to imagine what fans saw in the posturing, wide-eyed, frizzy-haired actress who moved like a sleep walker. At one preview in Riverside, Irving Thalberg journeyed into the back country to test the reactions himself. "You could feel the electricity. People sitting all around me were enthralled."

The demand for prints of *The Torrent* exceeded supply as the word spread through the Loew's Distribution Company, MGM's parent corporation. This was just the sort of reaction Louis B. Mayer hated. A star had been born without his guidance, but, more importantly, without the careful control the studio had over such home-grown stars as Joan Crawford and the obedient, fawning Norma Shearer.

A summit conference was held to deal with Greta's obvious public relations problems. And it was at that meeting that the Great Garbo Hoax was born. The conditions that led to her status as the most elusive, alluring star in Hollywood history were actually calculated as intricately as the studio budget.

It started with William Daniels, the ace MGM cameraman whose photographic talents had camouflaged the all-too-obvious faults of Joan Crawford and Norma Shearer. He noticed immediately that Greta was so unsure of herself, so jumpy, that even the presence of the crew drove her into a corner. He called up the prop department and ordered huge sheets of black canvas and maroon velvet to seal off her sets. The curtains and the secrecy were never abandoned during her long MGM tenure.

Shortly after Daniels closed Greta's sets, chance threw her in with a man who was to shape her and guide her with a Svengalian touch that altered the nature of star power forever. While making *Flesh and the Devil* with screen lover John Gilbert, Daniels introduced her to a nondescript, somewhat shy agent named Harry Edington. Over dinner one evening at Gilbert's mansion, Edington listened to Greta's chronic complaints about her paycheck (still about $500 a week) and the fear she had that her stardom would fade.

"You need an agent. Let me help you," he said.

Greta agreed and pleaded with Edington to deal with Mayer and Thalberg. "I don't like them, they don't like me," she said bluntly. "You talk to them."

A week later Edington met with Mayer and Thalberg in a three-hour session. "There's one thing I think will work," Edington said. "Since Greta can't deal with the press anyway, why don't we cut her off completely—from the press, the public, and even her fellow stars. We will fashion her into an unknown commodity. The less people know about her the better. Nobody can resist that strategy."

Edington even suggested a title—"the woman of mystery."

Bingo! Greta Garbo vanished from the public eye of Hollywood. Edington scoured Beverly Hills and found a house as secluded as a Spanish nunnery. It had a walled garden and a private road sealed by a gatehouse. Even the studio wasn't given the address.

It was also Edington who devised the Garbo costume that prevails today—gray and brown sacklike clothes, a battered old hat that came from the MGM costume department, and dark glasses on the order of Gloria Swanson's rococo frames in *Sunset Boulevard.*

Within a year Greta Garbo had turned her private life into the greatest performance she would ever give. There's absolutely no doubt about the chilly calculation that transformed a somewhat friendly, cheerful Swedish girl into a lonely legend. "Under the guidance of Edington and MGM loneliness became Garbo's most important product," said Howard Dietz, Metro's New York publicity executive for three decades.

Before the transformation, *Photoplay* magazine hired a team of private detectives to reconstruct a week in the life of Garbo, following her to gay public dinners in Mexican and Russian restaurants, shopping trips in downtown Los Angeles, and afternoon visits with fellow members of Hollywood's Swedish colony. *Photoplay* reported that they were never able to trace her this way again. "The new, hidden Garbo is a hoax," said the magazine in an editorial. "This is simply another creation of the dream factories."

Mauritz Stiller, her original Svengali, was perhaps the ultimate victim of the transformation. When they arrived together in New York and during their first weeks on the MGM lot, it was obvious to everyone that they were in love. "You could tell by the way they looked at each other," said Adela Rogers-St. Johns. "He was particularly smitten."

Stiller was a free-swinging director, running on intuition, with some degree of freedom on the set. MGM was a factory, and the Swedish director never finished a film there. He was forced to turn to Paramount for his only complete American film, *Hotel Imperial,* with Pola Negri.

As his fortunes disintegrated, Garbo's headed for the heights. But she continued to live with Stiller for several months (before Edington entered the picture).

Then Gilbert stalked into Greta's life. MGM legend (probably another of their fabrications) has it that the two fell in love during their first scene. "It was mad, passionate love, not acting," said an MGM publicist who had good reason to view it that way. Gilbert did make an immediate play for her, following her around the lot in his hussar's costume and begging for dinner dates and nights on the town.

She later told a friend that she had been "in love with Jack Gilbert for about fifteen minutes before the fleeting sensation evaporated."

There was nothing unusual about Gilbert's insistent passion. He had made a sexual play for all of his co-stars, marrying three of them. It seemed

Greta Garbo didn't emerge, gloriously beautiful, from the sea on a conch shell.

These MGM portraits show her before and after the studio worked its magic.

to juice him up for the breathless, thrashing love scenes for which he was famous.

Garbo remained cool, continuing to share the hotel suite on Santa Monica beach with Stiller. One night after dozens of martinis, Gilbert drove down to the beach, crashed his car into a post below the Garbo–Stiller balcony, and began calling for Greta and challenging Stiller to a midnight duel (with what weapons he intended to fight it was uncertain).

There was silence above. Finally, Jack pulled his way up a thorn vine on the side of the hotel, reaching the balcony just in time for Stiller to push him over the side.

Jack's rival was soon to disappear. Even Paramount felt he was one foreign genius too many. They bought out his contract and shut down a film he'd barely started. He booked passage back to Sweden and spent a wrenching weekend at the beach with Greta. "There was visible pain in his eyes," said a fellow Swedish director, Victor Seastrom. "And Greta seemed equally torn. She had once told him her career depended on his, that he was her life force. But she answered the pleading in his eyes with silence."

He sailed back to Sweden in defeat. Two years later he was dead.

Then, for an actress who prided herself on a disdain of the financial rewards and trappings of Hollywood, Greta did an incredible thing. Since her two-year pact was drawing to an end (although MGM had options to hold her for several more years), she went to Mayer's office and told him she wished to go home.

"Six hundred dollars a week is insufficient," she told Mayer. "Especially for a star of my standing." The speech reeked of calculation, probably Edington's.

"What would you consider?" Mayer asked.

"Five thousand dollars a week will do," she answered.

Mayer began screaming. "You ungrateful bitch," he said. "Such a salary is out of the question. Just who do you think you are?"

"Greta Garbo!" she answered coolly.

"Well, Miss Greta Garbo, I brought you to this country, gave you a chance to star in American films and built you into a star. And this is how you repay us."

Greta continued to stare over his head. She slowly pulled up out of the chair, turning her back on Mayer.

"Where the hell do you think you're going?" he said.

"Home. To Sweden," she answered.

She was on the next boat. As the months passed with no word from Greta, the MGM brass in New York panicked, discovering that they didn't even have her address. Reaching her through the U.S. embassy in Stockholm they began a series of offers starting at $2,000 a week and, finally, over the groans and protestations of Mayer, she was given $5,000 a week plus the privilege of going home each day at 5 P.M.

This time, she docked in New York to crowds of reporters so thick that she finally decided to take an exit ramp designed for the crew, slipping through customs and taking a cab to catch the Santa Fe express.

It was a newer, slimmer Garbo who reported back to MGM—as the queen of the lot. Unfortunately, she had begun to believe her own publicity—much as Marilyn Monroe would do twenty-five years later. The press depicted her as a lonely, melancholy personality, so she became just that.

In her secluded house Greta ran a bare-bones establishment that drove her Swedish retainers to distraction.

"She told me I was to do all the buying for the house, but that she expected us to keep the bills down," said her principal servant, Gustaf. "I couldn't believe it when she handed me a hundred dollars and told me that was the monthly allowance.

"We had kept house long enough to know that it would take a lot of scheming to do that," said Gustaf. "So twice a week I drove to the Central Market in Los Angeles—a distance of about eight miles—where I bought a supply of canned goods, fish, meat, and fruit."

The Central Market, which still exists, is a giant warehouse store where most items are sold at rock-bottom prices. "By careful buying I kept the food bills as low as eighty-five dollars a month."

But when he turned the accounts over to Greta, she grabbed her forehead and yelled. "This is too much. We eat too much. Cut back, and I don't care how you do it."

Only two rooms of the house were ever furnished and those quite sparsely.

The fifteenth of each month Greta handed Gustaf and Sigrid a fifty-dollar bill to meet all her personal expenses. "That had to cover everything from magazines and drugs to pajamas," said Sigrid. "And she demanded all the receipts at the end of the month. Don't ever let anyone tell you that Greta Garbo couldn't keep track of money. She watched pennies fall as if they were bars of gold bullion."

It's no wonder that Greta, the most gilded lily of all the early screen stars, looked like hell at home. Even starch and laundry soap were rationed. This led Thalberg to quip one afternoon, "Maybe we should take her from in front of the camera and put her in our accounting department."

One thing she never skimped on was the energy she poured into her physical fitness program. For hours she would cavort in the sun, sometimes nude, tossing a medicine ball (weighing fifteen pounds) in the air, frequently bouncing it off the wall.

"She would romp all over the garden with it," Gustaf said. "Rosebushes and hedges would lie crumpled in her wake. Then she would come whining in to me, 'Look at these poor rosebushes. What is the matter with them?' "

MGM treated her like a rare orchid on the lot. Each of her directors had to organize his shooting schedules as if they were crucial battles. When she arrived, all her gowns were ready to be slipped over her head by two maids who attended her permanently. Her movements and positions in each scene had already been plotted with chalk marks on the floor —much like a road map drafted by a kangaroo.

Her sets were more sequestered than Peking's Forbidden City, which they resembled in many ways. There was an hour-by-hour protocol that was never violated. When slight things went wrong, like lighting failures, Greta would walk off the set, order her car, and disappear. Director Clarence Brown, a frequent Garbo helmsman, told friends that the studio had created a monster when they caved in on the issue of her salary and contract. "Ever since she got her way, she has had the big head," he told Louella Parsons. "But if she can get away with it, more power to her. She's got them all scared around her. They don't dare scold or find fault with her for fear she'll turn around and go home."

Her paranoia increased over the years, and she frequently imagined spies on the set when there were none. "I know somebody is here. I can feel it," she complained to Clarence Brown.

"I assure you, Greta, there's nobody here."

"I don't believe it. Turn on all the lights," she demanded.

Not until the set was fully illuminated so that Greta could count each technician did she agree to continue the day's shoot.

One afternoon a party of bigwigs from Washington was touring the studio as guests of Mayer. More than anything else they wanted to see Garbo. A junior executive, with twenty-eight people waiting for him outside, came over to the actress and pleaded, "We can't keep these people standing outside."

"All right, let them come in," Greta answered. "And I will go home." The subject wasn't mentioned again.

Often Greta's high-handedness was not only rude but cruel. In one instance she managed to hurt Marion Davies's feelings—an almost impossible feat.

Both actresses were filming on the same sound stage. Garbo's was sealed off with the usual canvas and velvet. Marion's was open, almost festive with a high English tea served during the breaks.

Marion was in the middle of a line when she saw the curtains part. Greta sauntered in, sat in Marion's own set chair, and watched for about half an hour.

Marion was delighted, flattered.

"Pop," she said to director Robert Z. Leonard, "have you got a scene you can do without me. I'd like to go over and repay the compliment."

"I'll give you five minutes," he said.

Marion found her way through the scaled entrance to the Garbo set and watched while Fred Niblo guided the actress through a scene.

Greta raised her hand, bolted upright, and shouted, "Stop the camera. Who's there?"

Niblo snapped at Marion to leave. "You know Miss Garbo allows nobody on her sets."

"I know," said Marion. "But Miss Garbo came on my set, and I thought I'd repay the compliment."

Marion used her considerable social graces to maneuver Greta into a friendlier mood, bantering with the actress as hairdressers worked with her hair.

"Oh, why don't you go back to your own set where you belong," Greta said.

With the slight stutter she always developed when she was nervous, Marion answered, "Well, I thought I'd like to come over and see you. I understand you're quite a wonderful actress. You were kind enough to come to my set. I just thought I'd repay the compliment."

Greta sneered back at her. "You're very funny. You make me laugh. I didn't come over to see you—I came over to see a really great actress, Jetta Goudal [a onetime silent star from Sweden who was supporting Marion]."

Tears formed in Marion's eyes.

This only fanned Greta's peevishness. "They're calling you on your set."

"I didn't hear any call."

Greta's face reddened and her tone turned nasty. "You're wasting my time. Get off before I have to kick you off. I won't act. I don't like anybody watching me."

"Well, that goes both ways," Marion answered. "Don't you come to my set either."

Greta laughed scornfully. "To me you're null and void."

The incident was forgotten by Marion, but Hearst, hearing of it from Louella Parsons, complained to Mayer at a party that evening.

Mayer drifted over to Marion. "I wouldn't let anything that slut said bother me if I were you."

"Mr. Mayer, how can you say something like that. That's horrible."

"I don't think so," Mayer answered. "What else would you call a woman who sleeps with Stiller, Jack Gilbert, and Lord knows who else."

Although Greta Garbo's friends defend her as merely slightly cranky, incidents like the Marion Davies experience abound. And her solitary nature concealed what might have been a more objective view.

The "profane nun," as Hedda Hopper liked to call her, often invited extravagently comical incidents. At one Beverly Hills house of ill repute, for instance, a Greta Garbo lookalike, dressed in an exact replica of Greta's ballgown in *Love*, was the toast of the midnight set. She would come down a sweeping staircase with drooping eyelids and say, "Dahlings, I never want to be alone." The going rate was $250 a night.

In another deliberate case of mistaken identity, the Hollywood press corps was led on a merry chase for several weeks. It began with a call to Louella Parsons from an anonymous tipster that Greta Garbo was at a ringside table at the Coconut Grove at that very moment. And to top it off, said the informant, she's making it hot with a handsome real estate salesman.

Couldn't be, Louella thought. Impossible. A Greta Garbo sighting was as rare as an albino chimpanzee. The columnist called Chico Sanchez, her inside man at the Grove. "Chico, will you look out in the club and see if Greta Garbo's there tonight." He laughed at the task.

Chico slipped past the hatcheck girl and gazed across the floor. My God, there was Greta with wild orchids in her hair and an elaborate, sensuous gown draped over her frame.

"Louella," he said, "she *is* here."

It was still too long a shot for Louella. With Greta, there was no way to verify the truth.

But a wire service reporter ran a small item the next day about the "elusive Swedish Sphinx out on the town." During the next six weeks, Greta was seen at a club in Santa Barbara, having brunch at the Beverly Hills Hotel, at the races, and openly shopping at the Farmer's Market.

It was driving Louella crazy until Joan Crawford solved the mystery.

Joan was having tea at the Hollywood Hotel when the very picture of Greta Garbo walked in wearing a cocktail dress the star had worn in *The Kiss.* Joan walked over and grabbed the girl by the arm. "It's you, Geraldine," she said, collapsing in laughter. "I never thought it could be Garbo, but I couldn't figure it out."

The lady with the stage name "Geraldine" was actually Greta's stand-in, a dead ringer who had been found only after a six-month search by Metro. Geraldine was chosen from one hundred and twenty-five finalists to solve an expensive problem at the studio. Greta had become increasingly petulant, complaining that the hot lights sapped her energy, that standing ruined her posture, that posing for closeups drained her face of color.

Using Geraldine to stand in for the star solved that problem. She became so good at imitating Greta's languid walk that she was actually used in many long shots whenever possible.

"God! She looks like me," Greta said the first time she saw Geraldine filming wardrobe tests—a tedious but necessary process. (Since Cedric Gibbons decreed that his artisans could only tell whether a gown worked if it were actually on the star, only Greta escaped the duty.)

But Geraldine considered it a favor. "All day long I was able to sit close to the star studying her every movement," she told Louella. "I would often daydream about what it would be like to be the great Greta Garbo."

One day she decided to step through the thin gauze that separated the reality from fantasy. Greta indirectly provided the opportunity. She was afraid of her own stardom and avoided its reality by slipping into her nocturnal rendezvous with her press clippings. The facade wrapped her more securely than any mink. Geraldine was entranced with the reality. When Greta shrugged off her gowns and jewels and crept home, Geraldine collected them for a few precious hours—returning them, like Cinderella, just before the metaphorical midnight.

Looking more like Garbo than Garbo herself, she basked in the seductive lights of Hollywood café society while Garbo, hidden in a rough tweed coat, her slouch hat pulled over her face, took to the darkened backroads of the sprawling, anonymous city.

The only thing Greta couldn't camouflage, or even hide from, was her bizarre love affair with MGM's ultimate male sex symbol, John Gilbert, a man of violent passions, paranoia, and flamboyance.

It shouldn't have worked. Gilbert drove the flashiest cars, and wore the crown of the nightclub circuit with considerable elan while keeping a coterie of Hollywood society around him at all times. Greta's wardrobe was aged and shapeless. Her habits were nocturnal and only four or five people even knew where she lived. (It was, in fact, a secret from her own studio.) As for the shallow, tinseltown nightlife, to her it was anathema.

In spite of the yawning chasm between them, they shared a rare, unspoken bond that emerged the first day they met on the set of *Flesh and the Devil.* There was even a rumor—certainly a bit of public relations silliness—that they remained in each other's arms for ten minutes after the director yelled "Cut."

When they did come out of the clinch, Jack (the nickname used by his friends) began to slowly break through the chilly facade that Greta presented to the rest of the film community. During the lunch hour, when it was fashionable to be seen at the MGM commissary, Jack and Greta strolled far onto the backlot and lounged under an oak tree, sometimes talking for hours.

Normally, Mayer would have unleashed the wrath of God to prevent an affair that might erupt publicly into a scandal. This time greed prevented him from intervening. The remarkable personal chemistry between the lovers showed onscreen. Audiences sensed it from the day *Flesh and the Devil* opened across the country. MGM was flooded with fan mail asking when Jack and Greta would be teamed again.

Clarence Brown, the film's director, had begun shooting the film at Lake Arrowhead while waiting for Mayer to assign a leading lady. "Finally we got the go ahead with Greta Garbo," Brown said. "And it just happened that the scenes we started shooting back at MGM were the ones in which Gilbert was introduced to Garbo at a train station. Their film love affair proceeded from that point," the director went on. "Suddenly I realized that I had a real love affair going for me that you couldn't beat any way you tried."

Jack had already been married twice when he met Greta—once to the silent screen beauty Leatrice Joy. As the successor to Rudolph Valentino, he had become a brooding romantic with his head in the celluloid clouds. When he played an Austrian hussar, his shoulders squared off, he strode around the lot as if he were on field maneuvers, and he jumped on his leading ladies with the dash of a lusty Napoleonic officer. "You would swear that he'd just rode in on a horse when he walked onto the sound stage," screenwriter Frances Marion said. "And when he looked, he didn't see Culver City, he saw Vienna."

The grand affair was like that, nurtured entirely on sets where amber lights, sweet music, and gorgeous costumes blended into a romantic tapestry. The Greta Garbo who walked onto the set wasn't the Greta Garbo who'd slunk into Makeup an hour earlier. They had sprinkled her with gossamer and turned her hair into a halo with backlighting.

"That's the Garbo Jack fell in love with," said Adela Rogers-St. Johns, who considered their relationship the most bizarre coupling in a city of unbelievable affairs. "Mix Greta Garbo and the camera and you came up with a mythical, sphinxlike creature. But a myth it was. Take away the ingredients and you had a shy, awkward, stubborn young lady who had absolutely no desire to be the Garbo created by the camera. She could not be that creature, and she never was," Adela said. "The Greta Garbo that enthralled the world was made up of brush strokes and careful etching which worked like a great painting."

On the other hand, Jack Gilbert took his screen identity home with him, kissing the ladies' hands, leaping on his horse in riding breeches, and preening like a peacock. "He was one of the few onscreen lovers who was also a big beau offscreen," said actress Colleen Moore. "So many of my friends were in love with him at one time or another that it was hard to keep count. I even had a small flirtation with him once myself."

There are so many versions of the Garbo–Gilbert interlude that it has become almost impossible to separate fact from fiction. They range from Greta's own assessment that "I loved him for about fifteen minutes" to Adela Rogers-St. Johns mushy depiction of heaven parting and lightning flashing. "It was an explosion," said Adela. "I have never seen two people so violently, excitedly in love. I mean, when she walked through the door—if he was in the room—he went white and took a great long breath, walking toward her as though he were being pulled by a magnet."

Others, closer to Greta, maintain that it was a dalliance for a woman whose heart was saddened when her mentor Stiller sailed home, broken and near death. Greta's housekeeper, Sigrid, said the star collapsed against a wall in tears when word reached her that Stiller had died in Sweden. "It seemed like she would break apart. Whatever momentary gaity she did have disappeared."

Jack, for sure, was obsessed. He assaulted her frigid nature with midnight interludes at the beach and champagne picnics in the still undeveloped foothills that lurched upward from the Hollywood valley. He tried to draw her out and prop her up socially with his unerring finesse. "It never had a chance to work," said Joan Crawford. "If anything, Jack was too strong, too insistent for Garbo. Like a frightened animal, she bolted."

Most of Hollywood got their first offscreen glimpse of Greta at a 1927 party given by the screenwriter Carey Wilson and held in a private room at the Beverly Wilshire Hotel. It took several days of coaching before Jack convinced her to go.

Her constant stage fright, however, paralyzed her at the last minute. "Jack, I'm not going," she said. "I can't."

"Give me one reason," Jack demanded.

"I don't have a dress . . . come look in the closet."

Greta had already dressed in an old-fashioned European garment that was more like a bathrobe than anything else. It had long, drooping sleeves and a neck that came up almost to her ears. The color, forest green, was its only flattering quality—a contrast to her alabaster skin.

Greta was still hesitating when the host, Wilson, came by to pick them up. He listened patiently to her story, then asked, "Have you got a pair of scissors?"

Gilbert produced them.

Wilson cut off the sleeves, sliced a low back in the felt-like gown, and lowered the neckline. "Basically it may not have been very much," recalled Colleen Moore. "But with Garbo wearing it—who noticed? She was easily the most beautiful woman in the room and there were a lot of lovely stars there."

Colleen remembers another of Greta's rare appearances, at the home of MGM director George Fitzmaurice. There was a buffet, drinks, and a planned adjournment to attend the latest Greta Garbo film. "Greta said at the last minute that she couldn't go to the theater," said Colleen. "We went without her to the theater in Glendale where it was being previewed. The film was greeted by cheers, and we rushed back to tell her."

When Colleen, Jack, George Fitzmaurice, and the others returned, Greta had removed all the furniture in the Fitzmaurice living room, rolled up the oriental rugs, and was using the floor as a sort of toboggan course. Sliding from one end of the room to the other, she was so enraptured, laughing infectiously, that she barely noted their return.

It was only months later that Jack began pressuring Greta to marry him. A man of the old, and decidedly macho, school, he was ashamed of continuing the torrid affair without making it legal. He may also have sensed the torment Stiller's return to Sweden had left in Greta's heart.

Jack must have proposed to Greta at least a hundred times. He was overheard pleading his case at the studio, during a private tennis match, and during a dinner held at Jack's house and attended by Jean Harlow, Paul Bern, Norma Shearer, Colleen Moore, and others. "She would never seem to understand what he was saying," said Joan Crawford. "I don't think she wanted to hurt his feelings."

One of Greta's house servants witnessed still another proposal from Jack and heard Greta say, "John, John, you're such a child."

Late one morning during the first year of their relationship, Jack extracted a reticent "Okay, we'll do it" admission. He ran out the door, drove several miles to a friend's house, borrowed his car (capable of greater speed), and returned within minutes to collect Greta.

For some unexplained reason, Gilbert decided that sleepy, stodgy Santa Ana, about thirty miles from Hollywood, was the safest place to arrange a quickie marriage. The Santa Ana City Hall was, at that time, the centerpiece of a town still favored with vast orange groves and not a few dirt streets. Jack pulled the open roadster up to the steps of the civic center and was about to escort Greta to the license bureau when the actress leaped out of the car and broke into a run. Greta was—and probably still is—a perfectly trained athlete. Jack, a drinker and resident of the fast lane, was no match for her.

About a mile away, hidden by a grove of date-producing palms, was a retirement hotel tucked away on a side street. The clerk, a taciturn woman with thick reading glasses, looked up as Greta, her hair flying, burst through the door and looked wildly around the lobby.

"The restroom . . . where's the restroom?" she asked.

The lady, beginning to recognize the world's most famous face, pointed to swinging doors in the corner of the lobby. "Hey," said the lady, "aren't you—"

"No," said Greta.

She hid in the lounge until she felt certain that Jack, who had already been drinking, was well on his way home. She hiked to the Santa Ana train station, bought a ticket, and sat there—a solitary figure in a slouch hat —until the early evening train for Los Angeles arrived to carry her home.

The actress retreated to the hideaway Harry Edington had found for her. Sigrid and Gustaf were told to admit no one and to ignore the telephone. But several weeks later Jack again broke down her reserve and the sorrowful romance was renewed. This time Greta firmly steered the relationship into that graveyard of love referred to as "the understanding friendship."

Was Greta frightened because of her close call with matrimony? Or was she simply tired of Jack's nineteenth-century style of courtship? Whatever the case, Hollywood agreed with her decision.

There had been two bizarre chapters in her story during the months preceeding the love express to Santa Ana.

Early one morning Jack ran through the front door of Colleen Moore's mansion (just up the hill from his), shouting, "She's going to marry me. My *svensak flicka* [little girl] said yes." Jack bubbled over. "We're going to be married in the pine grove above my house. She says it's like Sweden there, and she gets homesick for the pines."

Before Colleen could complete her congratulations, Jack was gone. Although many film historians have discounted this first, fledgling step toward the altar, Jack also spread the news to Carey Wilson and John Barrymore. (Of course it reached Louella, who virtually machine-gunned the MGM publicity department for failing to inform her.)

Nobody knows what happened in the days following the aborted ceremony. Colleen believes that Jack, on his round of celebration, was roaring drunk by the time he got back to Greta. And she bolted.

It's also important to note that Stiller was still in town, a safe harbor to which she ran again.

The next false alarm was so public, so stunning, and so disastrous to Jack Gilbert's psyche that it has gone into the Hollywood history books —although there are as many versions as there were Hollywood cliques at that time.

King Vidor, Jack's favorite director and the man who made him a superstar in *The Big Parade,* was set to marry the beautiful Metro star Eleanor Boardman in one of those posh affairs that were de rigueur during the twenties—a king's ransom in roses, fountains of champagne, and Parisian gowns. It was all part of what Colleen Moore likes to call the "early-silent-movie-star-style," a style all its own.

The story goes that Gilbert had extracted a promise from the reluctant Swede, and had coerced Vidor and Miss Boardman into making the ceremony a double wedding. All Hollywood was there: Marion Davies (a bridesmaid), Irving Thalberg, Louella Parsons, and, to give the occasion the monarchical blessing, Louis B. Mayer.

It was an outdoor event, allowing for some flexibility in the schedule. Vidor, as handsome as most movie stars, was resplendent in a dark suit —as was Jack Gilbert. Jack nervously told Vidor that Greta was "undoubtedly late," as was her bent. Almost ninety minutes past the planned nuptial hour, there was still no Garbo.

"Jack was getting very nervous," said Eleanor Boardman. "In fact, he was getting rather violent."

Mayer ordered the wedding to proceed and, so the story goes, went with Jack into the men's room to calm his ire. "So what if she doesn't come?" he asked. "She's the kind of woman you sleep with, not the kind you marry."

Jack went crazy and grabbed Mayer by his vest, slugged him, and knocked him down.

"I'll get you for this," Mayer is supposed to have said.

There are other versions, of course. One of them, believed by Joan Crawford, portrays Mayer as pulling himself up and then decking Jack in return.

Leatrice Gilbert Fountain, Jack's daughter, said, "My father's career was officially over at that point."

The silent screen lover's hold on stardom did collapse several years after the incident, but mainly because his florid style of romantic acting didn't make the grade in the talkies. The talkies brought an entirely different type of hero into fashion—the rough-and-tumble school of lovers like Gable, Cagney, Robert Montgomery, and Frederic March.

One thing's certain. Whatever words of love Greta had been whispering in Jack's ear ended with the Vidor wedding. He found her house abandoned and dark. It was over. Any remaining romantic link was forever broken when Garbo stubbornly fled back to Sweden during the 1927 contract disputes.

Jack didn't pine away, however. He married actresses Ina Claire and Virginia Bruce in rapid succession, and was well into a cozy arrangement with Marlene Dietrich at the time of his premature death in 1936.

One of the most unlikely analyses of the affair came from Adela Rogers-St. Johns, who believed that Greta's refusal to continue her career after marriage was the true cause of Jack's failure. According to this version, Jack was berated by Greta for "loving Garbo, not me." Adela quotes Jack as telling her, "I told her yes, I am in love with Garbo. I want to marry Garbo. Adela, she wants to leave the screen, buy a wheat ranch, and have seventeen children."

"Jack told me he wouldn't marry her if she did leave the screen. So there it lay," the journalist-screenwriter said.

It's possible that Greta was leading Jack Gilbert on, then coyly backing off. She was the one who stayed at MGM, making no protest as Stiller was forced out of the studio and finally out of Hollywood. And her career zoomed as Jack's perished when sound pictures, the "talkies," came to town.

During and shortly after the Gilbert epoch, Greta surfaced long enough to reveal her peculiarities. It was again Colleen Moore who witnessed perhaps the most amusing of all Garbo anecdotes.

It happened during one of Jack's lazy brunches, to which Colleen brought a guest, the eminent illustrator James Montgomery Flagg. Colleen had been shooting six days a week, so she allowed her husband and

Flagg to mingle in the social mainstream while she sought a place to nap. The deep, red velvet sofa in Jack's empty living room was perfect. She buried herself in the deep cushions and was about to nod off when she heard voices at the other end of the room. Shielded by the tall back of the couch, she lay still and listened.

"You're my dream girl, I've drawn your face all my life," said Flagg in the vibrant voice of a young lover. "And here you are—come to life."

There was a lengthy silence, then, "All I want is to come and live in your studio." Greta gave every impression that she was deadly sincere. "Give me a little cot in the corner with a small curtain. I'll pose for you all day long."

"It sounds impossible after such a short time, but I'm in love with you. You're the most perfect woman in the world; the ideal woman. You would make me so happy." So ardent was Flagg's tone that it sounded like the track of a bad movie.

"My only interest in life is art," said Greta, egging him on.

Before the session was over Flagg was practically on his knees. The twosome finally drifted back outside, allowing Colleen to vent her laughter.

James Montgomery Flagg never saw Greta again. He sent her letters, telegrams, and flowers, which were left on her doorstep to wilt. Then he sent emissaries to her house and to the studio.

Still no answer.

"After awhile he wondered if it had happened at all," said Colleen. "I wanted to tell him that it had happened and that I had heard it. But I never could bring myself to do it."

One evening soon after, Jack persuaded Greta to attend one of Marion Davies's receptions at the beach, and they arrived after dinner, finding the mansion crowded with three hundred guests.

"Hullo, I'm tired," was the first thing she said to Marion. She took off her high heels, tossed them down the hall, and rudely asked the hostess, "You got a pair of bedroom slippers?"

"Sure," Marion answered. As she went to get them she hard the most frightful noise from the bedroom. "I found her jumping on my four-poster bed, testing the mattress. At one point she was jumping so hard her head was hitting the canopy."

"Ah, good mattress," she said.

Greta grabbed the slippers from Marion and asked her to get a knife. "Then she sat right there and slit the backs out of my slippers, put elastic bands around them, and slipped them on."

Garbo as the stricken ballerina in *Grand Hotel*, one of the few films that pleased her.

Luise Rainer, here with William Powell in *The Great Ziegfeld*, was imported to scare Garbo—to let her know there was fresh foreign talent on the lot. Luise won two Oscars but no fans.

"Thank you," she said over her shoulder as she padded down to the party.

"I never saw anyone so peculiar or so shy," said Marion. "And that's saying a lot for this town."

Another dimension of Greta's medieval mind showed itself to, of all people, Joan Crawford. Joan, who had to work every day for years to develop her screen persona, held Garbo in great awe. Longtime Hollywood reporter and author Bob Thomas, a favorite of Joan's who had interviewed her many times, said Joan went through a "Garbo phase" during which she emulated and worshiped Greta as much as any fan in America. She even fashioned her hair into a straight Garbo bob and tried to lower her voice several octaves before abandoning the imitation for the tough-cookie image that would dominate the latter part of her career.

Joan's dressing room was located a bit down the line from Greta's, and Joan bellowed out a hearty "Good morning" every day as she walked by. There was never a reply.

"Then one day Joan was in such a hurry that she forgot the ritual," Thomas said. "Greta threw open her door and said, 'Allooooo.' "

When Joan and Greta were in the all-star cast of *Grand Hotel*, Joan managed to obscure herself so that she could watch Greta's work. "Isn't she wonderful?" she asked an assistant director. "She's a genius."

A week or so later Joan passed Greta in the hallway. Greta stopped her, held Joan's face in her hand, and said, "What a pity. Our first picture together, and we don't work with each other. I'm so sorry." Then, as an aside, Greta said, "You have such a marvelous face."

If Joan had only known the hidden financial details of the MGM films of the thirties her feelings of inferiority would have vanished. In terms of return per dollar invested, Joan Crawford was the most valuable of all MGM's female stars. Her films returned about four dollars for each dollar invested—a profit margin equaled only by Clark Gable early in the decade and by Mickey Rooney during the last two years of the thirties. Joan's prime vehicles, *Letty Lynton*, *Possessed*, and *The Bride Wore Red*, cost the studio from $200,000 to $450,000 and returned profits in the $700,000 to $850,000 range.

Greta's films, with high overhead not unconnected with the star's demands, were more prestige items than anything else. For instance, it cost $1,144,000 to make *Queen Christina*, which returned $632,000 in profits. *Anna Karenina* had a price tag of $1,152,000 and brought only $320,000 in net profits.

Greta was well aware of her precarious economic position on the MGM scale of greed. "My range is really rather limited, and my audience is fragile," she once told Irving Thalberg. He tried to violently disagree. But she shushed him. "You know it's true. I know it's true. Without your support my career would have ended long before."

To protect herself, Greta reduced her work schedule to one picture a year after 1933 and exercised near-total control over her co-stars, screenwriters, and directors.

Much earlier than this, she had been so frightened by the advent of sound, (and the loss of her savings in the market crash), that she moved at a snail's pace at a studio that turned out films as regularly as a doughnut factory punched out doughnuts. When MGM converted to sound in late 1928, Greta came to Thalberg's office and talked quite honestly about ending her tenure at the studio. "Silent, I'm a star all over the world. How will it be with dialogue? Can I handle it?"

Thalberg tossed it off lightly while keeping to himself the serious reservations he had about her survivability in the new market. He knew that virtually the entire population of big foreign superstars was finished overnight the minute that Al Jolson appeared on the screen, saying, "You ain't heard nothing yet." (Pola Negri, for instance, made a few more silent pictures then headed back to Europe. Vilma Banky, Samuel Goldwyn's biggest moneymaker, wouldn't even test. With her thick Hungarian accent, she knew better. Emil Jannings, the Academy Award winner for *The Way of All Flesh*, didn't even bother to inform his agent that he was returning to Germany.) The most dangerous thing about the talkies was the imagination of the public. "We suddenly realized that the audience, in their own minds, had formed definite opinions about the way their favorites talked," said Thalberg. "They heard their voices in their heads as the titles flashed on the screen." When stars like John Gilbert and Norma Talmadge didn't sound the way their fans wanted them to, their careers collapsed. Even Gloria Swanson's massive following rejected the somewhat brittle tone of her voice.

With the star system turned upside down by the electronic earthquake, Mayer and Thalberg both agreed that Greta should continue making silent films until they could find a vehicle that would ease her into the new era. And this is what she did for almost two years. Then screenwriter Frances Marion suggested Eugene O'Neill's *Anna Christie*, which boasted a foreign heroine. The story department worked for six months on the adaptation of O'Neill's somewhat stentorian dialogue.

Frances Marion warned Mayer that Greta would need inspired support from the actress who would play her drinking crony during the film's bar scenes. There was a certain bit of calculation to her advice. Her old friend Marie Dressler, once a big success on Broadway and in the early days of the silents, was out of work and living on the generosity of friends. The screenwriter sidled up to Thalberg one afternoon and suggested Marie. "Out of the question," Thalberg answered her. "Let her test," Frances answered.

The rough test footage was sensational, and, nervously, the studio began filming, with the Garbo set so well guarded that special passes were required of even the loftiest MGM executive. Thalberg himself was turned away one afternoon, having left his pass back at his desk.

At the preview, audiences were ecstatic, "Why, her voice is almost perfect for this role," said Mayer. "She has just the right Swedish accent."

"I have no idea what they thought would come out when Greta opened her mouth," said Frances Marion. "They were addled by the smell of fear wafting through the industry."

By the fifth preview the studio realized it had not just an adequate talkie but a runaway hit. Their ad campaign was unprecedented. "GARBO TALKS" was the slogan, reproduced by the thousands on billboards, flashing signs in New York and London, and on life-sized cardboard facsimiles of Greta in her tawdry "Anna Christie" gear. However, the insecurity born at the start of the sound revolution always remained with the star.

Her staying power finally began to fade in the late thirties after her artistic triumph in *Camille*. (The figures still weren't very impressive. The $1,486,000 film earned profits of only $388,000.

"Greta Garbo did the greatest thing for a company that any star, living or dead, has ever done," said director Clarence Brown. "She had a fanatical following of fans in the United States, but, unfortunately, those fans were not enough."

Greta's swan song was *Two-Faced Woman*, a financial and critical bomb. The end was near.

But her career wasn't killed by bad films. It was killed by Adolf Hitler. By throwing Europe into war and cutting off all distribution channels for American movies, Garbo became a has-been.

"Her pictures opened to bigger grosses than any other pictures we handled," said Brown. "But they didn't hold on in the extended run or in middle America. The box-office takes collapsed after the third or fourth week of release."

In Europe, however, Greta was queen—the box office champion in

France, Sweden, Italy, Germany, Spain, and Britain. With that market closed, MGM couldn't afford to continue making Greta Garbo films. Her contract obligated the studio to pay her anyway. It was Greta who agreed to let the studio out of its pact. Some say it was her idea. In any case, MGM paid her $250,000.

And it was over.

MGM's greatest publicity stunt—the hoax of the elusive, solitary Greta Garbo—was no longer of any use. As Howard Dietz said, "Loneliness was her most important product, and it was planned and calculated every week she was on the lot."

Silence made her, and silence protected her loneliness. Like Charlie Chaplin, who walked away from his best films with his back to the camera, Garbo did the same.

Her final check was picked up by a messenger service.

5

Her Most Exhalted Majesty

THE STORY OF NORMA SHEARER

The "Queen of MGM" had finally been deposed, toppled from her platinum throne by a series of unprecedented disasters. And for Joan Crawford, a personal, degrading reign of terror was over, and she knew just what to do about it.

For fifteen years Joan had toiled in the shadow of Norma Shearer, who was, for most of that time, the wife of the boss, Metro production chief Irving Thalberg. Norma appeared in the studio's most expensive productions, had her pick of co-stars such as Gable and Robert Taylor, and relaxed during paid vacations that lasted for months. But most importantly, as far as Joan was concerned, Norma expropriated and sometimes extorted the best films—including at least three that had been written especially for Joan.

Then Thalberg, only thirty-seven but the victim of a lifelong heart condition, died in 1936, leaving his widow several million dollars and a film career that was plummeting at the box office. It was just the opening Joan had been waiting for. Nobody at MGM doubted that there would be a vicious confrontation. The only question was: When?

Although Mayer had told several associates that he was glad as hell to be rid of Thalberg, he moved quickly to protect his widow, telling directors, "Shield her, she's still a valuable investment."

The first explosion came on the set of *Mannequin,* a Crawford–Spencer Tracy melodrama. Norma was holding court across the lot, preparing to film makeup and wardrobe tests for an upcoming production. All morning a covey of artisans worked on her hair and face while others assembled a consort's ransom of gowns.

Shortly after noon she glided onto the sound stage and was introduced to a young cinematographer. Norma smiled sweetly, said a few vague words, and then abruptly walked off the set. "There's a problem," she told an executive in charge of her films. "I never, never make tests without Bill Daniel. And I don't care to make an exception."

William Daniel, considered the best cinematographer on the lot, was the darling of Norma, Garbo, and Crawford, whose demands on his services sometimes resembled a cat fight in a New York alley. As Crawford's luck would have it, Daniel was the principal film technician on *Mannequin.*

Norma took the junior executive by the arm and said confidently, "Ask if I can borrow him for just this afternoon. I'm sure it can be worked out."

The young executive left Norma trying on her Adrian gowns and dashed back to the executive office building. "What should I do?" he asked Mayer's secretary, Ida Koverman.

"You'll have to ask Joan if she'll loan Bill to Norma for the afternoon," Ida answered.

He was stopped at the door of the *Mannequin* set. Not only was filming in progress, but Edsel Ford and his family were looking on and were due to have tea with Joan and Spencer Tracy. The security man at the locked door said he would signal the film's director, Joseph Mankiewicz, that the executive was waiting and had some urgent business to discuss.

"What the hell does he want?" Mankiewicz raged at a young assistant director. The visitor quickly explained Norma's unusual request.

"Uh, I don't know if that is possible," the assistant director said.

"Sure, it is," the executive answered. "It's done all the time."

"Not to Joan Crawford it isn't," said Mankiewicz's assistant.

Mankiewicz was chatting with Edsel Ford when the young man interrupted him again. "We're in for trouble," he said.

"Why is that?" the producer asked.

The assistant explained Norma's request. "Well, you'll have to ask her," Mankiewicz said, pointing to Crawford's tightly sealed dressing room. There was a breathless pause on the set as the crew tried to keep an eye on the visiting Fords and on the door of Crawford's trailer.

About a minute elapsed. Then the door was flung open, the assistant tumbled out, and Joan appeared wearing only bra and panties.

"And you can tell Miss Shearer that I didn't get where I am on my ass!"

A half hour later Norma Shearer threw off her clothes in a rage. There were tears in her eyes as she called for her car and, still in makeup, headed home.

It was a key moment in the history of MGM. As unkind as Joan appeared, she was speaking for a large MGM contingent and hundreds more Hollywood outsiders down whose throats the imperial, pretentious Miss Shearer had been forced since 1927, when the Shearer–Thalberg love affair had first blossomed.

It had been a great love story, perhaps the prototype Hollywood love story—played out in front of the world. But along with the aura of romance, a nasty little rumor grew up among the dissatisfied, the vicious, and the incompetents to the effect that Norma had slept with Thalberg and then married him—on the condition that she become MGM's biggest star. Her career, they said, was born in bed.

The reality was far different. Norma had been a short, somewhat unphotogenic starlet when she arrived at Metro with a contract guaranteeing her $150 a week and eighteen weeks to prove herself. She couldn't act, had never been taught how to apply stage makeup, and her movements onscreen were awkward. "Personally, I didn't think she'd make it," said King Vidor, an eminent MGM director of the twenties. "There were a thousand girls like her already in town."

Norma, a Canadian, had already been in New York for two years, storming the casting agents and taking small modeling jobs to support herself and three other members of her family. The less interest she received from New York producers, the more she wanted a job in Hollywood, no matter how its rough-and-tumble style might offend her "finishing school" nature.

One afternoon, with absolutely no preparation, Norma reported to the stage door entrance of the Ziegfeld Follies. An old doorman looked her up and down, noting her thick legs, her minuscule height, and the eerie cast in one of her eyes. "Forget it, kiddo," he said. "Even if you could sing and dance like Fannie Brice, you're too short for this show."

"Please, I want to try anyway," she pleaded.

The stage at the Ziegfeld Theater was awesome in size with its empty black cavern and mammoth sets required to hold the lavish productions featuring the Ziegfeld Girls. When Norma auditioned she couldn't see

Ziegfeld and the others out in the dark. This made her even more jumpy. But she did the required dance, tried a few choruses of "Who's Sorry Now," and then stood in the silence waiting for an answer.

Finally, Ziegfeld yelled from across the footlights: "Go back to Canada and forget about the stage!"

The actress had, by now, learned to block these pessimistic reactions from her mind. That very afternoon she took the long trolley ride over to Vitagraph Studios to test for the Lillian Gish movie *Way Down East*. D. W. Griffith, the first great director of the cinema, looked her up and down before saying, "You'll never be a movie actress. Your eyes are too blue."

After months of working as an extra (when the pay was $5 a day), she was noticed on Fifth Avenue by an advertising artist. "You've got the kind of look I could use right now," he said. "Come on up to my studio tomorrow. We're doing a hat advertisement." While she had failed miserably before the cameras, advertising seemed to come naturally to her. Her picture was suddenly all over New York City.

A portrait of Norma with orchids for a perfume billboard caught the eye of Standford Strachn, the major marketing executive for the Springfield Tire and Rubber Company. His company had been seeking a symbol for their new tires, which wore longer, they said, than any in the business. Strachn decided it had to be Norma.

They called her into the studio and made portraits of her diving through tires, cuddling them, and sitting sweetly inside the rim much as if she were the adornment for a huge Valentine. "Miss Lotta Miles," they called her. When the photo of Norma appeared above New York's Columbus Circle, traffic slowed to view the lovely brunette sitting in a tire nine feet around. Then there was the familiar show business query, "Who is that girl?"

An MGM contract was in her hands two months later. The studio sent her a train ticket, provided a small advance, and told her somebody would be there to meet her at the Santa Fe station.

To Norma the train ride was like "The Night Before Christmas." While her mother had been dazzled by the enormous amount of gold to be mined in the Hollywood studios, Norma had heard the Circe call to glory. She never read fewer than five fan magazines a week. And she kept some of them until their pages were frayed. She took the box out in her compartment and imagined the royal arrivals in Hollywood. She read of Pola Negri's first day at Paramount when five hundred studio employees met her with a new Rolls Royce and a red velvet carpet that ran from the gates to Pola's five-room bungalow on the lot. As her train neared the Santa Fe station, Norma excitedly put on a new afternoon dress and hat to match. She imagined herself stepping gracefully down the platform and into the arms of adoring movie moguls.

The train jerked to a stop when it arrived, throwing Norma down three steps and into a hillock of dust. Some entrance, she thought. She looked up and down the tracks, seeing only two greasy switchmen. There was no band. No arms full of flowers. No handsome young aide to escort her out to the MGM studios in West Lost Angeles. She started to cry, then stopped herself. The amazing power to sidestep disappointment, which she shared with her enemy Joan Crawford, had already made its appearance.

A taxi was hailed and Norma watched the last few dollars in her purse whittled down mile by mile. Then she was deposited, suitcases and all, at the gate of MGM. She was walking toward a stern guard at the front gate when she heard a lion's roar. "What on earth is that?" she asked the guard. "Just what you thought it was—a lion," he said. "We gotta zoo here."

Then came the final indignity. They wouldn't let her inside the studio gates. "But my name was left here. I start work today."

"Sure, that's what they all say, lady. . . . There's no Norma Shearer on my list."

Norma was trying to remember the name of the man she was supposed to meet. "Thalman . . . Thalber . . . something like that."

"You mean Irving Thalberg, the production chief. I'll ring him."

Still dusty but beginning to get a mite put out by her treatment, she was directed toward the administration building. After all, she thought, they asked me, I didn't ask them.

A pale, extraordinarily handsome young man took her hand. "Oh, good, Miss Shearer. We've been expecting you."

Finally, she thought. I hope the rest of the studio isn't this poorly run.

Thalberg was wearing "preppie" clothes that day—hand-tailored chinos, an Oxford shirt, and a tweed coat. Norma decided he must be the office boy—too young to be anything else. He directed her to an imposing office and sat down at the large desk in the center of the room.

"Then—you're not the office boy?" Norma said.

Thalberg, then only twenty-four, laughed. "No, Miss Shearer, I'm Irving Thalberg, vice-president of the Mayer Company. I'm the one who sent for you."

Joan Crawford and her set always believed that the favored status of Norma Shearer began there in that office on the first day, that it was love at first sight. On the contrary, Thalberg, not any more interested in Norma than the twenty-five other starlets on the lot, almost dropped her contract several times.

The first time was only weeks after she arrived. MGM executives, having viewed footage of the bit parts Norma had played in four films made back East, decided she would be perfect as the ingenue in *The Wanters,* to be directed by John Stahl. Somehow the wardrobe department decided, all on its own, that *The Wanters* needed a gutsy, brash dame to give the film that little extra touch. A filmy dress of exploding color was run up on the sewing machine along with several pounds of fake pearls and a strange hat.

The screen test made by Stahl was schizophrenic—Norma playing the perfectly proper young Canadian while looking like the girl who ran the "Shoot the Duckie" booth at the Santa Monica Pier. Stahl immediately dropped Norma, giving her another bit part as a consolation prize.

Assigned to still another picture, Louis B. Mayer began hearing protests after the first day of shooting. "She simply won't act," said one assistant director. "It's like she was sleep walking." Mayer saw it differently. He had become good at picking up the scent of fear. He sent for Norma.

"You know what your problem is," he yelled as she sat in front of his desk. "You're yellow. Here you are given a great chance, the chance of your life, and what do you do? You throw it away because maybe you don't like the director. So he scares you. We don't have time for this out here. I'm through with you." Anyone who ever had to deal with Mayer remembers the ungodly fury he could call up at will. This was one of those times.

Then Norma started yelling. "I am not yellow," she cried. "I'll fight it out! I'll show you what I can do."

She was instantly redeemed in Mayer's eyes. Anyone who stood up to him, honestly and fairly, could ask the moon and receive it—not without strings, of course, but receive it all the same. So she got a second chance.

Several Norma Shearer films later, Irving Thalberg did begin to notice Norma in a more personal way. The first offstage contact came on Christmas Eve, 1924. Norma had been working on the set of a film that had to be finished before January 1, so she had worked until nine. It took her almost an hour to get out of a complicated costume and heavy makeup, and when she had, she found the sound stage deserted. So she went back to her dressing room for a thermos of hot chocolate.

Thalberg, who could see Norma sitting quietly inside the dressing room, dialed the extension there from his second-floor office. "Norma, I see you worked late?"

"Yes," Norma replied, a bit shakily.

"Well, I worked late, too. I just wanted to wish you a Merry Christmas." Then he hung up.

Several months later Thalberg's secretary called Norma off the set of a picture with a message. "Irving would like to know if you could go with him to the *Gold Rush* premiere tonight."

At first there was silence. Norma had never been asked for a date by an intermediary before. What the hell. "Sure, tell him I'd love to."

The date was a success and the Hollywood gossip columnists began looking for signs of a full-blown affair. They were disappointed. Irving and Norma, both seeing others, continued their flirtation in the Victorian manner in which it had begun.

Sometime later, Norma received a second call from Thalberg's secretary, who asked her if she would go to an informal dinner party that evening. This time Norma detected someone else on the line. She took a chance: "Irving, why don't you ask me yourself?" There was a click as Thalberg instantly cut the connection.

But she went to the party.

All through the mid-twenties, Irving had been trying to convince the silent comedienne Constance Talmadge to marry him. But Connie (known as "Dutch" in the film community) had successfully dodged him. Finally, in 1926, she formally turned him down.

Norma had moved one notch higher.

Studio executives noticed that Thalberg was showing an inordinate amount of interest in Norma's career. "He had already put her on a pedestal which would cripple her later career," Louella Parsons said in a 1946 story.

One afternoon Irving and other MGM executives were having a casting session, trying to fill a difficult part in the movie *The Great Divide*. The part called for a Boston girl who is almost raped in a Western mining camp. Screenwriter Lenore Coffee told Irving, "You've got the perfect girl right here."

"And who is that?" Irving asked.

"Norma Shearer."

Irving's jaw immediately set. "No one would believe she would allow herself to be raped no matter what the circumstances. She looks too well able to take care of herself."

If Thalberg had stars in his eyes when it came to Norma, Louis B. Mayer wasn't blinded by her. When Norma became the first of a long series of actresses who pushed for higher pay and won, Mayer thought he'd led Norma down the garden path. Norma presented a plan calling for $1,000 a week to start with, but gradually working up to $5,000 a week. Mayer quickly agreed. "She has no staying power," he told Conrad Nagle. "We're getting a good actress at a bargain price."

Once she and Thalberg were married, her status at the studio changed overnight. All of her films were now overseen personally by Thalberg. And he gave her the pick of directors and scriptwriters, and even let her adjust shooting schedules to her own whims and needs.

Overnight, she had become a superstar. The rough edges were buffed off. Her thick, slightly bowed legs were covered with long, flowing dresses that came to be known as "Norma Shearer nightgowns." Cameras were positioned so that only part of her face would show most of the time, to hide the slight cast in one eye, and the settings were designed to set off Norma's dark hair and willowy body.

The other actresses had to make do with leftovers.

Joan Crawford got Norma Shearer "hand-me-downs," stories she refused to do. But Joan decided to be quiet about it, vowing to bust the situation open only as an emergency measure. Her thoughts, however, were vicious. Shortly after the Thalbergs were married, Joan told columnist Dorothy Manners, "She doesn't love him, you know. She got married for the sake of her career much like a nun who gives herself to Christ to fill her inner needs. Irving is just filling one of Norma's needs."

"Oh, come on, Joan. She fell in love with him."

"I don't think so," Crawford snapped. "Why else would she marry a man as sick as Thalberg is? She knows he's going to die on her, and she wants to make sure she's a big star first."

Dorothy Manners answered, "Let's not talk about this anymore."

"Okay," said Joan. "But you know I'm right."

Joan finally decided to make her move. By the end of the twenties, she realized that her hits had all been soap operas about the Jazz Age. "Hell, they just keep me around to dress up the set and dance a couple of steps," she said. "But Norma's parts are getting bigger every year."

The "jazz baby," as the fan magazines called her, decided to storm

Thalberg's office. "Why do you save all those good roles for your darling Norma?" Joan demanded. "Don't you think I deserve some consideration?"

Irving answered her in icy tones: "Joan, your career is coming along nicely. You still have much to learn. If you tried something too ambitious, it might be disastrous. You wouldn't want to be laughed at, would you?" Then he dismissed her with a terse "I'm busy right now, Joan."

Joan had done the unthinkable. She had bypassed the byzantine court system established by Thalberg and Mayer to keep the actresses (whom Mayer referred to as "the meat") in their place. Ten days later Joan received a memo from the production office telling her she was set to appear in a Tim McCoy Western, one of a series of C-class pictures sent out to fill double bills.

"Damn them," she told Dorothy Manners. "They can't do this to me."

"Well, honey," Dorothy answered. "They can and they have."

So every day for the next four weeks a studio limo carried Joan out to the dust and sagebrush of the San Fernando Valley to complete her sentence. At one point, she told Tim McCoy, "I'm going to enjoy working with you and your cowboys if it kills me."

Then talking pictures hit, changing the entire hierarchy of Hollywood. For one thing, Warner Brothers, whose *The Jazz Singer* was the first talkie, became the premiere studio in town for a year or so—pushing MGM into the second spot. To make matters worse, Nicholas Schenck, chairman of the Loew's Corporation, which owned MGM, decreed that "talking pictures won't last more than a couple of years. This is an oddity. Nothing more." So MGM wasn't prepared when the public deserted the silents for even the most poorly made talkie.

Thalberg took no such chance with Norma. He brought the famous classical actress Mrs. Leslie Carter from England to coach her. While Marion Davies was trying to cure a stutter with pebbles in her mouth, Norma started learning to speak all over again. The lessons were so painstaking that Norma was ordered to speak a simple word like "mother" over and over.

When Thalberg thought she was ready, he set up a voice test and ordered a blanket of secrecy thrown around it. He didn't want the results to ruin his wife if the verdict was bad.

Norma went before the microphones late one afternoon.

As Irving stood by, his wife recited several lines from a play MGM had purchased for the screen. Then both sat down to hear the playback.

Thalberg gave a whoop as the tape ran out. Norma's voice was perfect for the screen.

Colleen Moore described the hilarious era of the secret voice tests. "I went to one party where several of the girls had heard that Norma Shearer's aristocratic voice had been tested and adjudged perfect. All of a sudden a dozen women were milling about—all of them talking in the 'Norma Shearer style.' "

Then several weeks later at another garden party the word was out that Garbo had been tested also, and that it was *her* voice, not Norma's, that was the most perfect style for the talkies. "You guessed it," said Colleen. "There were those same girls ambling about and whispering in the sultry tones of Greta Garbo. It was ridiculous."

However ridiculous, the test convinced Mayer and Thalberg to cast Norma Shearer in the studio's first all-talking drama, *The Trial of Mary Dugan.* It had been a stage hit the year before, and Thalberg was pleased that it had only one set.

Norma brought in her brother Douglas, an engineer, to create a sound system for the film. MGM's earlier adventures in sound had been fuzzy at best. Voices came out garbled; there were bleeps—like some whacky Morse code—on the musical tracks; often the sound recording would drag, stretching a "hello" into "heeeellooo."

Thalberg didn't wish to have Norma's voice sound as if it had come through the Holland Tunnel. He gave Douglas Shearer a blank check to develop a system that would at least tape actual sounds. Shearer spent about six weeks producing a camera and recorder sealed in an airtight closet, which had barely enough room for the director, the cinematographer, and Shearer himself.

In this case, Norma suffered through torment to get *The Trial of Mary Dugan* on the screen. Because of truck and car traffic outside on Washington Boulevard, the MGM air-conditioning system was shut down and all openings to the set were sealed with heavy flannel ticking. The main studio door was replaced with an airtight, cold storage door.

"Sometimes the temperature in there reached 95 degrees," Norma said later. "I couldn't get my breath. It was a nightmare. The director could only give directions a scene at a time before sealing himself up in the camera booth. We were left outside to fend for ourselves."

But it worked, making Norma MGM's first truly bankable star in the age of talkies.

✳   ✳   ✳

Shortly after the sound revolution, Mayer and Thalberg locked horns over money. Thalberg felt he was doing all the work while Mayer was getting all the money. Bitterness suddenly tore the studio apart. Thalberg was finally raised to Mayer's level and given the option to buy Loew's stock at prices far below the market value. (Exact figures aren't available, but Mayer was the highest paid man in America in the thirties, earning about $1.4 million each year.) Since the fight had to be arbitrated to the top of the Loew's organization, relations between the two studio principals were never the same again.

"They all liked to say that Mayer was upset because he had treated Irving like a son," Hedda Hopper said. "But it was really Mayer's greed and pride that caused the rift. He couldn't stand the fact that Irving, so much younger, was earning as much as he was. It just consumed him with rage."

This battle was barely over when Norma began to exercise her newly discovered will on her husband. He had designed a series of pictures for her in which she played one slick society girl after another. None of the characters she played had any bite to them. But she had read and liked a screen treatment of an Ursula Parrott novel, *Ex-Wife*, about a divorced woman who believed in sexual freedom. MGM had bought it and tentatively cast Joan Crawford in the role.

Irving was reading scripts in his office one afternoon when his secretary buzzed. "Mrs. Thalberg is here," she said. Irving jumped up. It had been a sort of unwritten rule that Norma wouldn't transact business with him in the public glare of the MGM compound. It would give the appearance of favoritism, he said.

Norma quieted him and blurted out what she had been hesitant to discuss at home: "Irving, the public is getting tired of me being the perfect lady in every picture. I've got to play something more daring."

"I don't want to talk about it," he snapped.

But Norma got her way and starred in *Ex-Wife*, which was renamed *The Divorcee* for the screen. It won her the best actress Oscar and the enmity of six or seven MGM actresses.

"The Oscars are rigged," Joan Crawford told Dorothy Manners, who was, by then, assistant to gossip columnist Louella Parsons. "Mayer and Thalberg decide who to nominate and then they tell the committee who should win. As long as I'm at MGM I'll never even get a nomination, much less an Oscar." (Her prediction proved true. Her first nomination, for *Mildred Pierce*, didn't come until 1945. And she won. She'd been off the MGM contract list for three years.)

Norma and Irving established themselves in a sprawling beach mansion in the old Santa Monica colony near the beach villas of Mayer and Marion Davies. The ocean air was deadly to Irving's heart and lung condition, but the beach colony was the chic place to live and to entertain. To ward off the worst effects of the dampness, double-thick glass was put in the windows to muffle the gentle surf, and a primitive air-conditioning system that relied on blocks of ice was installed. Norma decorated the house in a sane style. It was a welcome relief from the tasteless rococo spread of Marion's mansion and from the heavy-handed costliness of Mayer's beach retreat. The marriage seemed idyllic: two careers proceeding upward, a son (Irving Thalberg, Jr., born in 1930), and a daughter (Katharine, born in 1935).

Beneath the pleasant surface, however, was a pervasive fear that spread into every corner of their life. It was the sort of terror known only by the families of the chronically ill. When Irving was five years old, doctors had told his mother he would not live to see thirty. Irving had passed that marker in 1929. He was living on borrowed time.

Thalberg's handsome, boyish looks stemmed from the enervating weakness of his system. "Look at it this way, Norma," said one of her husband's physicians. "A chest cold could kill him if he weren't careful."

Death was around every corner. "I try not to think of it too much," Norma told Louella Parsons. "Irving seems so vibrant, energetic. But underneath is . . ." Norma hesitated. "Is a constitution so delicate a breath of wind could blow it away."

Fear became a reality shortly after Irving's new contract was negotiated. He suffered a massive heart attack, hovering near death for more than ten days. Doctors ordered a rest of at least six months—as far away from the clutching, greedy atmosphere of MGM as possible.

Norma canceled all of her projects for two years and, with her friend Helen Hayes and Helen's husband, Charles McArthur, took Irving on a tour of Europe.

Mayer raged about the trip, told Irving not to go, predicted dire results if he were gone from the studio that long. "Would he rather have a dead production chief?" Norma answered.

So the party sailed.

The trip itself wasn't so interesting. Other than a minor brush with Nazi anti-Semitism, it was the regulation tour of watering holes.

Back at Culver City, however, Mayer gingerly reached down and pulled the rug out from under the boy he had once called "the son I never had." Always able to ignore his own strident, cruel nature, Mayer believed

The beginning of an idyll. . . . Norma Shearer and husband Irving Thalberg when the movies were young (1936). *Below:* Norma Shearer was 36 when she played the 14-year-old Juliet in her husband's production of *Romeo and Juliet.* Here with Violet Kemble-Cooper (who played her mother), Norma's performance was perhaps a greater handicap than her advanced age. She hoped for an Oscar but had to watch as fellow MGM star Luise Rainer won for *The Great Ziegfeld*

he had been betrayed by Irving. "I gave that boy everything," he told an assistant, Eddie Mannix. "And he creates a scandal throughout the company. He could have come to me."

In a complicated maneuver, Mayer abolished the empire over which Thalberg had ruled, breaking the studio into a number of fiefdoms, all under the executive control of Mayer. Thalberg's fiefdom, of course, was the richest and the largest. But he was no longer MGM's crown prince. His only consolation was that he had first call on the services of Norma, Greta Garbo, the Marx Brothers, Clark Gable, Jean Harlow, as well as the best directors and writers on the studio payroll.

The trip seemed to have healed his tired body and revived his sparkling energy. With the entire studio watching for reactions, Thalberg settled into his lower-class empire and turned out some of the greatest films in Hollywood history—*Camille*, *The Good Earth*, *The Barretts of Wimpole Street*, *A Night at the Opera*, and *The Great Ziegfeld*. In addition, Irving made a quick flanking movement to protect Norma, gaining her a contract unprecedented in Hollywood. She was to be paid $150,000 a picture, was given script and director approval, and had the first pick over any properties coming down the line. MGM surrounded her with pliant sycophants, whispered golden words of praise in her ear, and sold her to the public, with a multimillion-dollar campaign depicting her as a saint.

In one quick week a monster was born. Norma Shearer read her press releases very carefully and came to actually believe them. She was what they said she was: a queen, the Sarah Bernhardt of the cinema, the classiest actress in the world.

To Irving there was only one role truly worthy of Norma—Shakespeare's Juliet. "It might have been written for her," Thalberg told Eddie Mannix. "She already has the Shakespearean meter in her speech. She is Juliet."

Mannix was much like those fat functionaries who served the emperors of China. His eyes narrowed and his placid face showed none of the concern he had at Thalberg's announcement. But as soon as Irving ambled down the executive hall, Mannix buzzed his secretary. "Get Mayer on the phone."

"Has Irving talked to you about *Romeo and Juliet?*" Mannix asked.

"What about *Romeo and Juliet?*" Mayer asked.

"He just came in here and told me he was going to make the play with Norma as Juliet. It'll cost millions, L.B. He's going to build the town of Verona on the back lot."

Mayer groaned and hung up the phone. It couldn't help but be a disaster, he thought to himself. Mary Pickford and Douglas Fairbanks had tried to sell their version of *The Taming of the Shrew* not so many years back, with dismal results. And the Warner Brothers' production of *A Midsummer Night's Dream* was currently bombing all over the country. Mayer realized that Thalberg could make *Romeo and Juliet* with or without his approval—that's how wide his powers were over his own MGM production department. Still, the old man considered taking the problem straight to New York, hoping they would use their veto power.

Thalberg's proposal seemed foolish even to his closest associates. "The language will have to be updated, of course," Thalberg told MGM's chief story editor, Arthur Marx. "But that can be done. With Norma as Juliet and Clark Gable as Romeo, it can't lose at the box office."

"Gable?" asked MGM publicity chief Howard Dietz. "Will he do it?"

"I think he will," said Thalberg.

Gable wouldn't hear of it. He had just been forced to wear the wig and tights of a navy officer in *Mutiny on the Bounty*. He found it an awkward and embarrassing chore. There was no way they were going to get him into velvet and tights to climb Norma Shearer's balcony.

"For me?" Thalberg asked.

"Not this time, pal," Gable answered.

Frederic March was Norma's second choice, but he wouldn't even read the updated script or agree to discuss the project. Finally, Norma and Thalberg convinced the British actor Leslie Howard to play Romeo, and the production was underway.

Leslie Howard found his costumes already designed when he reported to the studio. They consisted of thin tights that had to be sewn on. While trying them on in the wardrobe department, Leslie looked at himself in the mirror and started to laugh. "Look at me. A man of forty wearing the clothes of a fourteen-year-old lover. Why am I doing this?"

For Norma, the age factor, if anything, was exaggerated. She was a well-preserved thirty-six, and her face, when carefully painted, was one of the screen's most radiant. But a fourteen-year-old Veronese girl in the first blush of love? Hardly!

Irving plowed ahead, promising the front office that he would bring *Romeo and Juliet* in for $900,000.

Nobody on the lot was prepared for the unnerving film that was brought into the developing rooms each night. Joan Crawford, sneaking in to look at some of the daily footage (thanks to a friend), burst out laughing when she saw Norma dancing in a young girl's dress at her first ball. "They must be kidding about this," Joan said. "She looks like she's playing dress-up."

Irving, insulated though he was, heard the backstairs laughter and called in the cavalry. Norma reported in to Makeup as early as 4 A.M. so they could work their wizardry, pushing her time frame back twenty years.

Word got around that they were going to shoot the famed balcony scene on a given night—but not the night listed on the official shooting timetable. Since the great outdoor set abutted against the landscaping gardens of the studio, dozens of people waited on the lot to catch a glimpse of Irving Thalberg's Juliet.

Just as Norma and Leslie Howard began the scene, a black limo pulled up to the side of the set, a back window was rolled down, and Irving Thalberg watched Norma, with tears in his eyes.

"Well," said Joan Crawford. "Maybe it was worth it—just for that."

Romeo and Juliet cost not $900,000 as Thalberg had promised, but over $2 million. The film, even after years of sales to television, is still $500,000 in the hole. But it gained another Oscar nomination for Norma, which is what Irving wanted.

Having played the world's most famous princess, Irving wished Norma to play history's most beautiful and tragic queen, Marie Antoinette of France. He moved through the preproduction work on this film with such zeal that friends later wondered if he had had a premonition of his own death.

Irving sent four buying teams to Europe to secure the actual furniture (sometimes including entire wall panels) and trappings of Marie Antoinette's France. They even managed to secure the wooden crib in which the dauphin had slept.

The wardrobe department, under the direction of Cedric Gibbons, found the royal dress patterns in the archives of France, and cut them to fit Norma's size. "I want the dresses to be so exact, so sumptuous, that Norma will have the same regal bearing as Marie Antoinette," Irving said. In one case an extinct form of brocade had to be produced on special order from a mill in Lyons, France, which had to build a facsimile of an eighteenth-century loom to work pure gold strands into one court dress.

During the first costume tests, Irving came down to watch Norma being photographed in the queen's wedding gown. He walked over and grabbed her arm. Then he kissed her hand. "This is a role worthy of you."

Then, tragedy struck. Irving came down with a cold while organizing a benefit at the Hollywood Bowl. When he collapsed in a dressing room

This artificial, vapid portrait was actually only a costume test taken far in advance of the 1938 production of *Marie Antoinette*. This is the way Thalberg dreamed she would be.

A shower of stars at Norma Shearer's birthday party indicated that she was emerging as queen of the lot as early as 1927. Norma is in the left foreground holding a doll. Among the stars are Mae Murray, Conrad Nagle, and Jack Gilbert. *Below:* Norma and Joseph Schildkraut wearing the costumes from *Marie Antoinette* at a Marion Davies party. The front doors of Marion's mansion had to be removed to admit the queen and her gown.

Norma Shearer brought to life the look and the great flair of the doomed queen in *Marie Antoinette*, with Tyrone Power playing the earnest lover.

Marion and Norma, ambitious rivals for the power and glory of MGM,
pretend for the camera at a San Simeon costume party. Marion is on
the left.

at the Bowl, he was rushed home. The physicians thought he would make it at first. Ironically, his heart was holding up fine. But the cold accelerated into a severe form of pneumonia. A few days later, Irving Thalberg was dead at the age of thirty-seven.

His death tore MGM and the film community apart. His friends and well-wishers were so numerous that tickets had to be issued for over fifteen hundred people. Thousands massed outside the chapel as virtually every major star in town attended the funeral. Norma moved in and out of the chapel as if she were in a dream state. Only once, when opera star Grace Moore was singing "The Psalm of David," did she smile, remembering a long ago moment. Then she pulled the veil down over her face.

After that day Norma Shearer backed into the shadows of Hollywood. She went back to the beach house and refused to take calls. Much of her fabulous spirit died with Irving.

Mayer didn't pressure her at first. He didn't dare. On the way out of the chapel Mayer had turned to fellow executive Eddie Mannix and whispered, "Ain't God good to me?"

Naturally, the remark moved slowly through the gossip channels to Norma, who was hurt. Screenwriter Frances Marion always wondered why Norma was so surprised at Mayer's callous reaction. Then Adela Rogers-St. Johns, a Hearst columnist, said, "Frances, Irving hid all the ugliness from Norma. That was probably the most important protection he offered her—protection from the envy, greed, and criminal ambition which blights this town."

With $400,000 spent on costumes and sets for *Marie Antoinette*, MGM wanted to get the expensive film back on its track. But who could approach Norma? And what was the protocol?

Finally Mayer asked Ida Koverman to call Norma—but just to chit chat, mind you, nothing else. Ida, who had watched Mayer and Thalberg ripping themselves apart over money, had a particularly soft spot in her heart for Norma. And she had seen Norma fight for Irving's health against the grueling demands of the studio. So when she called Norma, she offered her shoulder.

"Ida, did you know that Irving wished me to retire after *Marie Antoinette*? He believed that I could really go no higher as an actress and that *Romeo and Juliet* and *Marie Antoinette* were to be my swan song. I'm committed to finishing *Marie Antoinette*, but right now I can't make a move. My lawyers won't let me."

"What do you mean?" asked Ida.

"You must know that Mayer doesn't want to honor the financial arrangements in Irving's will. I can't return until it's all settled."

When the probate court took over Thalberg's assets, they had capital, property, and investments amounting to about $6 million. The estate and other California taxes reduced Norma's share to slightly less than $2 million. Norma and most of Hollywood knew that Irving had intended to take care of Norma in grand style, deeding to her the proceeds from the movies he produced, with bonus payments for films like *Camille, The Good Earth,* and *Marie Antoinette,* which were due to be released after his death. So airtight were the clauses in Thalberg's will that he must have felt death already coming.

"Irving told me that, no matter what happened, we would be well taken care of," Norma told the columnist Louella Parsons, who had begun to hear ugly rumors about MGM and the Thalberg estate.

Louella heard right. In a burst of greed unequaled in old Hollywood, Louis B. Mayer decided that Thalberg was entitled to his stock options and percentages only up to the time of his death—no matter that the will said otherwise. When MGM lawyers in New York expressed their concern over the dirty deals, Mayer began yelling at them.

Since Thalberg had produced the lion's share of MGM box office hits and because overwork at the studio had led directly to his death, Norma's lawyers said they'd take their claims as high as the Supreme Court. To help their cause, Norma, in chic black, gave several interviews depicting herself as "the destitute widow."

The battle was long, bitter, and ugly. Both Mayer and Norma came out of it with scarred reputations. She made demands far in excess of reason, and Mayer seemed a doddering old Scrooge who refused to give Norma a farthing.

While the battle raged, veteran MGM director Victor Fleming called Nick Schenck in New York. "Nick, are you aware of the damage this battle is doing at the studio?"

"Partly," answered Schenck.

"Well, it's tearing the studio apart. Almost every actor, prop man, director, and technician is lined up behind Norma on this one. Mayer's trying to cheat her out of what the studio owes Thalberg's estate."

Schenck flew to the Coast, ordering Mayer to reach an agreement, "and get this thing settled fast." Coincidentally, while Schenck was in town, Norma appeared on Louella Parsons's radio show to announce her return to the screen. "As you know, Louella," she said, "Irving had wanted me to retire. And this idea appealed to me also. But now I'll only receive fifteen thousand dollars a year. I must go back to work—or to the poor-house."

Louella chatted and tried to make light of it. But the message was strong.

Norma received word of MGM's capitulation the next day. Under the new pact, the Thalberg estate would get the profits from all the films made during his tenure and those not released before he died. This meant that Norma was to receive 10 percent of the future net profits of Thalberg's MGM films from 1924 through 1938. In addition, she was able to buy MGM stock at below market price through 1938.

Triumphantly, she returned to finish *Marie Antoinette* at MGM and to make three pictures a year for $150,000 each. This pact put her price tag even higher than Garbo's.

Norma Shearer glided onto the closed stages where the Palace of Versailles had been recreated and came out another person—publicly at least. As the shooting progressed, she became more and more like the doomed French queen. She no longer walked through the studio, she glided regally as if she were heading for the coronation. She no longer merely said hello to her friends; she fluttered about them, her hands posing and gesturing.

She even took the huge dresses home where, alone before her mirror, she tried on gowns and wigs that were exact duplicates of Marie Antoinette's wardrobe.

Then the final step. She went public.

At a birthday party thrown by Marion Davies for her lover, William Randolph Hearst, the guests were ordered to dress in authentic early American clothes. If help were needed, Marion had purchased five hundred costumes that guests were free to use. To her friends, Marion pointed out an unpleasant incident that had caused Hearst to be kicked out of France. "It has left him disgusted with Europeans and particularly the French. I hope Louis XVI doesn't show up."

Louis XVI failed to show but Queen Marie Antoinette did. And what an entrance it was.

Norma, in a court dress stretching out from her feet in all directions, was greeted by the butler, who ran back and whispered to Marion that "there's no way we can get Miss Shearer through the entrance into the party."

Marion dashed to the front and ordered servants to remove the huge front doors. Finally, Norma was able to sweep in—a birthday cake apparition that drew giggles from dozens of guests.

Trying to pass Norma in the hallway, Hedda Hopper couldn't resist taking her down a peg: "Norma, how dare you come to this party as Queen Marie Antoinette? You know that Mr. Hearst has been chased out of France. Now you go right home and change."

Marie Antoinette decided to remain, taking up three full chairs at Hearst's formal dining table.

"I know she didn't mean it as an insult," Marion told Hedda. "You know, Irving told me she had a little something wrong in the back of her head. . . . I guess that's it."

At the premiere of *Marie Antoinette*, Norma Shearer experienced, for the last time, that great roar of fame so precious to Hollywood stars —there were to be only dismal films and an early retirement in the future.

Somehow Norma came to see *Marie Antoinette* through rose-colored glasses. The audience of her peers was cool to it. But at the end Norma cried copious tears into a handkerchief that had originally belonged to the real queen.

Tyrone Power, who played Queen Marie Antoinette's lover in the film, and had been making the film *Suez* with his French wife, Annabella, in the California desert, dropped in to the premiere for a second or two. Their eyes were still irritated by the desert sands.

Norma, in *Marie Antoinette* black velvet, twittered over, grabbed their hands, and said, "Ah, I see you were as deeply moved as I was."

Ty and his wife had to rush to an outside terrace where they collapsed in laughter. "Moved?" Tyrone said to Anabella. "Moved? By that old turkey?"

Norma's imperious ways increased after her husband's death. Since she failed to get the deference she had come to expect as a divine right, she tried a series of childish maneuvers to get her way. On the set of *The Women,* for instance, she battled with Rosalind Russell over closeups and control of their scenes together. In one scene Roz was to approach Norma as she was being fitted for a designer dress. Director George Cukor told Roz to circle Norma and "buzz, buzz, buzz" in her ear. Norma immediately realized this would reduce her to a well-dressed prop.

During a coffee break, Norma slipped away. A half hour later, she entered in Marie Antoinette's court dress, a monstrous boatlike garment. "I just decided to put this on," Norma said sweetly. "It's never been worn."

"Now, bear in mind that the set was a tiny dressing room with a platform," said Roz. "Once Norma was in the gown with the hoops, I wasn't about to get anywhere near her ears."

Cukor circled the set several times and then called over a prop master.

"Rosalind," Cukor said, "I want you to stand on that platform."

The property men wheeled in huge folding mirrors. "Now pull these full-length around her," he said. "And Norma, you go stand next to her as close as you can get."

It took a while to light the set since the glare from the mirrors hit the camera straight on.

Cukor turned to Norma just before the cameras rolled. "Now, Norma, instead of one Sylvia [Rosalind's character] you've got four."

Shortly after, Norma went to the front office and demanded that Roz Russell's name be listed below the main titles. Since it was written in her contract that only a man could be billed above her, MGM and Mayer dropped Rosalind's name to a small credit, "with Rosalind Russell."

"I can't settle for that billing," Roz complained to Cukor. "I've already starred in a number of films, and I don't care to be demoted by Norma Shearer."

"Agreed," said Cukor, shrugging his shoulders. But there was nothing he could do about it.

"When it comes to a fight with management, the only thing an artist can do is refuse to perform," Roz said. "And if an actress simply walks out of a production, the studio can force her back or sue her in court. But, if a performer gets sick, what can his boss do?"

Five weeks into the shooting schedule for *The Women*, Roz got sick. "You couldn't pull that trick at the beginning of a film. They would just replace you," Roz said. "I never attempted a ploy like this ever again, but I had a feeling I could make it work—just this once."

Several days into Rosalind's sick call, Norma still refused to budge in spite of personal requests from Louis B. Mayer and Cukor.

"I lay out in the garden, looking up at the sky," Roz said, "and every day Benny Thau, who was in charge of talent, would phone me and ask how I was getting along. I'd say 'I'm not feeling very well.' "

The fourth day of the strike, Thau called up and said, "Oh, Roz, something has happened this afternoon. Norma Shearer says you're so good in this film that she's going to allow you to be starred too."

"How perfectly lovely of Norma," Roz answered.

There was a long pause on the other end of the phone. "Do you think," he said gingerly, "you'd feel well enough to come to work tomorrow?"

"Hmmm," Roz answered. "I'll call my doctor and perhaps make a stab at it."

Finally, even Norma came to see it as a great lark, allowing her frosty spirit to open up a bit. At the completion party for the film, Roz was dancing with George Cukor when another director, Ernst Lubitsch, danced by and said, "If you want more closeups in this picture, never mind dancing with your director, you'd better dance with Norma Shearer."

And she did. But she complained later that Norma tried to lead.

6

Imperial Concubine

MARION DAVIES AT MGM

A gleaming Phaeton limousine pulled up to the back entrance of a darkened sound stage and honked once. A chauffeur in full livery left the motor running and headed for a small door with an amber light over it. The chauffeur knocked twice.

"Ready, Miss Davies?"

"Gimme a minute, okay?"

The chauffeur stood at attention and waited.

About fifteen minutes later, the door opened and a lovely blonde woman, still dressed in a sequined, bejeweled costume, stepped out of the door, took an armful of marten furs, and then settled into the luxury of the limousine's interior. There were peach-colored roses in a crystal vase and a mink lap robe.

"The champagne?" she asked. The chauffeur handed back two thermos bottles that had been chilling in the front seat.

It was a dreadful November night in 1924. The fog had crept up from the ocean and blanketed Hollywood with a thick mist. "How long to get to the harbor?" the blonde asked. "Half an hour, ma'am," he answered.

The car glided up the hills of East Los Angeles and through the already sleeping community of San Pedro with its harbor spreading out below. Finally the car pulled to a stop in front of a private dock, leading to the largest private yacht on the West Coast. The chauffeur helped the blonde out. And Marion Davies, one of the most famous stars of the silent era and certainly the richest, walked out to the yacht and through the fog to infamy.

Marion's lover, the rich and powerful William Randolph Hearst, had scheduled a languid cruise out onto the calm Pacific and toward the balmy sun off the Mexican coast. By the time the *Oneida*—Hearst's yacht and once the crown property of Kaiser Wilhelm of Germany—returned five days later, Marion, Hearst, and Charlie Chaplin were tainted by a scandal that would dog them until their deaths. The stage was certainly set for a tragedy of classic proportions.

Hearst, then sixty-one and the most powerful newspaper publisher in the world, had fallen for Marion Davies while she was still a teenager (sixteen years old, exactly) and the toast of the Ziegfeld Follies. A vibrant, warmhearted blonde, Marion first noticed Hearst when he bought two tickets to her show for each night of the run—attending every night and flooding her dressing room with peach-colored roses. He was married but separated and had reached what used to be called "the dangerous age."

Within months, Marion Davies had become his mistress, and Hearst, determined to set her up on a pedestal for the world to worship, had poured an estimated $20 million into her movie career. At the premiere of one of her early films in New York, he had draped the stage and the sides of the theater with 100,000 pink roses. The implausible happened. Marion fell in love with Hearst, never asking for anything and agreeing to bear the ignominy of being the all-too-public mistress of a married man.

Hearst moved Marion and her film company to Hollywood in 1922, affiliated her with the still germinating MGM, and established her as a major star.

Hedda Hopper once described Marion Davies as "a butterfly with glue on her wings," an obvious reference to Marion's youth (twenty-six in 1924 to Hearst's sixty-one) and Hearst's aging, settled nature. "But the only thing she really wanted was to be 'Mrs. William Randolph Hearst,' a prize forbidden to her," said Hedda. "To compensate, W.R. lavished her with diamonds [$1.5 million worth in 1919 alone] and an extravagant career." (Marion's films cost an average of $1 million when silent movies, good ones, were brought in for under $300,000.) Marion, never happy as a movie star, fought back by flirting and cavorting, somewhat innocently, while Hearst attended to his vast empire from a New York office.

In 1923 Marion went to a formal gala at the home of Mary Pickford, the self-anointed queen of movie society. Mary, probably on purpose, placed Marion next to the lustful Charlie Chaplin, a devastatingly handsome man offscreen. The flirtation was on.

Marion and Charlie drove through the wild, Prohibition-era streets of Los Angeles without caution. But in spite of Chaplin's reputation as a cocksman, there may have been little more to the alliance than flirtation. But Hearst didn't think so. He was worried enough by January of 1924 to move his business headquarters to the West Coast, linking up with his Eastern papers through the first "hot line" phone service in California.

So the stage was set for that mysterious journey on the *Oneida*. The *Oneida* was a walnut-paneled, Victorian monster, with stained-glass windows, a gold service for forty, velvet wallpaper, and a wine cellar that was the envy of the Hollywood establishment.

Among the guests on the cruise were novelist Elinor Glyn and Thomas Ince, a motion picture director who ranked second only to D. W. Griffith. (It's of not slight importance that Ince bore a startling resemblance to Charlie Chaplin.)

Hearst was already on board when Marion entered their suite and wrapped her arms around the old man's neck. "This should be a lot of fun, huh?" she said. Hearst stared straight ahead, convinced of her infidelity yet fearing to bring it up because of his own inability to make her his wife. The boat, with its fifteen or so guests, began moving out of the harbor as Marion took off the elaborate costume and began the task of washing the heavy grease makeup from her face.

A muffled gong announced that dinner was ready to be served in the yacht's main dining room. Lobster salad, hearts of palm mushrooms in wine sauce, and prime rib were on the menu.

Thomas Ince, who was being wooed by Hearst to direct a series of Marion's films, announced that it was his birthday. A cake was produced, and Hearst made the toast himself.

Marion, fond of drink but forbidden by Hearst to indulge the habit, giggled and pointed out that it was bad luck to toast with water. "It must be liquor," she said to Hearst. "It really must."

The servants were finally ordered to bring wine and a case of harder spirits to the salon off the dining room. Some of it had been brought from Europe but some of the case came from a bootlegger who personally handled Marion Davies's orders. Ince, already suffering from an ulcer and a heart condition, consumed enormous amounts of the rich spread, and then finished off a bottle of the bootleg bourbon. (Elinor Glyn said two

These two scenes from Marion Davies' first major classical drama, *Quality Street*, proved she had the deftness to handle heavy duty parts. MGM, unimpressed, refused to give her class-A properties. Conrad Nagle is the ardent suitor.

313~

A glowing Marion Davies as her lover William Randolph Hearst wanted
her to appear—a sun-dappled ingenue.

shots of the same bourbon sent her running to the deck where, to quote her, "I had a little sicky.")

One by one the crystal lights on the ship were dimmed, and Hearst ordered the captain to head past the San Clemente Islands toward the warmer waters off the booming Mexican resort of Ensenada. Even Ince, a heavy drinker, finally staggered to his stateroom and went to sleep.

By 7 A.M. the next day, the *Oneida* had drifted into the silvery waters off San Diego. Wisps of fog still surrounded the boat and masked it from the sun. Marion and Seena Owen, a close friend, were on deck throwing the crumbs of last night's sponge cake to the seagulls. At 8 A.M. a school of propoises circled the boat, entrancing both Marion and Seena. A blistering Mexican sun finally appeared just before noon as Hearst, Marion, and the guests changed to more formal attire for a seven-course lunch. But Ince remained in his cabin.

An hour later a cabin boy entered the dining room and whispered a couple of sentences to Hearst. "Oh, my God," he said, excusing himself from the table. In the cabin he found Ince in a state of shock and obviously suffering from great pain. "What's the matter, Tom?" Hearst asked.

"My ulcer," he moaned. "My ulcer. Get me to a doctor."

The captain was ordered to turn toward shore and the nearest hospital, which was in San Diego. Marion and Elinor Glyn were told nothing more than that Ince was suffering from acute indigestion and had to be taken to a hospital.

In San Diego harbor, hospital attendants carried the almost lifeless Ince to an ambulance and sped off. Marion approached Hearst, but he refused to talk about it.

Ince was rushed up the coast by train to Del Mar, California. Physicians there treated him for an ulcer and okayed his train trip back to Hollywood. Two days later, he was dead.

But there's another version of this story—which many believe to be the true version. Or was it simply a mirage?

Fans of this other version, and there were many, described a horror story in which Hearst, a power close to the White House and the Justice Department, shot Thomas Ince in a fit of rage, mistaking him for Charlie Chaplin. Millions changed hands, they say. And Mrs. Ince agreed to bury the truth in an avalanche of innuendo.

Witnesses said they had seen Marion, still in her costume for *Zander the Great*, drop by the Chaplin Studios to pick up her lover, Charles Chaplin, and Louella Parsons.

With Chaplin on board, the *Oneida* sailed into the fog bank where a murder was committed.

The story goes that Marion, an insomniac and incurable gossip, sat up through the night talking with Ince, who found it equally hard to sleep. As the boat headed into the choppy waters off the Mexican Coast, Hearst, they say, was awakened and began prowling the boat in search of Marion. Walking quietly on the deck slats he heard Marion's distinctive laughter coming from the lounge. Seeing the Ince shadow against the window and believing it was Chaplin, Hearst pulled out his pistol and shot Ince in the head.

The legend depicts Louella Parsons as running to the scene, trained as she was to recognize disaster. Then and there, say the gossips, Louella and Hearst concocted a coverup that involved huge payoffs to Nellie Ince, Tom's widow, and the coroners of both San Diego and Los Angeles counties. The legend has it that Louella Parsons was promised her lucrative position as the major Hearst columnist in Hollywood and that Mrs. Ince pocketed $5 million, which she used to build apartments and purchase great hunks of land to assure her future.

But it must have been only a mirage.

Louella Parsons was in New York, attending the opening of a Broadway play when the accident occurred. In fact, she didn't settle in Hollywood until late 1925.

As for Chaplin, he had dinner that evening with Mary Pickford and Douglas Fairbanks at their famed estate, Pickfair.

While Ince was being carried home by rail, the *Oneida* continued the cruise and returned to Los Angeles harbor on Sunday afternoon. By then, the New York *Daily News* had issued an extra edition claiming that Thomas Ince had been shot by William Randolph Hearst in a fit of rage.

"When I read that story in the New York *Daily News,* I was as mad as I'd ever been," said Marion later. "Why would Hearst shoot him? There were no weapons aboard, and Tom didn't die until late Monday."

Two days later many papers were calling it "The Marion Davies Murder." Coroners in both San Diego and Los Angeles counties ruled natural death, but the rumor has refused to die—even sixty years later.

In an interview shortly before she died, Nellie Ince said, "You know, there was really nothing to it. Tom had a heart condition, had suffered with it for some time. The doctors told him not to drink. But he did. The feast on the *Oneida* was just too much for him."

However innocent, the "Thomas Ince Affair" made Marion's entrance as an MGM Girl a spectacular one. Hearst couldn't give Marion his name but he was determined to give her almost everything else.

*   *   *

After her first MGM picture, *Little Old New York,* Hearst contracted to build Marion a dressing room that would outshine even the Gothic studio palaces of Gloria Swanson and Pola Negri. The studio population watched in amusement as three construction firms, working on double and triple time, constructed a fourteen-room bungalow on the backlot. It was equipped with its own kitchen, screening room, and a dining room built to seat thirty. The gossip called it "Trianon," after Marie Antoinette's hideaway bungalow at Versailles.

Nobody ventured a guess as to what it cost. But MGM's art director, Cedric Gibbons, who was a world authority on French antiques, estimated the value of the French art and furniture at $10 million. The wine cellar alone contained fifty vintages, including brandy more than a hundred years old.

All of this was merely show, as if the trappings alone would convert Marion into an actress of the top ranks. Hearst knew better, of course. He had brought Marion to MGM because the greatest concentration of talent was there. In effect, he told Mayer to make her the biggest star in films.

By turning Marion into an MGM star he was trying to balance the scale a bit in his favor. (In 1919 a New York financier told Hearst at a party, "There's money in films." Hearst replied, "Yes, mine.") MGM was to pay Marion $10,000 weekly, fifty-two weeks a year, plus a bonus of $100,000 annually. Cosmopolitan Films, the company built around Marion, had been operating at a deficit. This had nothing to do with Marion. Hearst simply spent so much time and money on publicity and trappings that profit was out of the question.

The Marion Davies bungalow became the social center of MGM. Charles Lindbergh was entertained there, as was George Bernard Shaw. The Prince of Wales asked for an autographed picture, and Herbert Hoover blushed when introduced to Marion at a luncheon.

Looking back through the mists of time, it's hard to pinpoint the power of Marion's charm. She was beautiful, no doubt about that. With her natural, platinum hair and willowy figure, she was the predecessor of Marilyn Monroe—right down to the laugh.

Frances Marion, the MGM screenwriter who fashioned stories for her, compared her to Elizabeth Taylor. "She was so alluring, so basically sexy that neither men nor women could resist her. She bubbled over with life."

Others were less kind. Irving Thalberg, the MGM production chief who was saddled with her films, said she was a modern-day Madame DuBarry—the lover-consort of Louis XV of France—and little more.

Thalberg grumbled a couple of times but was quickly silenced by Mayer, who prized the "Hearst Connection" above all his achievements. Mayer, never forgetting his rock-bottom beginnings, was flattered and blinded by his association with Hearst, one of the most powerful men in the world. It opened doors Louie never thought he would enter.

A year after Marion became an MGM star, Mayer had to move quickly to prevent a rift. During the filming of *Tillie the Toiler,* Thalberg received more than five hundred telegrams from Hearst—all of them describing how a "Marion Davies production" should be run. One wire alone ran a thousand words and dealt solely with the tailoring of Marion's costumes.

Irving protested to Mayer. And Mayer answered, "I'll take personal responsibility for all the Cosmopolitan Productions."

Marion's talent wasn't all in her bedside manner. King Vidor, who directed her several times, still calls her one of the five greatest comic actresses in film history. "She had a gift which I've seen in only one other actress, Marilyn Monroe," Vidor said. "But Hearst—he wouldn't leave her alone. He smothered her with turgid productions. The more expensive they became, the worse they were."

In 1929, at a meeting of theater owners affiliated with MGM, there was an outcry about Marion Davies pictures. "Why do we have to keep taking these turkeys?" said Herman Klein, owner of a theater chain that stretched from New Orleans to Chicago. "People are complaining."

All Mayer could do was placate the angry exhibitors. MGM operated through a system that required theater owners to take the whole catalogue of studio productions—the good with the bad.

"Why do we have to put up with it?" Thalberg asked Mayer.

"Do you realize the amount of publicity we're getting from Hearst because of Marion Davies?" Mayer asked. "We're guaranteed space in Hearst papers which reach twenty million readers."

"I still wonder if it's worth it," Thalberg grumbled.

Stardom meant nothing to Marion. She only wanted one thing—to become Mrs. William Randolph Hearst. In 1930 Hearst tried one more time. He offered his wife, Millicent, who had also been a chorus girl when Hearst met her, a cool $10 million to grant him a divorce. One friend told her: "Mrs. William Randolph Hearst is a very important name in America and the world. What would you gain if you gave it up?" On the advice of such friends, Millicent refused.

Hearst continued to hope that film stardom would fill in the gaps. But Marion told Louella Parsons, "I'm not crazy about making pictures.

It was alright once we got started. But to me it was a big waste of time. You only live once; you've got to have fun and and not work all the time."

There was little chance of that. Hearst considered Marion not only his hostess but the mistress of all his castles. And he provided her with clothes, jewels, and mansions in such a lavish manner that her wealth became a public-relations problem.

Jealous of Mary Pickford's domination over Hollywood society, Hearst determined to give Marion a showcase that would make "Pickfair" look like Hansel and Gretel's cottage.

He picked her up on the MGM lot one afternoon and told the chauffeur to drive to Santa Monica beach. In between the growing row of movie mansions was an acre of prime beachfront. Hearst, stumbling through the sand in a full business suit, began drawing a huge outline with a piece of driftwood. "Do you like it here?" he asked Marion.

"It's fine," she said.

"It's yours. And this is where I'm going to build the house."

Marion smiled absently, visualizing a beach house on the order of Mayer's fifteen-roomer down the way.

Within a week, construction crews moved onto the site, where they would work more than a year on a $7 million white Georgian house with thirty-seven fireplaces, a parlor paneled in gold leaf, crystal chandeliers from Tiffany's, the largest private motion-picture screen in the world. A porcelain room was imported from Peking, where it had decorated the boudoir of a Chinese princess. Oriental rugs worth $900,000 were imported from Turkey. And the pool was lined with Carrara marble.

It was so large that Marion once told Louella Parsons there were parts of it she had never seen. She said she was kind of awed by it. "It hasn't a feeling of a home, does it?" she asked Louella. "And that feeling is what I really want."

She was never to know that feeling. No sooner was the beach house complete than Hearst began to construct the incredible castle at San Simeon, a palace twice the size of Versailles. The weekend parties began, and Marion became hostess to the world—entertaining the rich and famous, the authors and painters, the intellectuals of an entire age, at the castle.

Gloria Vanderbilt, Sr.—a jaded society figure hard to impress— called Marion's touch "light and beautiful."

"It was Marion Davies' personality [she said] that has made the Rancho Casa Grande's house parties rare. She has the deep intuition which is a gift, of asking groups that partition well with other groups. Besides that she has the tenderest heart to be found on this globe."

During the same epoch (from 1927 to 1933) Hearst showered on her caskets of jewelry that included a platinum marquise solitare ring of 21 carats, a 17-carat emerald solitaire ring, a necklace of 46 baroque pearls, a diamond and emerald choker of 281 diamonds, and emerald and diamond bracelets with 22-cabochon emeralds, and a pear-shaped diamond pendant of 29 carets.

Many wondered how Marion managed to keep her career afloat since she and Hearst entertained an average of three nights a week, and three-day weekends were required for the cavalcades to San Simeon. The answer, of course, was that exceptions were made for her at MGM. They worked around her rather than the other way around. There was also her sense of organization, which led to fewer retakes on a Marion Davies film than on those of most other stars, some of whom required endless retakes.

So the idyll continued until talking pictures exploded into Marion's world, promising ruin and devastation. Moviegoers were unaware that Marion suffered from an almost incurable stammer. It made no difference to her silent career. But the talkies? Horrors.

She and Hearst tried to ignore it, sticking their heads into the ground like celluloid ostriches. Mayer comforted Hearst. "I think it's a passing fad," he said. "We aren't even planning to gear up for it."

"That's a relief," Hearst answered.

Nobody, however, could ignore the profits generated by *The Jazz Singer* and its Warner Brothers sequel, *The Singing Fool.*

Louella Parsons was the first to bring Hearst the bad news. "It's going to take over the industry," she said. "How do you know?" Hearst questioned. "I can show you the sacks of mail I'm getting each week if you like," the columnist answered. "People are actually complaining about stars who are continuing to make silent movies." (Included on that hushed list were Garbo, Douglas Fairbanks, Sr., Gloria Swanson, Pola Negri, and Clara Bow.)

Marion decided to see for herself, attending an afternoon showing of *The Singing Fool* with a Hearst columnist, Maury Paul.

When Jolson broke into song, Marion began to moan and then to cry openly. "I'm ruined. Ruined!" she told Paul, grabbing his arm.

When she returned to her New York penthouse, Hearst immediately asked her what was up. "Talking pictures, that's what's up," she answered.

But it was surely nothing to cry about, Hearst scoffed.

"You'd be crying, too, if you'd seen it."

By the time Marion returned to MGM, Mayer's prediction had been disproven. The studio was importing Broadway stage talent by the trainful, and had built a sound stage outside the grounds of MGM to begin testing all of the studio's silent stars. Norma Shearer and Buster Keaton were the first up to bat. And both passed.

Marion was up next.

The sound engineers had turned the process into a nightmare. Suddenly it seemed as if the inmates were running the nuthouse. The technicians, with so much power thrust into their hands, became little tyrants, reserving the right to rule on both stars and studio product. Sometimes the tests lasted for two or three hours. While a star was in the sound box, the other stars gathered in frightened little groups to await the verdict. After an endless period a technician would appear at the door and yell, "Keaton talks!" Not even Thalberg or Mayer were allowed inside during the testing process. The technicians had the moguls over a barrel and they knew it.

Marion's test partner was the proven comedian George K. Arthur. Marion's biographer, Fred Lawrence Guiles, says the dialogue the actress was given was absurd beyond belief. So the actress decided to ad lib. She informed Arthur of her plan. And he blanched.

"Look," said Marion. "When you get stupid dialogue like this, what difference could it make? It's just a test. I don't care if I live or die."

"What about me?" Arthur asked.

"Just follow me," Marion answered.

As the sound cameras rolled, Marion took a swallow of champagne from a thermos and literally said the first thing that came into her head.

"This is a dinner party where there're ersters . . . Brooklyn ersters. Sit down."

"But there's no chair," Arthur answered.

"Well, then, fall down. What's the difference?"

Her humor was forced, however, and she thought she had failed the test.

"I think I'll just go back to Europe. I don't like this climate out here," she told sound engineer Douglas Shearer, Norma's brother, who became Hollywood's most proficient sound technician.

"It's all right," Shearer answered. "You better go home now."

"But first I'll make a reservation on a slow boat to China."

She rushed to the beach house, ignored her family, and went right to bed. "I hope I never wake up," she snapped at her sister, Rose.

Irving Thalberg called her the next day about noon. Marion still wasn't out of bed. Before Thalberg could say a word, Marion blurted out, "I want my contract broken right now, Irving, I'm not coming back to the studio."

"Marion, listen to me," he said. "I don't know what you did in there, but the test was fine. You stunned the other people with that test. You're one of the few who's getting a new contract. Your test was the best. Do you want to see it?" he asked.

"No, absolutely not," she answered.

The studio still had to deal with Marion's stammer, which appeared whenever she was nervous. It never showed on the soundtracks, and rumor has it that her scenes were done in very short takes of three or four minutes.

Hedda Hopper, as close to Marion as Louella, always believed that the confidence Thalberg had in her got her over the hump. "She only joked about her confrontation with talking pictures," Hedda said later.

On one occasion, she turned to the columnist and said, "Hedda, somebody told me I should put a pebble in my mouth to cure stuttering. That goes back to the Greeks, you know. But during the first day, I swallowed the pebble, and that was the end of that cure."

Another, more sinister bit of gossip, depicted Marion as mouthing her words while another actress, theater trained, spoke into the microphones. There's no doubt that Hearst would have paid anything to keep Marion in the movies. But technically it was almost impossible to fake a track in the very early days of sound when Marion made *Marianne*, her first talkie. In any case, Marion's voice was so intimately known to the Hollywood establishment that any deviation from her normal, silvery tone would have been detected.

Several years later Marion's status as permanent companion to Hearst almost blew up into a national scandal because of the Internal Revenue Service. She was audited down to the amount of money she spent annually on nail polish. One IRS commissioner told Marion he didn't consider her an actress in the technical sense, hinting that her paychecks came because of her status as Hearst's concubine. He told her she owed a million dollars in back taxes and threatened to make a nasty public issue of the case if she didn't give in.

There was a small grain of truth to the claims by the IRS. Marion didn't, in fact, have many expenses. The bills were all paid by Hearst. On the other hand, friends estimate that the actress gave away more than $500,000 a year to friends and needy charities. "She would hear of an operation needed by the son of a lighting man," said Hedda Hopper.

"And that very day she would drift quietly over to him with twenty thousand in cash, telling the man she didn't want to be paid back."

Naturally this meant absolutely nothing to the IRS, and the commissioner laughed out loud when Hedda and others tried to intercede for her. The commissioner finally told Marion secretly that he would let her off if she paid $900,000 in cash.

She hadn't the heart to sell the jewelry Hearst had lavished on her. And the old man would have interceded if she sold any of the property.

In desperation, she turned to Mayer. Quickly and with no questions, he gave her $900,000 in cash. And she accepted, with the provision that Hearst never be told. (The secret was kept from Hearst through tricks of accounting where paychecks were recorded when none actually existed.) To pay the money back, she worked twenty months without pay.

Almost every two years Hearst, Marion, and a coterie of friends toured Europe in grand style—all expenses paid. On one occasion both Marion and Mrs. Hearst were more or less on the same tour. How that worked has never been precisely explained.

Since Hearst could never get enough of churches, statues, and paintings, Marion's sense of fun kept the tours afloat. She concealed fine wine in thermos bottles, hid from Hearst in the catacombs of Rome, and climbed over a fence into the secret and inaccessible palace of the Duchess of Alba in Madrid.

One prank, however, backfired.

Marion and Hearst were guests of honor at a luncheon in Paris held at the Elysees Palace. She was chatting with a handsome young French colonel in the dining room. "I noticed a half-opened door," Marion said. "And I wanted to find out what was behind it."

Slipping into a confining closetlike room, Marion noticed that the room's major fixture was a huge safe, one door of which was half-opened.

"I just happened to look through. Something was in there—a fancy document written in French. I thought: 'Just for fun, I'll sneak this thing out.'"

She stuffed the document under her slip and went back to the luncheon. "I thought it might be fun to read it. Then I could mail it back anonymously with a note, 'You left this hanging around.'"

Marion quickly forgot about it and plowed through an afternoon of shopping before returning to the hotel. "I started to take a bath and the darn thing fell out. I thought: 'Oh, what a nuisance.'"

She took it to Hearst who exploded. "What did you do that for?"

"You know me," Marion answered. "Curiosity."

"A butterfly with glue on her wings" was the way Hedda Hopper described the MGM star. "She was wistful, unselfish, and witty—rare commodities in this town," said Hedda.

Who was the most beautiful film star of the twenties? Many claimed the title, but Marion Davies stood in a class by herself. William Randolph Hearst, her lover, spent thousands blowing up this photo to promote the latest Davies film.

Hearst, using his Paris office, had the document translated and was thunderstruck at what Marion had stumbled upon. It was a French proposal for a pact between France and England—and it discussed the need for a pact because of the growing threat of Nazi Germany.

Journalistically, it was a bombshell.

The document's loss became a scandal in France, where suspicion was focused on Hearst even before his papers printed a detailed story about it. Hearst was ordered by the president of France to leave the country. Gendarmes, supported by members of the French secret service, blasted into the hotel room and tore it apart "We will give you exactly one hour to leave," he was told.

"W.R. never said a word about it afterwards, and I didn't either," Marion wrote in her diary. "When anyone would ask how he got hold of it, W.R. would say, 'I haven't the slightest idea.'

"He did say to me, 'Thanks for the scoop, Marion.' A newspaperman just loves that kind of thing. And W.R. remained a reporter all his life. He also told me it was okay because the pact was against America— although I could never understand what he meant. But I never did anything like that again."

Back in Hollywood, Hearst's anger focused on MGM in general and Irving Thalberg in particular. Hearst was convinced that Thalberg's obsession with Norma Shearer's career was preventing Marion's emergence as a major actress.

No sooner had the Academy Awards been established than Hearst decided Marion had to have one. First, he tried a project of his own, *Peg o' My Heart*, a terribly old-fashioned story that had the all-too-adult Marion playing a very young girl. He decided that the honored screenwriter Frances Marion would fashion the script into an award-winning vehicle for Marion. "I was appalled," Frances said. "I loved Marion, but he was trying to sink her with these trite old stories."

Frances Marion, however, was too frightened of Hearst's power to protest. "Luckily, Thalberg wanted me for another project . . . very badly. I lucked out."

Marion Davies always claimed that it was Hearst himself who thought up the Oscars—though clearer evidence pegs the idea to Mayer. "He wanted me to win the Academy Award in the worst way. You bet your life he did," Marion wrote. "He suggested the idea to Mayer at a party. But I missed out by a mile—or should I say by twenty miles. I never won, and I thought several times of cancelling my membership. I used to say that it was a plot."

Both Marion and Hearst came to hate both the Academy and its awards—a fact that was to have dire results later. "I thought the Academy Awards were designed to create an incentive. But they were bound to create jealousy. You would go to the show and think you were going to win, but somebody else did."

Hearst was so heavy-footed in his attempt to make a serious, saintlike actress out of Marion that a vicious legend was created—that Marion had absolutely no talent and was in films only because of Hearst's bribes of MGM. The evidence proves otherwise. King Vidor, who directed Marion in several silent comedies, called her "the most talented comic actress in films. The only problem was Hearst."

Everyone also took it for granted that Marion's pictures, weighted down with special effects and costumes ordered by Hearst, lost MGM millions of dollars over a ten-year period. It was a myth. Marion's MGM pictures cost the studio $10,007,000 and earned $14,401,000, which outdistanced Norma Shearer's overall earnings by about $200,000.

Hearst and Thalberg first clashed over the successful Broadway play, *The Barretts of Wimpole Street.* The publisher knew that MGM had purchased the property and felt that Marion would be the perfect "Elizabeth Barrett Browning," the long-suffering heroine of the piece. Hearst even made Mayer sit through another showing of Marion's performance in *Quality Street,* a weepy classic not unlike *The Barretts of Wimpole Street.*

Mayer agreed. "I don't see why Marion shouldn't play the role," Mayer told Thalberg. MGM's crown prince was immediately offended. "If you remember, it was purchased for Norma, and she expects to do it," Thalberg said, also pointing out the great dissatisfaction of the theater owners over Marion's turgid attempts at drama.

After a struggle of two months, Mayer informed Hearst that Norma had already been assigned the role and that "it would be a violation of her contract to cast Marion"—which was not strictly the case.

Two years later, when the Hearst party was once again in Europe, Hearst asked Marion to pose for photographers in the lush surroundings of Trianon, Marie Antoinette's hideaway at Versailles. In her billowing, floor-length dress and a Parisian hat, Hearst commented that she was "the very picture of Marie Antoinette." He purchased an armload of Stefan Zweig's 1932 biography of the French queen and assigned Marion and some of his associates to read the book.

Back at MGM Hearst once again stormed Mayer's offices, carrying his copy of *Marie Antoinette.* "This is just the sort of project for Marion," he said. "Can you object to this?"

Mayer nodded in mute agreement, waiting until Hearst was gone before calling Thalberg. "Irving, we've got trouble with Hearst again. He wants Marion to play Marie Antoinette."

Thalberg snapped back, "I bought that book for Norma more than a year ago, and we have already started planning the production." Thalberg told friends that *Marie Antoinette* was to be Norma's swan song. "First she will make *Romeo and Juliet* and then *Marie Antoinette*," he told Mayer. "Then she'll retire. How could she follow those achievements?"

The studio head was on the spot. Assigning the film to Marion could cost him both Thalberg and Norma Shearer, since both worked under fairly freewheeling contracts. He called Hearst up at San Simeon. "Marion can do it," he said. "If you guarantee to fund it yourself." Hearst choked into the phone, saying he would get back to Mayer later.

Hearst funding of the film was out of the question, and he knew it. The depression had taken big bites out of his publishing empire, leaving Hearst hanging by a thread. "We pass," he told Mayer.

These negotiations became so well known during the thirties that all sorts of gossip surfaced about Marion Davies's career. She would never have made a picture, it was said, if Hearst hadn't paid her way. She was a tragic, giftless performer without redemption, according to another story. They dubbed her voice. Her entire face had been created through surgery. She had started as a whore. Hearst found her after drinking had forced her off the Broadway stage. All these stories, and many more, became a part of the Hollywood legend.

These rumors resurfaced in a devastating manner in 1941 when Orson Welles unveiled his masterpiece, *Citizen Kane*, about a newspaper magnate of withering ego and his drunken mistress. In the Welles film the mistress was called Susan Alexander, and Welles dwelled at length on her drunkenness, lack of talent, and stupidity. Dorothy Comingore, who played Susan, resembled Marion in a fleeting way, and was devastating in her hesitant, stammerlike pattern of speech. The film was finished and ready for release before the word got back to Hearst. And even then it was by accident.

Hedda Hopper, who had been tipped about the contents of the film, called the executives at RKO Studio, producers of the film, and demanded a private showing. Three days later, with Orson waiting for a verdict, Hedda viewed the film portrait. In one scene, where Susan Alexander tried to perform on stage to derisive reaction, Hedda openly cried, "You son of a bitch. How can you do this to them. You bastard, I'm going to have your hide for this."

Welles was greatly disturbed. His plans called for full distribution of the film on the grounds that parallels to the Hearst–Davies relationship were slight.

Hedda stopped at a phone booth and called Richard Berlin, a major Hearst executive. "You better get somebody over there to see *Citizen Kane*," she said. "There will be hell to pay if the film is released without a report to Hearst."

Louella Parsons, the Hearst columnist, had heard the same wild rumors as Hedda. But she didn't believe them since she had asked Welles about it and received a strong denial. "The main character is a publisher," he told Louella. "But it could be one of several people. As for the girl, she's an opera singer." Louella was appeased.

After Hedda's report she was ordered to see the film by Hearst executives. Louella was equally tearful during the screening. "How can you do this to them?" she screamed at Welles, who was starting to get alarmed.

The filmmaker knew the basic power and quality of his film, which many still believe is the best movie ever made, but he was up against Louella (and her twenty million readers), Hedda (and her ten million readers), and all the power of the Hearst empire.

Louella first appealed to Mayer. "I haven't seen it," said the MGM chief. "Well, I suggest you do," she replied.

The afternoon *Citizen Kane* was screened for Mayer he called RKO and offered to pay the studio the $800,000 the film had cost if it wasn't released. No dice, said RKO.

But the going was rough. No major distributor would touch the film, and it had to be released on a theater-by-theater basis, making it a little-viewed picture. And although it was nominated for ten Academy Awards, the pro-Marion Davies coterie in the closeknit organization prevented it from taking any major awards. (It received only one, for best screenplay.)

Despite the damaging characterization of *Citizen Kane*, it was the clash between Hearst and Mayer that led to the devastation of Marion's career and ended the star's tenure at MGM.

"Marie Antoinette was the straw that broke the camel's back," Marion wrote. "W.R. had his heart set on it. I decided that I was going to try my best. I wasn't sure I could make the grade. I read all the histories about Marie Antoinette, and I went through the whole routine. Finally, I could visualize myself as Marie Antoinette with a big white wig and upturned nose. It was a big disappointment to both of us."

Several months after Mayer's refusal, a crew of workman paraded onto the MGM lot at dawn. Using two cranes and four bulldozers, the fourteen-room bungalow was split into three pieces. Two days later, at the height of rush-hour traffic, the three sections were driven through the heart of Hollywood and over the hill to Burbank where they were set up on the Warner Brothers' lot.

Police all along the route stopped traffic, and crowds gathered to view the crystal and rich brocade that decorated the little palace. It was a visible defeat for MGM and for Mayer.

And although MGM wouldn't let her play a French queen, she certainly exited like one.

BOOK THREE

Damsels in Distress

Harlow at her first publicity session. Her overt sex appeal would later be toned down. But privately she carried the burden of an image she couldn't live up to.

7

The Tragic Muses

JUDY, JEAN, AND THE OTHERS

Judy Garland clung to her stand-in and shivered in the darkness. All around her, unseen, were the hundreds of dancers, singers, and stars (including Gene Kelly and Walter Slezak) who were supporting her in a lavish new musical, *The Pirate*. Five times they had started the music, and five times they had waited in vain for Judy to burst on the scene in her $125,000 dress and sing a frenetic production number called "Voodoo."

For the scene the sound stage (the size of two football fields) had been blacked out, its doors sealed with tape and guarded by a phalanx of studio police. A roaring fire had been lighted, and dozens of native drummers were stationed in a semicircle, where they pounded out an authentic voodoo call—a call to the spirits of evil, the spirits of the dead.

Judy, bone thin and tight as a crossbow, had spent four hours in Makeup and another being sewn into her billowing dress. Her husband, Vincent Minnelli, was directing with love and care, fitting his schedule carefully around his drug-crazed wife and her bouts with paranoia. Realizing his role was as a father figure as well as a husband, he had coaxed and coddled Judy, painfully drawing out her performance minute-by-minute. But now the pressure was on. It was costing $20,000 an hour to keep the "Voodoo" cast assembled and waiting for the singing star to appear. So he did what was necessary. "Let's move it, Judy," he said. "We've got four hours to get this number on film—and four hours only."

★ 165

She looked up at him through a drug haze and nodded. "Bastard," she said through clenched teeth. "He's as bad as the others."

Judy had already recorded "Voodoo" almost a week before, producing a strident, hysterical vocal track that was almost painful to hear. But it was "Voodoo," after all, and therefore not completely out of character.

So for the sixth time Minnelli signaled for the playback. The towering fire was stoked and a two-story door opened to the darkness of a midnight sky for ventiliation.

This time Judy leaped into camera range, reproducing the movement of a Haitian rite with chilling accuracy. Then she moved within two feet of the fire. She stared into the flames, and her eyes opened wide with terror. "I'm going to burn to death. They want to kill me," she shrieked. "They want me to burn to death. It's a trick. Don't you see? It's a trick. They want me to burn to death." Tears ran down her face, streaking the makeup that had been so carefully painted on. She ripped her dress, tore off her earrings, and began running from one extra to the other.

Her voice came out in a croak. "Do you have any Benzedrine? You must have. Give it to me, please. Give it to me. They won't let me have any." She repeated the pitiful plea over and over again, alternately sobbing, laughing, crying, and, finally veering completely out of control. She was led off the set. The production number was junked.

In the MGM front office, Louis B. Mayer accepted the news with much anger and not a little guilt. He would tell the world that Judy had been coddled, pampered, and supported emotionally as if "she were my own daughter." But, privately, Mayer expressed his shame at the greed that had made him push Garland to the breaking point.

When the crackup came, and everybody knew it was only a matter of time, Mayer told his secretary, Ida Koverman, "We should have given her more time off. We should have put her in fewer films."

Those were hollow words. In the three years after Judy's breakdown on the set of *The Pirate*, Mayer pushed her into one quick production after another until, finally, she was a broken star and never again able to function as a competent performer.

Thus MGM lost one of its most valuable assets. In just ten years, from 1938 to 1948, Judy Garland films brought in $180,000,000 at the box office. For four years she was in the golden circle of the top-ten box office champions.

Instead of ensuring care, this only resulted in greed that would eventually sop every level of her considerable talent. Mayer and his seedy lieutenants merely stood by and squeezed every last drop from her professional abilities. This was hardly an isolated incident, because MGM was a throwaway organization. As soon as the bloom was off the rose of any star, Mayer shoved him or her into a creative trash compactor and then kicked the star out the front gates. He had practiced this cruel method in the Roaring Twenties, perfecting it with each succeeding decade until his touch was as chilling as an oriental despot's. Mayer made the MGM Girls, and he could break them at the slightest whim.

Jean Harlow had died because of this attitude, as had Barbara La-Marr, "the most beautiful girl in the world." Silent star Alma Rubens was coaxed onto morphine by studio physicians and then fired when her addiction became a problem. Still other stars, such as Mae Murray and Hedy LaMarr, were consigned to poverty simply because they incurred Louie's wrath. And their ordeals didn't end at the MGM gate. Easily the most powerful man in old Hollywood, Mayer saw to it that the MGM rejects were blacklisted at every other major studio as well. Since Warner Brothers, Paramount, Columbia, and Twentieth Century-Fox all relied on star loans from the MGM stable, they were loath to hire MGM's outcasts.

Judy Garland's life was the ultimate Hollywood tragedy. She was literally reared on the MGM lot from the age of eleven, when she was still a pudgy, awkward adolescent.

The week she was hired, a producer asked Mayer, "Are you sure she can make it in pictures? She's so chubby and gangly."

"Don't worry about it," Mayer answered. "You won't recognize her in six weeks."

How right he was. Within two months he had changed the playful, cheery (but plump) young girl into a sullen, nervous (but slim) young lady. She photographed better, danced better, but cried herself to sleep each night.

For the first time, Ida Koverman contradicted her boss. "You can't do this to her," Koverman said. "You can't destroy this girl's childhood." Mayer told her to mind her own business.

Several weeks later Ida was shocked at the apparition that was once babyish Frances Gumm. The childish figure was gone, replaced by the slim body of an older woman. Her eyes were dull and staring. Her skin was waxen. "They're starving me to death," she told Ida. "Please make them give me more to eat."

Mayer's secretary knew it was impossible to countermand Mayer's stern directives to the studio commissary cooks that Judy was to be given tomatoes, light chicken broth, and a two-ounce hamburger patty. Every

This was a publicity shot. Judy was rarely allowed the bounty of a large
steak and fries. Mayer ordered chefs to ration her food and report any
violations directly to him.

The casting call for "Toto," the errant dog in *The Wizard of Oz*, involved hundreds more dogs than these. The heartbreak on the yellow brick road didn't show yet in Judy's face.

Mickey, Judy, and the MGM orchestra in a number from *Babes on Broadway,* the first of the enormously successful series that left both performers drained. *Below:* Busby Berkeley directs Judy and Mickey Rooney in the final production number from *Girl Crazy.* It was during this grueling film that pills became a necessity, then a habit, and finally, an obsession for Judy.

Judy as the world loved her. The poignant tramp. The bittersweet clown whose dreams didn't come true.

Judy Garland, on the comeback trail after her drug-ridden MGM years.
Director George Cukor coaches her.

night Koverman would whip up thick vegetable soups and thin, top-grade steaks and sneak them into Judy's dressing room. Even the technicians were in on the secret, making sure that neither Mayer nor Judy's mother ever got word about the subterfuge. Since the star's figure continued to decrease, nobody was the wiser.

But Ida could do nothing about the pep pills administered to the teenager as if they were penny candy. These pills, so much a part of the Garland legend, have been discussed and dissected so many times that they've become one of Hollywood's givens. Still, so many books and doubtful memoirs have clouded the truth that a quick look might prove enlightening.

In 1938, when the studio was trying to groom Judy for *The Wizard of Oz*, Mayer's secretary received the following order one morning: "Have her mother get the studio doctor's prescription for sleeping pills. She's reporting to the set so tired she can't work." Ida took the memo but debated whether to put it into effect. Then Mayer popped back out of his office again. "While she's at it, she can also lay in a supply of that stuff they use to pep you up in the morning." He noted Ida's disapproval. "By the way," he told her, "I'll tend to the rest of Judy's diet. You let it rest."

Frances Marion, the noted MGM scriptwriter of the thirties and forties, remembers Judy's mother doling out the pep pills on the set every few hours. Starting a conversation with the young star, Frances asked her about the pills. "I have to take them, but I hate them," she said. "I hate the wake-up pills the worst, because they make me hop around like a Mexican jumping bean."

The writer got two Cokes and strolled with Judy across the vast backlot. Stopping before the Andy Hardy sets, where Judy had toiled upward of sixteen hours a day, Judy suddenly blurted out, "I love to sing, but I don't want to be a star. All of them seem so unhappy. You know what? I'd like to sleep until noon every day."

There were plenty of signals that a tragedy of great proportions was developing. But Mayer couldn't afford to heed them. The quickie black-and-white musicals for which Judy and Mickey Rooney were so famous had to be made in an assembly-line fashion. It finally reached the point where each extra Garland pound cost the studio thousands in new costumes, retakes, and special editing to make her look the same in each frame.

During the filming of *Strike Up the Band*, Mayer noticed more poundage on the screen and called her into the office. "Let's get it straight, you have to follow my orders letter by letter."

"But, Mr. Mayer, I am. I try to."

"Don't take that tone with me," he said. "I hear you eat cream puffs and chocolate cake on the sly. No wonder you're still shapeless. Then it's reported that when we do use you in a scene you arrive late and walk around like a zombie."

Judy began to cry. "That's because I've been in vaudeville since I was five, Mr. Mayer. We never went to bed until after supper at midnight. So I got used to sleeping late. I can't break the habit."

"From now on, you follow those orders or I'll fire you—you and your mother both," said Mayer, dismissing her coldly.

This approach couldn't have been easy on a seventeen-year-old whose entire family depended on her for support. And so began the horror of pills and paranoia that ended with her death at forty-seven, many years later.

MGM apologists such as Dore Schary, who succeeded Mayer, claim that the studio would "never have given that girl pills which would have interfered with her career." And he was right—to a point. The adult Judy Garland no longer needed the studio to provide the chemical haze in which she was used to functioning. A dozen doctors, a score of willing pharmacists, and even friends provided her with the steady main-line train of drugs that slowly eroded her physiology.

Her husband, Vincent Minnelli, says he could never plug up most of these sources. But at least he tried. Several times a week he would conduct drug raids on the house he shared with Judy. Once she was gone, Minnelli searched every crack and cranny of each room. There were pills sewn into the hems of drapes, hidden in underwear drawers, and stuffed inside dummy pill bottles. Finally, the marriage dissolved in the tidal wave of chemicals that destroyed Judy's movie career.

The legacy of greed was eventually reaped on the set of the biggest musical in the studio's history, *Annie Get Your Gun*. The Broadway smash had been purchased for and tailored to Judy Garland. It was meant to be the crowning moment of her career. She, however, was beyond immediate hope.

Gulping Benzedrine by the handful, Judy reported to the MGM recording studios to dub the musical track. It took six tortuous weeks to produce fifteen mediocre tracks. Never released to the general public, the Judy Garland *Annie Get Your Gun* album is a pitiful souvenir of a woman coming apart. In the song "I Got Lost in His Arms," Judy's voice emerges as a terrible moan, drifting off key dozens of times. "I Got the Sun in the Morning" is virtually unplayable.

Still, Mayer and the MGM brass decided it would do and ordered filming to commence under the baton of Busby Berkeley, as cold-hearted a genius as the movies ever produced. He and Judy were particularly antagonistic as a result of the grueling shooting schedules of the Mickey Rooney–Judy Garland musicals—a condition for which Berkeley was not to blame.

But Judy didn't complain. She was past caring. She did tell executive producer Arthur Freed, "I don't think we're a very good combination right now." (Berkeley was then in the midst of a drinking cycle that was to effectively end his own career.)

Down to ninety pounds, Judy faced her first day before Berkeley's cameras in a wilted condition. For the better part of three hours she merely stood leaning against her makeup trailer—her eyes dull and unfocused.

Then the director began shouting at four children and a group of extras hired to support Judy as she sang "Doin' What Comes Natur'lly." Judy shuddered, remembering, perhaps, the tearful encounters on the sets of the Andy Hardy musicals. Her eyes met Berkeley's, and she turned and walked to her car. She was not to make an appearance for three days.

The actress was undergoing the trial by pills and rejection that would eventually make her one of Hollywood's folk heroes, a fragile victim of big business and the race for bucks.

Her nights became long journeys through the ups of Benzedrine and the downs of Seconal. (A makeup artist at MGM tallied Judy's pill intake during the day alone at "more than one hundred.")

If the nights were hellish, the dawns were tortuous. Just before sunrise at about 4:30 A.M. she would call one of several assistant directors. "What kind of day do you think this will be?" she would ask. "If only the sun would shine." Then she would call a second, third, even a fourth time. Assistant director Al Jennings noticed that what little optimism she expressed at 4:30 would disappear by five or six. "Al, I don't think it's going to be a nice day. It's just awful. There's going to be fog, maybe even rain." By 7 A.M. Judy would begin discussing the real enemy—her own inability to function. "Al, I don't think I'm going to be any good today. I don't think I should come in today."

"Judy, Judy, listen to me. You're going to be fine."

You're going to be fine. They had been telling Judy that for more than ten years, psyching her up to work unendurable hours and make unendurable films. But somehow, through the intervention of her mother, her husband, Vincent Minnelli, and the strong arms of Ida Koverman, she had always been pulled back from the brink of complete nervous collapse. This time the reserves were all used up.

She rarely appeared on the set of *Annie Get Your Gun* before noon after the first week and usually left before 4 P.M. She appeared more like a sleepwalker than anything else, mouthing her songs as if she were in a perpetual dream state.

Three weeks into the shooting schedule Judy showed up at MGM's executive projection room to see the first prints of her "Doin' What Comes Natur'lly" number. Watching the screen with horror, she slid further down in her seat as the embarrassing footage rolled by. "Jesus Christ," she said at one point, rushing over to a water fountain and gulping down a fistful of Benzedrine capsules. "How could you make me look so bad?" she hissed at Berkeley.

One afternoon, when executive producer Arthur Freed came to the set, Judy seemed to lose all control. While playing a simple love scene with co-star Howard Keel she suddenly collapsed and slid out of his arms and onto the ground. Her eyes blinked and tears stained her face. Although fellow cast members were also crying, Freed rushed over to her and shook her as hard as possible. "What the hell's the matter with you? Get up off your ass and let's film this scene." Fortunately, Judy was too far gone to notice this indignity.

Several days later the actress began rolling her eyes during "I'm an Indian Too," a number with seven Indian actors. Alex Romero, a character actor, had to support Judy by grabbing her under the arms. She couldn't stand up, didn't know where she was, and, finally, couldn't open her mouth. "I've never seen anybody so far gone on drugs," he told Freed. "I don't think she even knew who she was."

The MGM executive offices were only eighty yards, due east, from the *Annie Get Your Gun* set. But they might as well have been in Peking. Louis B. Mayer, Dore Schary, and the other Metro moguls had gradually built up an entire monarchical court around themselves, making them as inapproachable as Louis XIV of France. Closest to them were the sychophants who sat around with their tennis tans and tight Beverly Hills pants and nodded yes whenever asked a question.

Mayer and others actually thought the musical film was headed toward a major Judy Garland success until the accounting reports showed otherwise. Seven weeks into the project, the books showed that more than $2.7 million had been spent on the production, including the price paid for the Irving Berlin play, but less than forty minutes of usable film was in the can.

"At first, Judy's failure to report on time and her absences from the set were interpreted as the willful tantrums of a spoiled child," said Vincent Minnelli. "And I was similarly innocent about drugs. Barbiturates and Benzedrine were, after all, a cure for the stresses of white-collar life. They were 'respectable.' Too late, I learned that they were more addictive and toxic than the opiates used by low-life junkies."

When the New York office received the reports of wasted film, unpardonable costs, and overtime, it took less than an hour for the execs to fire Judy. Most of the supporters of the actress assumed that this callous act was an isolated incident—dictated by the collapsing economy of the film industry in 1949. There was potent evidence to support this belief. MGM box office revenues had plummeted from $17.9 million in 1946 to $4.2 million in 1948—a condition directly related to the rise of television. And the studio, which was releasing more than fifty films a year in the thirties, produced only twenty-four in 1948. The $2.7 million already spent on *Annie Get Your Gun* could, quite easily, make the difference between profit and loss for the lumbering old studio.

Still, it wasn't money that dictated the cavalier treatment of the studio's most popular star since Joan Crawford. Judy Garland was a victim of a perverse heartlessness that was bred into the soul of MGM by the unforgiving, vindictive Louis B. Mayer. Since MGM's creation in 1924, Mayer and his lieutenant, Irving Thalberg, had had a chilling, impersonal attitude toward the studio's stable of stars. The MGM Girls were treated like cattle—fattened and groomed to luminous sleekness. But as they grew older and lost their bloom MGM put them out to pasture—usually informing them of the action in a memo delivered by one of the front office flunkies. Only Katharine Hepburn, Greta Garbo, and Norma Shearer (Mrs. Irving Thalberg) were exempt from the grim studio reaper.

This callous treatment was meted out to MGM's very first international star, Barbara LaMarr, whose last days at the studio were wrapped in a drug haze ironically similar to Judy Garland's. They called Barbara LaMarr "the most beautiful girl in the world," a title she had carried since her adolescence. Raven-haired and ivory-skinned, she was discovered by Douglas Fairbanks, Sr., and his wife, Mary Pickford, and cast in a supporting role in the first version of *The Three Musketeers*. But her fame predated her tragic movie career.

In 1916 (when she was fourteen) police hauled her in after a raid on a gin-and-burlesque dive in downtown Los Angeles. She was charged with violation of the city's work permit statute and sent to Juvenile Hall. She wasn't Barbara LaMarr yet; she was Rheatha Watson of Imperial, California, a sparsely populated desert furnace known for its date palms.

She appeared before Judge Jonston Hall at 9 A.M. the morning after her arrest, wearing a severe white dress and her hair falling in a cascade around her shoulders. "Miss Watson," said the judge kindly, "do your parents know you're here performing onstage?" Rheatha shook her head.

Judge Hall looked at her for a few seconds, sighing as he made his ruling. "Technically, Miss Watson, you haven't broken any criminal statutes appearing here onstage. But you're too beautiful to be without constant protection in this city. Your beauty could be a ticket to tragedy . . . you go back to your parents and stay there under orders as a ward of this court."

News of the judge's ruling quickly reached the city desks of the three Los Angeles papers, who dispatched reporters to intercept the girl on her way to the bus station.

Adela Rogers-St. Johns, headed her off with a phone call made from the judge's very chambers. Adela talked Rheatha into detouring to the Hearst paper's city room long enough for portraits to be taken.

"When I took her into the city room everything stopped," said Adela. "I remember city editor Jack Campbell staring at her and then saying to me, 'Helen of Troy, I presume.' "

Three full pages of pictures ran in the morning editions under the headline, "THE GIRL WHO'S TOO BEAUTIFUL." Notoriety notwithstanding, Rheatha Watson disappeared into the barren Imperial Valley, not to reemerge until she was seventeen.

Then she changed her name and made a second try at the relatively bright lights of Los Angeles. It was as public as the first—in fact, Barbara LaMarr was never again to make a move without the blinding glare of the press. This second time she called Adela from the train station, where she'd arrived with a wedding dress under her arm. "Can you come to my wedding, Adela?" she asked. "I'm going to be married tomorrow."

The journalist, with two photographers at her side, attended the nuptials of the "too beautiful bride." The bridegroom was a handsome and well-heeled young lawyer who blanched when he saw the reporters enter. And with good reason. The next morning, after his photo made the front pages, he was arrested for bigamy—the very married father of three young children.

From jail he told Adela, "I had to have her. It was like I went crazy for two weeks. I just knew I had to have her."

It was back to the Imperial Valley for Barbara.

Two years later, armed with a work permit signed by her parents, she stormed the casting offices and was hired on her second day in town. Her first film, *Harriet the Piper,* attracted the attention of Mary Pickford, who alerted her husband. And the rest was history.

The movies were still in their first decade when Barbara LaMarr became a household word. Hollywood Boulevard was little more than a dirt road winding among dusty orange groves. Movie money was not only new, it was big. And the stars were on their own to sink or swim in a town that resembled the Sacramento gold fields of sixty years earlier.

By 1923 Barbara was earning $6,500 a week. She drove to work in a Phaeton with peacock-colored seat covers. Her Russian wolfhounds wore collars of sapphire laced with pearls. And there was, of course, the obligatory mansion. Like all the early silent stars, she poured her soul and her physical wealth into a pile of stucco with eaves that lay wrapped in the Pacific fog.

The house is still there—owned by a disco star who also seems likely to leave it behind. The entrance is off a storybook street in what they used to call "Hollywoodland." There is a Hansel and Gretel gate house with a set of flagstone steps off to one side. The steps are lined with tulips and jonquils. But they only stretch halfway up the hill, ending there in a pile of rubble and weeds. A road to nowhere! Only two rooms in the mansion were furnished before the needle tracks engulfed her life.

Barbara took the first shot of morphine from a studio doctor on the set of *Souls for Sale.* She had sprained her ankle during a Charleston scene and was due to be recuperating for more than a month. "Look, Barb, we're already over budget—we can't wait," said a solicitous executive producer. "Take a little something to keep you going for the next few days. Then you can take a nice, long vacation."

The vacation never materialized, and Barbara's life was already running out. Morphine was her closest friend by the time she became an MGM Girl in 1924. Its ravages, however, were well hidden. When the first stills for Barbara's first major Metro film, *Thy Name Is Woman,* reached Louis B. Mayer's desk, he shuffled them over and over until they were dogeared. In gowns that clung to her breasts and hips like liquid, she had the lush European looks that appealed to Mayer's latent but obsessive lust.

Barbara was the first of a series of MGM stars whom Mayer would place on a pedestal only to destroy them completely when they showed the slightest flaw. He viewed these women much as a wealthy dowager views prize crystal that she tosses at the slightest sign of chipping. "Here was a man," Clark Gable said of Mayer, "who wanted to hide in the shadows and peep out at virginal women who were controlled, body and soul, by him. But somewhere inside of himself was a voice that said, 'Destroy them. Destroy them!' "

It didn't take too much to crush Barbara's slight hold on reality. On the set of *Thy Name is Woman* the star was making it through the grueling schedule with the help of brandy in a silver flask and morphine administered by needle in her dressing room. Faint rumors finally reached Mayer and Thalberg, who wrote her off immediately—despite the fact that *Thy Name Is Woman* became a major box office hit.

Barbara LaMarr presented problems of a particularly delicate nature for Thalberg since his first sergeant, Paul Bern (later Jean Harlow's star-crossed husband), had developed an obsession for the doomed woman. He sat at Barbara's feet on the set, smuggling in her booze and negotiating midnight deals to continue her morphine flow. On one occasion, he provided his own apartment as a love nest for Barbara and her latest one-night stand. He even entertained her husband as the dalliance proceeded.

MGM's hot screen lover at that moment, John Gilbert, came to Thalberg's office in the uniform of a Russian hussar, slung his booted legs over a chair, and said, "Look, Irving, Bern's in real trouble. He's spending all his time nursing that slut Barbara LaMarr. I think he's going over the edge."

"What's the attraction?" asked Thalberg.

"Easy, Irving, he's got a Magdalen complex. He's out to save the whores of the world. But he's the one who needs the protection, not LaMarr."

It's interesting to note that the front office, including Mayer, spared no expense in saving Bern, one of their own, while Barbara was allowed to career downward to addiction and death.

Five days after she finished *Thy Name Is Woman*, MGM canceled her contract. She died, in the agony of morphine withdrawal, two years later.

There was no room at MGM for weakness and fragility. The studio was not so much plagued by tragedy as it was the cause of tragedy. It was no accident that the survivors among the MGM Girls, such as Debbie Reynolds, Greta Garbo, and Jeannette MacDonald, were women of iron.

Barbara LaMarr slipped quietly out of sight. No mess. No bother. But it wasn't always so easy to throw smoke screens around the damsels in distress. Many of them broke out of the MGM closet and into the headlines, causing orgies of embarrassment. One of these was Alma Rubens.

While she was still an MGM star, Alma's life drifted out of control and into the limelight in January of 1929. On that day, dressed in a Parisian nightgown, she ran frantically out into the traffic on Hollywood Boulevard with two uniformed attendants chasing her. "I'm being kidnapped. Save me. They're going to kill me," she screamed.

It was the same old story. Alma had suffered a series of almost crippling migraine headaches on the MGM lot. Naturally, she consulted one of a number of physicians off and on the studio payroll. "They told me, 'Just take this. You'll be okay,' " she told her friend Joan Crawford. "It was only later that I learned what a terrible poison it was."

By the time she crashed completely, MGM had already written her off. The screenwriter Frances Marion remembers a conference held during the hysteria over sound pictures. "They were deciding, at a table, the fate of silent stars who were faced with the trauma of sound pictures," Marion said. "Somebody finally said, 'What about Alma Rubens?' "

"Nothing," said Mayer. "Her contract's almost up. Let her go. She's too sick, anyhow."

"We who were fond of this actress knew the reason for her halting memory and glassy eyes. We wondered why she didn't heed the lesson of Wally Reid [a silent superstar] when he died of drug addiction. Alma's name was scratched off the list without any evidence of pity," Marion concluded.

In one of those touches of irony for which MGM was to become famous, Greta Garbo was shoved into *The Torrent* and became a superstar when Alma became too ill to continue the picture.

Many MGM veterans, including Joan Crawford, came to feel that there was a measure of deliberateness about these tragedies. "Some people on the lot, and I'm not going to say who, almost licked their lips when these actresses were counted out."

Deliberateness certainly seems to have played a part in the unnecessary death of the studio's biggest box office draw of the thirties, Jean Harlow. A week earlier she had been on the set, lively and in fine form, filming *Saratoga* with Clark Gable, when suddenly she collapsed. After only one afternoon in the hospital, she died, stunning the film world. Even the studio's Nazilike publicity department was caught off guard for once. They weren't even able to publicly announce her illness before she was dead.

Like so many other disasters, Harlow veered toward her death with not a little help from Mayer, (who had been jilted, according to agent Arthur Landau, by the blond bombshell).

Jean, only twenty-six, incurred Mayer's displeasure when she accepted an invitation to appear at a White House benefit organized by Eleanor Roosevelt—a woman high on Mayer's hate list. For the first time in her MGM career, Jean disobeyed not only Mayer but her mother—the iron-willed woman behind her career.

To get even, Mayer devised a shooting schedule for *Saratoga* that called for seven-day weeks and eighteen-hour days. Jean met all the demands and even slept on the lot several nights so filming could resume the next dawn. The *Saratoga* sweatshop was a drastic contrast to the treatment MGM afforded Garbo and Norma Shearer, who went home at 5 P.M., and Joan Crawford, who had contract-mandated vacations between each film.

But Jean never complained . . . said nothing, in fact, except that she needed ice-cold showers each morning to brace her for the day. Hairdressers noted that she was listless, practically dozing through the sessions.

On Saturday morning, May 29, 1937, the *Saratoga* crew was filming the key bedroom scene between Jean and Clark Gable. The actress was lost in a daze. All traces of her vitality were gone. She even snapped at director Jack Conway when he tried to get the weekend shoot underway. "Come on, kids, speed it up," he said.

Clark picked Jean up, kissed her, and was ready to drop her onto a chaise lounge, but they were to nuzzle each other affectionately first. The cameras rolled and nothing happened. For the first time in their years as screen lovers, the magic simply didn't happen. "Jean, Jean, what's the matter with you?" Gable asked.

"Gimme a second," said Jean, frantically reaching for a glass of ice water. "Okay, Jack, ready," she said.

Gable gathered her in his arms a second time. He looked down and saw that she'd broken out in a cold sweat. As he eased her onto the chaise, Jean slipped into a coma.

"Jesus Christ, this girl's really sick," Gable yelled at Conway. She was carried into her dressing room to wait for the studio doctor, one of those who practiced medicine by the bottle. There, under the gray-green makeup light, Gable suddenly saw the terrible condition she was in. The bones on her face, normally covered by the baby fat that made her so popular, jutted out in an angular fashion. Her face was bluish-white.

Jean revived an hour later and began the wisecracking banter that was her trademark. Conway heaved a sigh of relief. "But I think she better have a long vacation after this picture is wrapped," he told Gable.

"You tell that to those bastards in the front office," said Gable as he helped Jean to her limousine. She looked at him one last time—her lips curved upward in an exhausted smile. "Tell Bill [her fiancé, William Powell] that I've gone to bed. I'll talk to him tomorrow."

Slowly, the gossip of Jean's breakdown filtered into the conversations at Mayer's poolside party where the execs frolicked as their stars toiled. "How bad is it?" Mayer asked vice-president Eddie Mannix.

"She's tired, L.B. There's nothing more to it than that," Mannix replied.

By this time Mayer had begun his prize collection of racing horses, all of them tended by a corps of stable boys. He was notified at the slightest drop in their temperatures, at the slightest hint of a sneeze or cough. This tender care, however, didn't extend to the stars in his stable. Collapses from exhaustion were a common occurrence on the MGM lot. In the early forties, Judy Garland developed anemia and chronic exhaustion during the "Andy Hardy" musicals; Myrna Loy was forced into court to obtain a rest after twenty straight pictures; and the mother of child star Margaret O'Brien simply ignored the studio rules and took Margaret to Tucson, Arizona, during the filming of *Meet Me in St. Louis.* "I don't intend for my daughter to become another Judy Garland," she said. "Margaret has made five films without rest. And I do not intend for this pace to continue."

Jean Harlow had no family knight to fight the battle against exhaustion. If anything, her mother, Mama Jean, and her stepfather, Merino Bello, urged a faster pace since their revenues depended entirely on Jean's output. So she left the studio forever in that limousine; her descent and death were already inevitable.

Her career at MGM lasted only five years but each month brought its own special torment. Arthur Marx, the studio's story editor at the time of Jean's death, said, "She was a girl who had lived a thousand lives and none at all. Onscreen, she seemed to be the essence of the American girl out for a good time in spite of the smothering economic depression. Quips dripped from her mouth in an acid fashion. Her platinum hair (which had resulted from a hairdresser's mistake), her white silk dresses unsupported by underwear, and her insolent sexuality became the rage for young girls the world over." Such diverse public figures as heiress Hope Hampton and Hitler's mistress, Eva Braun, surrendered themselves to her quicksilver image, parroting even her walk and smile.

She was a victim of scandal from the start of her MGM career in 1932.

Without a champion in the studio, Jean Harlow was immediately adopted by MGM vice-president (for the story department) Paul Bern, a diminutive, shy man of forty. MGM was trying to cast a blockbuster film, *Red-Headed Woman*, and Bern decided to test Jean, who was languishing on the studio's contract players list.

"Are you crazy?" asked Bern's superior and closest friend, Irving Thalberg. "Just look at her. About all she can play is jazz baby, 'cheap women' roles. She's no comedienne. We need somebody like Joan Crawford for this role."

Crawford herself had turned it down, going over Thalberg's head to Mayer, who granted her request. The studio, in fact, had tested more than thirty actresses for the comedy, creating an industry joke about "The Red-Headed Woman Syndrome." The studio's huge, sixty-year-old superstar Marie Dressler slapped a red wig over her jowled face and persuaded cameramen to shoot a test that was delivered to Thalberg's screening room.

Bern and Harlow made a test of their own, directed by Bern after more than a week of coaching Harlow. The minute Thalberg saw it, he said, "She's it. You were right."

Jean Harlow became a superstar with that first picture—the ultimate blond bombshell who burst on the scene as a redhead. In the last frame of the comedy, Jean walked away from the screen, stopping just long enough to wink out at her audience. "Gentlemen prefer blondes. Sez who?"

She became Paul Bern's Eliza, fashioned into a sexpot by the retiring, plain-faced executive. He helped her select a movie star house, took her shopping for designer clothes, taught her how to talk like a lady—a talent she would rarely have a chance to use.

Then began the dates, the secluded weekends, the nightclub hopping that scandalized MGM. The word was out. Jean Harlow was a gold digger, a lady who owed her career entirely Bern. And who knows what she had to do in return.

Nobody noticed that this Pygmalion fixation was a life pattern for Jean. She had been discovered and nurtured by Howard Hughes, was passed on to Bern, and would be under the thumb of one dominant man or another until the end of her life. Paul Bern was simply the first one to insist on marriage as part of the unspoken contract. Until Jean entered his life, Bern had been considered a confirmed bachelor, a Casper Milquetoast whose persona was buried in culture.

Thalberg, the first to be informed of the impending marriage, was horrified. He told his wife, Norma Shearer, that Bern needed protecting, that he would have to be dissuaded from going through with the wedding. "Paul, this will be a terrible mistake," he told Bern in the presence of Norma. "Where can it lead? Personally, I think Jean is only using you."

For the first time in their relationship, Bern turned on his heel and walked out on his friend. The wedding would occur with, or without, his approval.

"The view common in Hollywood at the time was this: Jean had latched on to Bern and was aggressively pushing him into the marriage," said silent star Colleen Moore, who was close to Jean and one of her confidantes in the months preceding the wedding. "The truth was that Paul was deeply in love with Jean. People assumed that the intellectual Bern couldn't exist side-by-side with the flashy Harlow. In fact, their opposing natures were a bonus."

So the wedding was held with a hesitant Thalberg and Norma Shearer both serving as members of the wedding party.

Bern took his bride to a hilltop bower lost among pines and eucalyptus groves. It was a strange and lonely house that was frequently lost in fog. There was an outdoor pool, a secret garden lit by a hundred Japanese lanterns, and a secluded entranceway that could be found only by those familiar with the layout.

The house itself was built and tailored for a man living alone. There were only three livable rooms plus a tiny kitchen, and the entire arrangement could have fit inside a castle turret.

This solitary house, with its hidden entrance and the tangled groves surrounding it, was to become crucial in the tragedy that began to develop only months after the marriage. A brief period of sunny happiness followed the wedding, but it was soon replaced by a tangible sadness. It was inevitable, since heartbreak always seemed to linger beneath the surface of Jean's life.

Like Marilyn Monroe two decades later, Jean Harlow had an aching void in her life that nothing could fill. While still an adolescent, she had been fashioned by her mother, Mama Jean, into a pouting and painted woman, exactly what Mama Jean wished she had been. Born Harlean Carpentier, she was a shy homebody as a child, a girl of quiet pleasures. Therefore, it took considerable energy to shape her into the hard-edged, brassy dame that was Jean Harlow. (Even her movie star name had been fashioned by and borrowed from her mother.)

Until she met Bern, she had drifted on the edges of the closed

Barbara LaMarr, the girl who was "too beautiful" to last, is held by screen lover Ramon Navarro in a scene from MGM's *Thy Name is Woman*, the last film made before Barbara sank into a hell of drugs and drinking, and an early death. Mayer, who refused to be bothered by her drug problems, wept publicly at her death. *Left:* An early MGM director (unidentified) gives Barbara LaMarr instructions for a Ziegfeld-type spectacular. She was Louis B. Mayer's most beloved star in spite of the tragedy that dogged her.

The world really knew Barbara LaMarr as "the girl who was too beautiful." The dress was "it" in 1925, a year before she died of drug abuse.

Jean Harlow at the height of her platinum fame, sound testing for *China Seas* with Gable, Mary Jane Saunders, and a kneeling Wally Beery.

Jean Harlow and husband Paul Bern at a premiere only four days before
Bern's suicide. The photo hardly depicts them as a doomed couple, and
there are no apparent signs of Jean's disgust with Bern, which would be
depicted so graphically in the press.

In a spirited session with MGM's corps of still photographers, Jean Harlow looked vibrant and healthy. But she told one of them, "This will be my last sitting." She died a week later.

Hollywood society of the time. She had too many of a scarlet woman's trappings to be accepted at Pickfair, the mansion of movieland's queen, Mary Pickford. Yet she was too unsure of herself to blend with the "jazz baby" crowd of Joan Crawford and Constance Bennett.

Paul Bern changed all that, bringing her into the glittering company of the film colony's bluebloods. She became a welcome party guest at the monstrous castle, San Simeon, built for MGM star Marion Davies by her lover, William Randolph Hearst. She lunched with Norma Shearer, had tea with Mrs. Louis B. Mayer, and was taken under the wing of the city's queen of gossip, Louella Parsons.

None of this filled the void between the reality of who she was and the fantasy of her screen image. Tensions ripped her apart. Hollywood columnist Dorothy Manners, probably as close to a best friend as Jean had, used to keep a secret case of gin hidden for the actress in her house. Protected from drink by her family and then by her husband, she would dash into Dorothy Manners' apartment on the way home from the studio and gulp glasses of gin before frantically rushing out again to rendezvous with Bern or her mother.

She dissolved in tears once during an interview with Louella Parsons. "I keep hoping for another type of role, another type of picture," she said. "But I know I'll never get it, Louella. I don't want to play the hard-boiled girls anymore. It's so different from the real me. I wouldn't speak to that sort of woman even if she was a guest in my own house."

As the weeks of her married life progressed she also grew tired of playing Eliza Doolittle to Bern's Pygmalion. "I feel like I should buy a grammar school dress and sit there with a pencil and paper," she told Dorothy Manners. "He doesn't talk to me, he lectures."

But on another occasion she told director Jack Conway: "He explains things and let's me know that I've at least got a brain. He's different and doesn't talk fuck, fuck, fuck all the time."

Arthur Marx, a close friend of Bern's, said that the Harlow–Bern marriage seemed idyllic. "At the wedding, the bride hung on the arm of her adoring groom. Whatever mysterious undercurrents were at play here, as biographers and columnists would soon claim, they were not discernible during the first weeks of the marriage."

The laughter and romance were actually a facade. Beneath the surface an emotional cancer was growing. Both Jean and Bern would soon slip and then fall into a chasm of infamy.

On the morning of September 5, 1932 (only three months after the wedding), the body of Paul Bern, nude and shot through the head, was found by his gardener. The gun he had used was lying near his right hand, and a carefully written note was found nearby—addressed to Jean.

Dearest Dear,
Unfortunately this is the only way to make good the frightful wrong I have done you and to wipe out my frightful humiliation.

Paul

P.S. You understand that tonight was only a comedy.

The gardener, Cifton Davis, had been well schooled by all his MGM clients. So he alerted the chief of security at the studio rather than the Beverly Hills Police Department.

Mayer was reached at his home immediately. He gasped, "Oh my God!" and called for his chauffeur. Thalberg and Norma were hosting their usual Sunday brunch and had left word with the staff that they should be disturbed only in a dire emergency. The butler held back for a few minutes and then wrote a note to Thalberg. When it was delivered to him his face turned ashen. He grabbed Norma and they both rushed to the death site.

The suicide note was pocketed by Mayer and might never have been given to the police if a publicity man hadn't insisted. He carried it from the death room, showing it to Thalberg and his wife. "What does this mean?" he said. "What's been going on between those two?" Thalberg, consumed with grief, merely shook his head. "This could ruin Jean's career. Do you realize that?" Mayer yelled. "Where the hell is she?"

At first, that seemed to be the big mystery since servants had seen Jean and Paul laughing and drinking wine near the swimming pool the night before. Norma, more tuned in to the MGM gossip mill than her husband, suggested that Jean was back home—with Mama Jean. "Why would she be there?" asked Mayer. "She spends many, many nights there," answered Norma. A quick phone call to Mama Jean confirmed it.

Irving drove through the ghostly quiet streets of Beverly Hills, hoping to reach Jean before the news spread too far. Mama Jean, her hair wild and her eyes red from weeping, opened the door and told him Jean was still asleep. It was left to Thalberg to break the news. Nobody knows what passed between the star and her boss during the half hour on an upstairs balcony of the mansion. Norma, who stayed in the car, could see only their heads and feet. She remembered that Jean almost collapsed when Thalberg broke the news. "She seemed to be both angry and full of grief at the same time," Norma later said.

Mayer, meanwhile, was talking to Mama Jean and learned that Jean's stepfather was on an early morning fishing trip with Clark Gable. Mayer let out a howl and phoned his publicity chief, Howard Strickling.

"Can you imagine what the press will do if they see Gable returning with Merino Bello?" he asked Strickling. "We've got to head them off."

Using maps and five secretaries from the MGM publicity department, Strickling mapped out a plan to block off the two intersections leading to Jean's home. "They will have to run over one of my girls to get to that house," Strickling told Mayer. And he kept his word. Gable's car was diverted, and Merino Bello had to sneak through backyards and leap a seven-foot-high fence to sneak into the house.

The studio had made it over that hurdle but still had the biggest potential scandal in Hollywood history on its hands. Details of the death and the contents of the suicide note were on the wire services four hours after the body was discovered. But MGM, on the advice of Louella Parsons and her boss, William Randolph Hearst, answered no questions and made no official release. In hindsight, this was disastrous for the studio and its star. Reporters, with nothing whatsoever to work with, printed crass rumors. Paul Bern was an impotent pervert. Jean Harlow was a raving bitch who drove him to suicide. He had been killed by Jean. He had been killed by gangsters hired by Jean's mother. There was a sex orgy the night of the death. The suicide note was a fake. The studio had bought off Los Angeles District Attorney Buron Fitts. All of these theories and dozens of others appeared in newspapers around the world.

Jean was secluded, cloistered. Mayer haunted his office and sneaked in and out of a rarely used back gate of the studio.

The police, however, began unearthing disturbing clues. There were two smashed brandy glasses at the edge of the pool and an overturned crystal bottle. There were footprints in the muddy grass at the edge of the pool—not leading to the house but to the end of the property's hidden driveway. It appeared as if someone had left the house in a hurry—there were tread marks from a very large car on the drive.

Fitts sifted through the evidence and then ordered an arrest warrant written up for Jean Harlow. "This was no suicide. This was a murder," Fitts told one reporter.

Word of the possible indictment reached Mayer. He quickly called a summit meeting in his office and said, quite seriously, that MGM might have to throw Jean to the wolves. "This may be one scandal too many," Mayer told Strickling. "We could end up with federal intervention into our operations."

Strickling disagreed. "She's obviously not guilty," he said. "Why not make yourself and Harlow available to the D.A.? He'll drop the charges immediately."

It was done.

But the public cloud over the scandal was never to disappear—not even a half-century later. Denied access to all information sources, Hollywood reporters and the city's establishment fashioned a legend entirely of back-fence rumor. Paul Bern, so the story went, was cursed with minuscule sexual organs that made him unable to have normal relations with any woman. Worse, said the gossips, Bern had nurtured within himself a perverse and masochistic hatred for all women, especially for Jean Harlow. So vivid was this hate that Bern repeatedly abused his wife with a military cane on their nuptial night. This in turn so damaged Jean's kidneys that she died after that tragic collapse in Clark Gable's arms.

The legend, which became accepted as fact over the decades, describes Bern, naked, making one last attempt to sexually satisfy his wife. (He supposedly used a dildo—allegedly scooped up by Mayer and destroyed.)

Almost everything is wrong about this legend. The L.A. district attorney was in the process of obtaining an indictment against Jean for murder. Mayer used considerable political clout to halt this proceeding. The D.A. himself said of the theory: "Nonsense. I thought, at first, that Jean had found Bern with another woman and shot him. We uncovered no sign of impotence in our investigation."

As for the savage beating inflicted on Jean only hours after the wedding, testimony from dozens of friends belies this. Colleen Moore, for instance, spent the afternoon after the wedding with the bride. "The reception was held the day after the wedding," she said. "Marion Nixon [a fellow star] and I arrived an hour early. We spent the time chatting with Jean in her bedroom.

"Now Jean never wore underclothes. She hated them," said Colleen. "I guess if I'd had her beautiful figure I wouldn't have wanted to bind it up in girdles and bras either. Anyhow, she took off her slacks and blouse, standing there as the good Lord made her (and what a job he did), while we helped her into her long garden dress.

"Now if she'd been covered with black and blue marks or had marks covered with makeup, we would have known it. You can't fool an actress with makeup. If anything," Colleen concluded, "she was happier on that day than I had ever seen her."

But what about the other woman? Neighbors, though far down the hill, told detectives that they heard Bern and a hysterical woman yelling at each other for more than an hour. Then there was silence. Then the sound of tires screeching down the hill. A guard further down the hill saw a long, black car speed out of the private drive, then head east toward Pacific Coast Highway, which, in 1932, was the only plausible route to Santa Barbara and San Francisco.

Fifty years later it seems obvious that the shrill, midnight visitor was Dorothy Millette, Paul Bern's common-law wife, who suddenly reappeared after reading about the Bern–Harlow nuptials in a New York newspaper. The argument was real, and it was fateful, leading directly to Bern's suicide.

Arthur Marx, Bern's closest friend and associate after Thalberg, says that Dorothy Millette, after living with Bern for the required time, suffered a peculiar form of mental illness that left her with amnesia. The costs of sanitarium care were borne permanently by Bern, who had been assured by doctors that hope of recovery was impossible.

In 1931, however, Dorothy Millette came out of her twilight coma with no memory of the years between. She began asking for Bern the next day, and finally reached him by mail at MGM. Somehow Bern, already enraptured with Jean, explained the circumstances and persuaded her to stay in the East and begin life anew as he had done himself.

The series of letters, checks, and transcripts of telegrams between the two have been in the MGM legal vaults all these years, under orders from Mayer. One letter, written two weeks before the suicide, wishes Dorothy well on her move from New York to San Francisco and promises to continue the financial support.

Arthur Marx believes that the woman had become obsessed with regaining Bern in any way possible. Bern told his secretary that Dorothy had called him from San Francisco and "might be on the way down here." Hysterical on the phone, she threatened to go public, a move that would have made Bern a bigamist and might have destroyed Jean Harlow's delicate hold on her career. (It's important to note that Jean Harlow, at the time of the suicide, was just coming into her own. She was in no way the superstar she would become after the tragedy.)

Marx says Bern agreed to meet her. He ordered Jean over to her mother's and then met with Dorothy Millette. "She refused to understand his predicament," said Marx. "If she brought a charge of bigamy, which she was legally able to do, it could finish Jean Harlow. In fact, all three principals would suffer. He could even draw a jail sentence."

Bern's friend says the "frightful wrong" mentioned in the suicide note was a "fake quarrel Paul picked with Jean to get her out of the way when Dorothy arrived. And his suicide made good the frightful wrong. Jean Harlow never admitted that her husband was impotent," said Marx. "And no one ever learned the truth from Dorothy Millette either."

The spurned wife returned to her San Francisco hotel room in the hired car that brought her to Beverly Hills, boarded a steamer headed up the Sacramento River, and jumped to her death beneath the paddle wheels. After she was pulled from the water, detectives who searched her hotel room found the word "justification" printed on a notepad by the bed.

It must have been painfully obvious to Jean Harlow that Mayer and Thalberg were interested in protecting the studio and not her. Otherwise, they would not so carefully have nurtured the legend that Bern was an impotent, emotional cripple and Jean a castrating bitch. Eddie Mannix said that his boss had worked out an arrangement whereby a physician would testify, verbally and by letter, that Bern's sexual organs were shrunken and nonfunctional. (Such testimony was provided to the D.A. and others.)

Jean returned to work with Gable in *Red Dust* two weeks after the tragedy, beginning her rise to superstardom. It was never to be the same, however. Thalberg, the snotty, creative, Victorian prince at MGM, was always glad to use the millions made by Jean's films (and Joan Crawford's) to finance the box office bombs he designed for his wife, but he was disdainful of Jean. He told one associate that she was cheap, obvious, "a money machine." And he was furious when *Time* magazine, in one of its first Hollywood covers, passed over studio pleas to use Shearer or Garbo, and slapped Jean, in nightgown, onto newsstands around the world.

This careless attitude and disdain led directly to her death.

After she was rushed home that May 29, unable to stand, MGM executives ignored pleas from several of Jean's friends to make an on-sight visit to Jean's home. Jean's lover, William Powell, personally suggested to Mayer that he check up on Jean himself.

What Powell and others knew about Mama Jean threw them into hysteria when they learned Jean was so ill that she had collapsed. A Christian Scientist to the point of fanaticism, Mama Jean believed herself to be a powerful healer on the order of Aimee Semple McPherson. It clouded her reality and made her view illness as if it didn't exist.

Gable, Powell, and even Joan Crawford sought admittance to the house and were stopped at the door. Mama Jean refused to open it more than a few inches, saying that she was in constant attendance at Jean's bed, "praying and serving." Phone calls were also spurned.

Gable and MGM character actor Frank Morgan, being unable to reach Jean for days, finally forced their way into the house and followed Mama Jean up the stairs to the white satin boudoir for which the star had become so famous.

"Doesn't she look better now than last Saturday?" whispered Mama Jean.

They were aghast. Jean was crumpled into a fetal position. Her face was blue, she was moaning in pain and drifting in and out of consciousness. She had recently vomited and was wracked with fever. Over and over again she called for William Powell.

Morgan, trained as a medic, took her pulse. Tears formed in his eyes. "Gable," he said. "I think she's dying. I wouldn't give her one more day."

Still, Mama Jean refused to allow Jean to be taken to the hospital.

Bill Powell was dispatched to break through Mayer's corps of eunuchs, forcing his way into Mayer's house at the beach. "Harlow's dying," he screamed. "Her crazy mother won't let us get her to the hospital or operate. You're the only one who can move her."

Mayer hesitated. Finally, an associated producer who arrived after Powell dialed Jean's phone and held it out to Mayer. "Don't you believe me?" he said. "She's dying."

"Give me that phone!" Mayer yelled.

Jean was at the hospital less than an hour later. But it was too late. Infection from her kidneys had spread throughout her body, even affecting her brain. There was no help.

Louis B. Mayer arranged for the funeral himself, sending a massive heart of white Italian roses that cost $5,000. And the statements from the studio were glowing—praise Jean never had while she was alive.

"She was," he said tearfully, "just like my own daughter."

A decade later, Judy Garland didn't die from MGM's heartlessness, she simply staggered out through the gates to face a broken life.

She had finally begun making an attempt to return to the *Annie Get Your Gun* set and was in fairly good shape one afternoon when an officious young man delivered a form letter. Your services are no longer required; get the hell out, it said in so many words.

She began screaming, "No, no, no. They can't. They can't."

When she came out of the door of her dressing room the sound stage had been emptied, and a car was waiting to drive her home.

As with Jean Harlow there was the last gesture. The studio found a nice, secluded hospital for her and even paid a part of the cost.

"Would you have treated one of your prize horses that way?" Judy's agent asked of Mayer.

The old man turned his back and terminated the interview.

Another casualty of the MGM studio system was Luise Rainer, the first actress to win two Academy Awards in a row—ironically, an accomplishment that effectively ended her career.

A discovery of Mayer's, Louise was imported from Vienna where she had achieved the status of a minor star. (Posters and billboards in Austria referred to her as "the Viennese teardrop.") Mayer told fellow executives that he had brought Luise to the studio to "scare Greta Garbo out of some of her arrogance."

"If Greta sees that her acting can be duplicated maybe she'll make more of the pictures I want her to make," Mayer told MGM publicist Howard Strickling.

But Irving Thalberg saw potential in the Viennese actress that eluded Mayer. Thalberg created a showcase for her in *The Great Ziegfeld*, in which she portrayed Ziegfeld's first wife, Anna Held. Although she was only on screen for sixteen minutes she was named best actress (beating out Mrs. Irving Thalberg—Norma Shearer—who had been nominated for *Romeo and Juliet*).

Thalberg immediately starred Luise in Pearl S. Buck's *The Good Earth*, with the same result—she won another Oscar and was picked as "the actress to watch" by 50,000 readers of *Photoplay* magazine.

However, when she failed to make even one other decent picture, gossip columnist Louella Parsons invented the term "Oscar curse" to describe Luise's troubles. Louella was trying to endow the Oscar with emotional power and superstition, but the actress' problems were really a case of the studio trying to strike too quickly and too often while she was still hot.

Two legends quickly grew up around Luise Rainer. One depicted her as a casualty of Mayer's casting couch. She refused to sit on the Mayer lap, some said, and was therefore deliberately given poor pictures in an attempt to drive her out of Hollywood. Others said she was actually a casualty of the Thalberg regime, which ended with his death in 1937.

The real story of Luise Rainer, who many felt was a better actress than Garbo, has remained buried in a slag heap of gossip—perhaps because it reveals a highly unflattering picture of the Academy Awards and the studio system that ruled them during Hollywood's golden era.

The week Luise was nominated for *The Great Ziegfeld* in the winter of 1936 also saw the Academy of Motion Picture Arts and Sciences at its weakest point. Hundreds of actors (virtually every big name in town) and scores of writers had resigned from the Academy. They were enraged over attempts by Louis B. Mayer and others to use the organization to bust up the fledgling unions and defeat fair-wage proposals for the thousands of little people in the industry. It was a complicated Hollywood dispute. But, in a nutshell, actors, writers, and directors felt that the Academy had sold them out during the National Recovery Administration's attempt to deal with Hollywood's labor problems. The Academy was forced to support the studios (since executives dominated its leadership).

As a result of this stance, the Academy was crippled, and its membership dropped to forty. Only a handful of regular members were involved in the process that selected candidates for the award, and pitted Luise against Irene Dunne, Gladys George, Carole Lombard, and Norma Shearer.

"They never planned for her to win," said a former MGM publicist. "You must remember that Mayer and his fellow executives believed it was *their* prerogative to choose the Oscar winners. When they lost control of the Academy, they didn't treat Luise with the same deference that went to such previous winners as Norma Shearer, Mary Pickford, and Janet Gaynor."

In Luise Rainer's own words: "For my second and third pictures in Hollywood I won Academy Awards. Nothing worse could have happened to me."

After winning the Oscars, MGM thought she could do anything. The studio shoved her into one ludicrous picture after another—including the multimillion dollar flops *The Emperor's Candlesticks* and *The Toy Wife*, assuming that, like Crawford or Garbo, she could transcend even the silliest vehicles. But audiences weren't impressed.

Only three years after *The Great Ziegfeld*, MGM pressured Luise out of her contract. "I was just a piece of machinery with no rights," she said. "They completely abused me. I was catapulted into the position of being a box-office champion. It ruined my career."

Rainer subsequently married playright Clifford Odets, then divorced him and returned to Vienna—finally fleeing to London where she married a publishing executive. When she was reimported to Hollywood in 1983 as an Oscar presenter few people knew her name. This was particularly true of the press, to whom Academy publicists carefully explained Luise Rainer's backstage history.

Perhaps the final touch of irony to her story was that Luise and Greta Garbo left MGM, disgraced, in the same month.

8

Friday's Child

LANA TURNER'S STORY

The pulsing life of Beverly Hills didn't miss a heartbeat during the moments of agony when Johnny Stompanato's life drained out onto the pink carpet of Lana Turner's boudoir. The Rollses and the Porsches glided past the big house on Bedford Drive without so much as a stutter of their well-kept engines. No screams rent the heavens. No cacophony of sirens shattered the dinner hour. Sable rubbed against cashmere, Baccarat crystal clinked softly against Wedgewood plate, and the first perfume of the California jasmine sent a seductive aroma through the April fog. Dry winds from Death Valley, which had set tempers flaring earlier in the day, had dwindled out as moist and comforting air off the Pacific pushed over the Santa Monica Mountains and into the foothills.

It happened shortly after dark, but the crystal prisms in the house on Bedford Drive remained unlit. An automatic lawn sprinkler was flooding the gardenia beds, and the garage door stood awkwardly ajar—as if one of the sleek cars had been readied to leave. Inside the house, at the top of a sweeping staircase similar to those in Lana Turner movies, time seemed to stand still as the ultimate Hollywood tragedy unfolded second-by-second.

Lana stood pressed against a bedroom wall. Sobs wracked her body. Her hands shook so violently that she couldn't dial the phone dangling uselessly at her side. Her eyes turned from the unwatchable. In front of her lay her mortally wounded lover, Johnny Stompanato. He gasped for breath as his life's blood poured from a deep wound in his abdomen. Lying five feet away, almost buried in the carpet, was a kitchen butcher knife.

MGM's most slickly packaged movie star was at the end of a desperate road that was forged by her own fame. Only this time there was no press agent to soften the blow, no makeup artist to blunt the edges of the nightmare. This was no script. The lover who had pursued her and then bullied her because of her allure, and her considerable fortune, had been killed by her own daughter.

But she was stunned, unable to move. Her feet and hands were ice cold. How long did Lana stand there, trapped by fear and indecision? How many precious minutes did it take Johnny to die? Where were the police? Or the ambulance with its battery of life-saving technology?

There were no answers then. There are none now. Gossip, the powerful weapon of camouflage, had entered that house to obfuscate the truth and cloud the news reports. Days later, months later, even years later, the best legal and journalistic minds would try to disentangle fact from fiction to no avail. They faced a puzzling maze built of deliberate, artful confusion—one of the last creations of old-style Hollywood gossip.

And it started with Louella Parsons, the plump, omnipotent empress of Hollywood's journalistic elite. She'd just returned from late Mass that Good Friday, 1958, and had settled into the welcome calm of her darkened office, a seventy-eight-year-old matriarch weary of watching the Hollywood she loved disintegrate around her.

By 1958 the days of electronic journalism had begun, spawning television reporters, like Rona Barrett, who could broadcast the juiciest of news hours before Louella could get it into the afternoon paper. This had made her and Hedda Hopper elegant dinosaurs, dishing out a brand of celebrity dirt that seemed banal. But the old fire lurked just beneath the surface, ready to erupt with a dazzling power and finesse that nobody else could imitate. Nothing in her five-decade career demonstrated her awesome power as well as the Johnny Stompanato killing.

She'd half finished a cocktail when the insistent ringing of her office phone broke the reverie. Louella toyed briefly with the idea of letting it ring. What time was it? she thought to herself. It was late enough that it almost had to be an emergency. Finally, on the phone's sixth ring, she grabbed for it.

A servant heard her say, "Hello, this is Louella Parsons," in that vague twang so familiar to radio audiences. Then there was silence.

The servant saw Louella sink back into the couch and heard her gasp, "Listen to me! Calm down!" In calm, measured tones she told the mysterious caller, "Here's what I want you to do. Stay right next to this phone until I call you back; it'll only be a couple of minutes. Don't move anything. And for God's sake, don't call anybody else."

Louella hung up and grabbed the phone that connectd her directly to the news desks of the Hearst papers downtown. She was about to ring through when her private phone again broke the silence. "I know all about it," she patiently told the second caller. "Yes, yes. You better get over to Lana's right now. I'll call you there."

A minute later she had the night city editor on the phone. "You better clear some space on page one. Somebody's killed Lana Turner's boyfriend."

The implication of this violent death was as shattering to Louella Parsons as it would later be to the world. Lana Turner, the first of a new wave of superstars that came in with the forties, lived her life on the very edge of the fast lane. In nightclubs from Acapulco to Monte Carlo, she had splashed her life with the finest champagne and lived in the alluring quicksilver of news camera flashbulbs. For eighteen years before that horrible night on Bedford Drive, Lana Turner's life and career had became an integral part of the warp and weave of Hollywood legend. She really had been discovered at a soda fountain. She really had sold $12 million in savings bonds in one day by selling her kisses on a Seattle dock. And her films, bad though most of them were, had sold more theater tickets than the films of Norma Shearer, Jean Harlow, and Greta Garbo put together.

The *Los Angeles Times* film critic, Charles Champlin, once described her thus: "She has been in a curious way all the Hollywood legends rolled into one, the ballad from which a thousand other ballads were derived, the original who gave rise to the typical. I mean, to be discovered at a soda fountain became almost as much a part of the American dream as to be born in a log cabin had been. But Lana Turner was the one it happened to in that malt shop outside of Hollywood High."

Like millions of other young women in the war years, Lana grew up too fast. "I was dancing at the Trocadero and Ciro's every night and going to Miss McDonald at the Little MGM Red Schoolhouse," she once told Hedda Hopper. "It was a cock-eyed situation. There were girls who were prettier, more intelligent and just as talented. Why didn't they make it?" she asked. "It's a question of magic. You either have it or you don't."

Her brand of magic leaped from the screen in an early MGM

movie, *Love Finds Andy Hardy*, that impressed Louis B. Mayer as no other juvenile performance had since Joan Crawford's *Our Dancing Daughters* in 1928. But even more than Joan, Lana was packaged by the studio. The alchemy learned in the creation of Harlow, Jeannette Mac-Donald, and Judy Garland turned her into a star molded to the point of brittleness.

"I was just a kid of sixteen when I went to Metro, and they took me over completely. I was educated, gowned, groomed and assigned to customized films.

"They brought me along slowly. I posed for the dumbest Valentine pictures, and God did I make some bombs," Lana said recently. "Then, when they felt I was ready, they put me opposite Gable, Tracy, Robert Taylor. Then they put me opposite a new male star, finally making me strong enough to carry a picture for myself.

"Sometimes, though, life sped by in a haze," she added somewhat ruefully.

Lana's personal life also careened by. Before her international affair with Johnny Stompanato, a mob-connected pretty boy, she had gone through five husbands and a score of front-page love affairs—most notably with Tyrone Power and Fernando Lamas. The specter of Stompanato lying dead in the pink glow of Lana's boudoir suddenly revived the horror of the loose and immoral twenties when the federal government had made noises about moving in to control public debauchery.

Louella, who would have Hollywood's biggest story to herself for several hours, was at first hysterical about the implications of the story. "I can't figure out if Lana did it or even if there was a fight," she told the Hearst editors. She demanded a rewrite man.

The servant noticed that Louella was silent for about five minutes. Her cheeks flushed red and her voice took on a icy tone: "No, now you hear me out! If you send other reporters out here, we'll lose the entire story. Every newspaper in town will be camped on that lawn."

Louella won her point. She dialed the number of Lana's unlisted phone in the fated bedroom. She was silent until she began sobbing in answer to questions from someone on the other end of the line. "I'm here to help you. And I'll be here on the other end of this phone as long as you need me." Leaving the line open, she picked up the phone to the Hearst city desk a second time and asked for Dick DeSick, the ace rewrite man.

"Mr. D.," she said. "You know that hood Lana's been wrapped up with for six months? He's dead. From the best I can tell, Lana's daughter stabbed him to death about an hour ago. I just wanted you to know so you can pull the clips and get an early start."

DeSick, the writer who had sculpted and tightened Louella's stories for almost a decade, suggested that he call the Beverly Hills police. Louella almost dropped the phone. "Dick, they haven't been called yet. As far as I can tell, I'm the first outside person to know."

With the presses on hold downtown and the old Hearst International News Service waiting for a bulletin, Louella was sure of only two things: Johnny Stompanato was already dead, and a superstar's career was hanging precariously in the balance.

Of the Macbethean tragedy unfolding on Bedford Drive she and the world would always have only tortuous hints. To this day only Lana and her daughter, Cheryl, know exactly what happened. Periodically, they have revealed tantalizing splashes. The Stompanato killing remains a jigsaw puzzle with a handful of the crucial pieces tattered or missing completely. What's left is a skeleton story, a poignant road map with sorrow as a guiding beacon.

The first rumbles of the tragedy appeared that midafternoon. With two friends listening in the game room of Lana's sprawling house, the movie star and Stompanato had rekindled a violent argument over slights he felt Lana was dealing him. At one point, grabbing her by the arm and shaking her up the stairs, he screamed, "I'm good enough to do your errands, good enough to sleep with you but not good enough to take you to the Academy Awards."

Lana's face flushed with fear and anger. The man she had taken to her bosom when she was once again between husbands had turned into a viper, threatening her with force in a manner that was becoming increasingly terrifying. She bolted upstairs with Johnny behind her. "We've been through all this," she hissed. "I can't take somebody like you to the Oscars!"

Johnny slammed his fist into the wall and Lana ran back down to her friends. Visibly shaken, she offered them drinks and then sat down.

Crestfallen for a moment, Johnny threw on a coat, muttering that he was going home and would be back to take Lana to dinner at about 8 P.M. Lana later told Louella that she had collapsed into the arms of her friends, telling them she'd become increasingly afraid for her life and that of her daughter.

The dark young man who stormed out of Lana's house was hardly unfamiliar to Louella or to the Beverly Hills police. As he moved from bed to bed in the gigolo-for-sale set, he had accumulated sizable bank accounts. More than a dozen well-heeled ladies known to the readers of society pages had been wooed by Johnny and then strong-armed into paying blackmail. In one case, detectives were able to prove that $8,000 was fraudulently taken from a compromsied matron. But she refused to prosecute.

At first glance Johnny Stompanato had the looks of a matinee idol, with his dark curly hair, Grecian face, and weightlifter's body. He could have passed for a shabbier Valentino or a backroom wheeler dealer from Vegas. Actually, he was a society parasite, a part-time errand boy for gangland kingpin Mickey Cohen. He had the muscle but apparently little courage. His fists were used only on women.

He had greased his way slowly up the ladder of Hollywood society —aiming for stars with big, mineable incomes. Lana Turner was perfect. Their stormy affair, spiced by her teenage-style love letters, had lasted eight months. It had been punctuated by public battles in London, (from which he was ejected by Scotland Yard), and in Acapulco, where Lana told police she feared for her life. It was during this supposedly frightening period of Lana's life that she wrote the scorching series of love letters to Johnny that would haunt her during the aftermath of the tragedy. It was not insignificant that she paid Johnny's passage to London and supported him there, temporarily, in fine style.

Back in Hollywood, Lana's career reached its zenith when she appeared at the Oscar show as one of the best actress nominees for *Peyton Place*. When she appeared on the arm of her daughter, Cheryl, tanned and in an evening gown, two thousand of her peers gave her an explosive ovation.

Mickey Cohen later said that Johnny never got over his shame at being left home on that night. "Johnny told me that he couldn't understand why he was good enough to be a lover but not good enough to share her professional life," Cohen told reporter Aggie Underwood.

There was a peaceful week after the Awards ceremony.

Ten days after they returned from Acapulco, Lana's mother, Mildred, called Louella late on a Friday afternoon—ironically, one week to the hour before Stompanato would be killed. "Louella," Mildred said, "I'm worried about Lana. This guy's started to beat her up, making nasty threats. I think he could kill her."

Louella, having already received an intelligence briefing on Johnny from Beverly Hills Police Chief Clinton Anderson, told Mildred to file a formal complaint. "And don't wait too long, honey. I've seen too many of these things turn into tragedy."

Mildred immediately visited Anderson's office. "He could kill her, you know," said Anderson. "Do something to help us," she pleaded. Anderson pointed out gently that only Lana could file a complaint and that she would have to do it in person. Lana demurred, fearing both Stompanato and the press.

The stage was set for the events of April 4, 1958.

That night, the guests had left, and Lana was upstairs dressing when Johnny stormed back into the house at 8 P.M. A running fight started, ending with a screaming match in Lana's bedroom. Cheryl, thirteen, was watching television in her upstairs playroom. But she was becoming more and more distraught as the fight progressed to the hall. Johnny, enraged and shaking Lana by the shoulders, threatened to disfigure her so that "you'll never act again."

Out on the second-floor landing, Johnny started slapping Lana's face. The movie star hurled expletives in his face. Then, noticing Cheryl standing outside her door crying, she said, "Please, baby, go back to your room. Don't listen to this. Please, baby."

The events that occurred during the next half hour have become so clouded with rumor, innuendo, and inaccurate testimony that no set of facts agrees with any other. With Louella, Hedda, a press agent, and a superstar attorney involved, gossip triumphed over accuracy, blunting the nasty edges and salvaging Lana's career.

The known facts speak for themselves. Lana and Johnny moved back into the pink bedroom. Cheryl crept downstairs to get a butcher knife. She ran back up the stairs and stood holding the knife, just outside the door to the bedroom. While Johnny and Lana both grappled at the door, Cheryl was pulled inside. The blade sunk deep into Johnny's abdomen, severing the body's most powerful blood vessel. Cheryl started to sob and ran back to her room while Lana, her face white, cringed against the wall and clawed for the telephone.

Her mother got the first call. "Mother, Mother, call Doctor Mac [Dr. John MacDonald]. Get him over here quick. Something horrible has happened."

"But what?" asked Mildred. "Tell me what!"

Lana's voice trailed off to an unearthly moan. "Just get him over here, Mother."

Then a second call was made—a call later omitted from all versions of the event. Was that call to Louella Parsons? She was the only journalist powerful enough to pull Lana's career from the ashes. And one thing seems clear. She received a play-by-play account of the tragedy in the bedroom.

Mildred and Dr. MacDonald were the first at the scene. The physician could see immediately that it was too late to save Johnny. The damage to the body's largest artery had already killed him.

Attorney Jerry Giesler was called to Lana's house right after Dr. MacDonald. He walked across the bedroom to Lana and took her hand. "Lana, tell me as calmly and as quietly as you can exactly what happened."

"Cheryl was trying to protect me," Lana said. "She had been listening outside the door. When I first saw her burst into the room I didn't see the knife . . . only seconds later did I find the knife." Lana held up the weapon for Giesler to see.

"Just stay where you are," the attorney said, following Stephen Crane, Lana's ex-husband and Cheryl's father, into the child's room.

A sedative had been administered to Lana by the time Police Chief Clinton Anderson came to question her. Lana grabbed him by the arm. "Let me say I did it. Please let me say that I did it."

"Lana, don't," Anderson said. "We already know it was Cheryl."

Those few sentences have dogged Lana to this day. In Hollywood crime there is always one factual version (often doctored by studio executives and willing police) and one falacious, rumor-ridden story. Lana's plea to the police chief would set in motion a headwind of gossip that portrayed her as the murderer and Cheryl as a sacrificial lamb who took the blame. There is no doubt that Johnny's friend, Mickey Cohen, believed the second version, which was later portrayed in a Harold Robbins novel, *Where Love Has Gone.* Cohen, who saw the body in the county morgue, said, "A girl of thirteen couldn't have done this. She wouldn't have had enough strength."

Recently, Clinton Anderson said in an interview that the unusual position of Johnny's arm—it was raised—and the fact that the parties were moving, allowed Cheryl to inflict the fatal wound. Anderson said he never learned any facts that would have caused him to change his initial theory—"that Johnny Stompanato was killed accidentally by Cheryl Crane."

Lana and Cheryl were taken to the nearby Beverly Hills police station, a Spanish Mission–style building hidden by vibrant bougainvillea and flowering vines. Sitting across from the police chief, Cheryl was asked what happened. "Don't ask her," Lana said. "Ask me." Anderson persisted in his demand.

As Cheryl depicted her version of the dreadful twenty seconds, Lana tried to get a grip on her version of it. "She had heard John say he was going to destroy my face," Lana later told her personal manager, Taylor Pero. "The knife in her hand was to prevent Johnny from doing any damage."

"Lana didn't often talk about the Stompanato incident," said Pero. "But when she did she always stressed that the killing itself was an incredible accident. She watched Stompanato lift his arms to take a jacket off a coat hanger. This put his abdomen in the path of the knife." Until that moment, Lana told Pero, she had no idea of the depth of Cheryl's protective feelings.

While the investigation was proceeding, privately, at the police station and Lana's house, the biggest journalistic coup in Hollywood history was taking place. Aggie Underwood, the tough woman city editor of the *Los Angeles Herald*, had been given a thumbnail sketch of the crime by Louella Parsons in the hope that Aggie could mine her long-standing relationship with Mickey Cohen. And it was Aggie who broke the news to Stompanato's friend.

"There is a rumor that Lana wrote Johnny hundreds of love letters," Aggie said. "What do you think?"

"She was crazy about Johnny," Cohen said. "He showed me a couple of those letters, and they were something."

"Did he save them?" Aggie asked.

"You kidding?" Cohen answered. "He's got them somewhere in his apartment."

"I'm calling in my chit," said Aggie, speaking of the favor Cohen owed her for some previous journalistic favor.

Cohen gave her the address of Johnny's apartment on Wilshire Boulevard, an apartment the police hadn't searched because they believed Johnny was living with Lana in the Bedford Drive house. Using a professional master key, he let himself into the apartment while Aggie was still on her way there. The mobster found the letters in a velvet jewelry box, all of them tied neatly with a lavender ribbon that still smelled of Lana's perfume.

For Aggie Underwood the letters were the mother lode—the simpering, adolescent scribblings of a passionate Lana. In many of the letters she signed her name "Little Lanita." And in others she cooed about Stompanato's talents in lovemaking. They covered a period of about nine months, the latest having been sent only weeks before the death.

By the time Anderson got detectives to Stompanato's apartment, the letters were already in the paper. An extra edition of the *Los Angeles Herald* had been printed with pictures of Lana, Stompanato, and Cheryl on the cover next to one of the letters blown up to an enormous size.

Such a breach of a crime scene would probably result in a jail term for someone today. But under the lenient rules of the cushy Beverly Hills

Police Department, Anderson didn't even administer a rap on the knuckles, because it was Lana's career that the letters endangered.

Lana was down for the count, with executives at her studios—MGM, Universal and Fox—already betting against her. Her plaintive midnight cry to her agent that "I'll never work again. Never!" was uttered in desperation. And it was the cry of an adolescent—as if the soul of a very young girl were buried inside the glittering shell of a superstar. "With Lana and Cheryl that night, it was hard to tell who was the mother and who was the child," Louella said later. "Cheryl, even with all her fright, seemed to be providing the security for her mother."

Cheryl was carried off to Juvenile Hall, Mildred Turner was sedated and put to bed, and Lana was left to her grief and her thoughts. The girl who had been pampered and protected by MGM every second of her professional life was now a scandal-plagued star—a virtual leper in the film colony. It was this sudden ostracism that caused her to do something she had never done, to search inside herself for a hidden strength. It turned out to be strong and deep, making her the first movie star to turn tragedy into a triumph.

Just eight days after the killing, Lana Turner walked into a crowded Los Angeles courtroom and vindicated herself before the world. Until then she had hidden from the glare of the cameras and the hostility of vindictive tongues.

The setting was the smog-stained, grimy old Hall of Records in downtown Los Angeles. It was 9 A.M. on April 12. A long, green Cadillac belonging to Jerry Giesler, Lana's attorney, rolled up the hill, pushed its way through a smothering crowd, and stopped at the foot of a long flight of steps. A chauffeur in black uniform (specifically rented for the occasion) leaped out of the front seat and swung open the rear door. Giesler, a compact man with an eagle's countenance, was a celebrity in his own right. The divorce and criminal attorney had been so gallant and successful in defending film stars that "Get Giesler!" had become commonplace in Hollywood.

The angry mob of reporters rushed toward him and began pelting him with questions. When the chauffeur lent his arm to the lady inside, the mob grew silent.

No entrance in a Lana Turner film had ever been so spectacular. She wore a gray coat and gray suit. Dark glasses shielded her eyes. Her only jewelry were single pearl earrings given her the Christmas before by Cheryl. Flashbulbs formed a stagy spotlight as she walked slowly up the steps, looking straight ahead. At the elevators she was surrounded by reporters, harshly shouting questions at her, finally pinning her to the marble wall. "Please," Lana said quietly. "Please." The journalists fell silent and moved away.

Up on the eighth floor, four hundred spectators crowded outside the doorway. It was a sideshow—a circus of scandal in a city starved for glamour. Cigarette smoke clouded the air.

Lana stepped out of the elevator, pulled her shoulders up, and removed the sunglasses. She looked the crowd in the face and saw sympathy. The girl who had almost everything suddenly reached out and found the hearts of her fans. The housewives from Culver City, secretaries from the nearby skyscrapers, bobby-soxed teenagers—all reached out to the woman who had bewitched a nation in the forties.

Nobody was ever quite prepared for the clarity of color or the handsome starkness of Lana Turner, a star who equaled and perhaps bested her screen beauty. On that day she showed another side. Lana Turner was human, a woman of flesh and blood who was fighting a tidal wave of bad press to keep her child from becoming a victim.

"Did you see her!" cried one plump matron. "It was her. Did you see her?"

"Poor thing," cried another. Lana looked into her face and smiled a thank you.

A camped army of photographers with blistering floodlights faced the actress as she entered the courtroom. Some said that Lana Turner gave the performance of her life during those few minutes. Most people who were there would agree. Her poise shattered only once—when she faced down Johnny Stompanato's friend and boss, Mickey Cohen. That was only for a moment. She leaned on Giesler's arm. He smiled. And it was over.

After what seemed an eternity to the spectators, Lana was called to the stand. There was a hush. Then a grapple for the best view. More than a hundred women took off their shoes and stood on the benches to see over the bank of photographers at the front. Then others did it. Soon almost the entire crowd stood on the seats.

There was only the clack and clatter of the cameras. The carefully cultured voice of Lana Turner seemed to operate in a vacuum, becoming the only sound in the room. She sighed, ran her fingers through her platinum hair, and recreated the terrible moments during which Johnny Stompanato was killed.

"I swear it was so fast . . . I tried to think that she had just grabbed him in the stomach." Tears were running down her face. "Mr. Stom-

Clark Gable entwined with Lana Turner in the eighteen-year-old's first love scene. When Mrs. Gable (Carole Lombard) saw this still she haunted the set for days.

Lana Turner took her first dip into the quicksand of bad-girl roles with
John Garfield in *The Postman Always Rings Twice*.

A glossy Lana Turner in an avant-garde scene from *The Bad and the Beautiful*. Her personal troubles and career agonies were just ahead.

panato grabbed himself . . . he started to move forward. And then he dropped on his back."

Reporter Jack Smith of the *Los Angeles Times* said, "Lana seemed to be tearing each word from her throat as if it were an evil thing. Her blue eyes were luminous in the floodlights and scanned the ceiling as if searching for some way to escape."

"I saw the sweater was cut," she continued. "I lifted it and saw the wound." One of the spectators, listening to Lana, bent his head and closed his eyes.

Lana groped for the glass beside her with a trembling hand. She gulped some water and went on. "I tried to breathe air in his mouth. . . . I begged the police—'can't I say I did it?'" The words had a wrenching, wistful quality. Then it was over.

The verdict came within hours. "Justifiable homicide," said the foreman of the jury. There was a shout from the room. Her eyes averted, Lana Turner reentered the green Cadillac and drove off.

Most people in Hollywood sighed with relief at the verdict. In a Hollywood scandal, the whole industry is on trial. And most of them wondered how it had all gotten so crazy for the golden girl of the forties, the MGM successor to Harlow and Crawford.

It had been twenty years since Lana had first greeted the press and the world on the set of *Love Finds Andy Hardy*. Reporters had been driven onto the MGM backlot to interview Mickey Rooney and Judy Garland, the stars of the film. They were treated to a lazy picnic lunch in a picture-book setting of Victorian house fronts dotted with bushes and old gas lamps. The chatty session was well underway when Lana, then demure and brown-haired, waited for a pause in the conversation then stepped forward and introduced herself with a curt, "Hi, I'm Lana Turner."

She looked seventeen and acted thirty. Hedda Hopper told Louis B. Mayer after the press luncheon, "You have a tiger by the tail this time."

Several weeks later Lana dutifully appeared with her mother, Mildred, on one arm and MGM's publicity director, Howard Strickling, on the other for one of those treks to Louella Parsons's journalistic throne. Strickling had stripped Lana of her makeup, dressed her in a frock with a Peter Pan collar, and coached her on the limited range of subjects she was allowed to discuss—"Men, no. Drama lessons, fine." Privately Strickling told his staff to monitor Lana's every move—even at harmless premieres and USO suppers. "God forbid," he said, "that we should have another Jean Harlow on our hands."

First time out, the facade fooled everyone—even Louella and Hedda. "This is one young star whose head is screwed on straight," pontificated Hedda in a paean to Lana on a radio special. Louella merely rhapsodized about her freshness and candor, calling her "an altogether likeable girl."

Then the rumors started: Lana with Mickey. Lana with Bob Taylor. Lana with attorney Greg Bautzer, a handsome Hollywood squire whose reputation stopped just this side of rakishness. And, finally, they were saying it was Lana and Gable.

Louella deafened her maiden aunt's ear to a lot of things: trysts and dalliances that scorched her puritan sensibilities, and blatant affairs that outraged her belief in the sanctity of marriage. But she who trod on the Carole Lombard–Clark Gable marriage committed the cardinal sin. Not only did Clark and Carole live snuggly close to her Marsons Farm out in the valley, but she and her husband, Dr. Martin, were poker buddies of the Gables. Carole was one of only two stars (Bebe Daniels was the other) who had access to Louella's sacrosanct boudoir. Gable was the only man besides Hearst who could tell her off and get away with it.

The malicious tidbits leaking from the set of *Honky Tonk,* a Gable–Turner film, could have been merely the result of studio hype. Louella decided to make sure, unwittingly adding to the Lana allure. "Now listen to me, Howard," she told the MGM publicist. "If you guys are putting out this dirt to help that lousy little film, then knock it off. You know how jealous Carole is."

Howard stuttered into the phone. "Louella, this is the first I've heard about any of this. Lana's just a kid. Lemme check it."

He called her the next day: "Honey, there's nothing to it. Nothing's going on here. This is just a little offshoot of the gossip about everyone who co-stars with Clark."

Appeased, Louella let Strickling off the hook. "There's nothing to it," she said to her assistant, Dorothy Manners, as she dashed off to lunch. "It's not even worth a mention."

Hedda Hopper was more persistent. She refused to drop the matter until she had lunch with Strickling, Clark, and Carole at the MGM commissary. Gable laughed it off, Strickling puttered about nervously with his chicken soup, and Carole walked Hedda to the front gate after waving bravely at Lana and her mother from across the lot.

Privately, Carole suffered each day of the *Honky Tonk* shooting as if it were her private calvary. The movie had been in production a month when she hiked over to Marsons Farm on a Sunday and tossed a pile of MGM stills onto Louella's couch. The columnist reached for her glasses and spread the proofs out carefully. They showed a sexy Lana Turner entwined with Gable in some of the most torrid stills ever to come out of the studio photo labs. The Turner eyelids were lowered languidly, the bust that was to make her world-famous was thrust into Clark's face, and their arms and shoulders grappled in Grecian poses.

Louella tried to make light of it. "So what, Carole?" she said. "I've seen stills of you that were highly similar." "I know," answered Carole, "that's what worries me." The Lombard laugh echoed through the Sunday stillness as Louella eased her guest out to the brunch table.

The columnist decided, right then, to make one of her royal visits to the Gable–Turner set. Dressed to the teeth in black and pearls, with the limo ready to roll, Louella called Ida Koverman at 9 A.M. "Oh, Ida," she cooed. "I thought it would be best to let you know that I'm on my way out to watch the *Honky Tonk* filming today."

There was a slight intake of breath on the other end of the line as Ida, secretary to Mayer, let the impact settle. "What's up?" she finally asked. "It takes more than a backlot Western to get you out here."

"You bet it does," Louella answered. "And you know as well as I do the rumors about Clark and Lana. See you in a couple of minutes, dear."

With Mayer out of town and Louella obviously at odds with Strickling, Ida hesitated for a second and then buzzed Sound Stage Seven. "Get Jack Conway [the director] on the phone," she said.

"Mr. Conway's directing a scene, the camera is running," said a young page.

"Never mind," Ida said. "Get him to the phone."

A disgruntled Conway finally reached the phone. Ida blurted out the news about Louella. "What are you filming this morning?" she asked.

"A love scene. What else?" he said. The director couldn't help laughing.

"It's not all that funny, Jack. Louella's out for blood—Lana's. What's she gonna see?"

"Nothing, Ida, there's nothing to see."

Louella was on the lot and headed for the sound stage when Ida intercepted her. "What's up, Louella? Don't beat around the bush with me. What do you expect to find?"

"Lana's only seventeen," Louella said. "She's vulnerable and unschooled. But I've seen the way you can make them grow up overnight on this lot. Without meaning to, she could do Gable and Carole a lot of harm."

Ida Koverman tried to deflect some of the gossip columnist's ire, chatting about the lovely sunshine, about Louis B. Mayer's trip to Europe, about the rush of bachelors competing for Norma Shearer's hand. It was like trying to deflect a NATO missile with Kleenex. Louella, very much the cobra of gossip ready to strike, had honed in on Sound Stage Seven.

"Morning, Miss Parsons," said a young security guard as he swung open the door to the normally closed set.

The mist of make-believe suddenly enveloped them all. Gas lamps of a century earlier flickered in a perpetual sunset, casting a rosy glow over a honky-tonk interior hung with brocade. Gable, in a Rhett Butler suit and white Stetson, was slouched in a canvas chair, his nose deliberately buried in a script. The heroine—or villainess—of the piece seemed absent.

"Where is she?" demanded Louella in a stage whisper not lost on Gable, Conway, or the twenty members of the crew.

Conway was twenty feet above the set in an overhead crane, which he ordered to deposit him at Louella's feet. "You're about to see your scandal, kiddo," said Conway. "Tell Lana we're ready," he said almost offhandedly to an assistant director.

The lights had been turned to a soft amber. Love-scene pink, they used to call it. Then the door to a dismally small dressing room opened, revealing a visibly shaking Lana, platinum hair blazing like a sconce, in a Helen Rose gown cut within a breath of her fabulous figure. She drifted past Louella as if lost in a personal fog bank.

Gable tugged at his waistcoat and ambled into camera range. He winked at Lana, but even Louella couldn't fail to notice his basic disinterest. He approached the *Honky Tonk* bower as if he were ready to escort a maiden aunt to a potluck supper.

Each tentative step toward Lana seemed to make her shrink further back on a settee. "Here's your story," said Conway. "That kid's scared to death of touching Gable. I can't even get her to take his hand. The suggestion of a kiss might dissolve her onto the floor."

Louella was fascinated and amused. "She is scared, isn't she?"

"It's been this way since we started the picture," Conway said. "Late last week when we stated rehearsing the love scene, I saw Lana look at me over Gable's shoulder and blanch. I swung around to see what had caught her eye. And there was Carole Lombard with her arms folded, glaring at the kid. Less than a minute later Lana ran to her dressing room sobbing—where she stayed until I could talk Carole into leaving. Now you!" he continued, accusingly.

Louella took the hint and backed into the shadows to watch the filming of one of the most reluctant love scenes in movie history.

Conway moved the cameras to within four feet of Lana and Clark. Still, Lana clung to the edges of the settee. Gable stood it for as long as he could before taking Lana gently by the shoulder. "Look, kid, snap out of it. It's just a kiss. I'm not going to rape you." He kissed her on the cheek and elbowed against her as if she were a baseball buddy. He winked at Conway as he eased Lana into the embrace. It was a one-take shot.

"This is another time I'm glad to be wrong," Louella told Conway.

Later that day Carole Lombard was informed, kindly but a bit curtly, that Lana Turner was "only a frightened young girl—no threat to you and of no particular interest to Clark."

After this inept beginning, Lana Turner was to quickly become Hollywood's champion love goddess, trading on the spectacular expertise she displayed in the clinch. "They saw something there that I never saw myself," said Lana, still as lovely as when she was MGM's most beautiful star. "From the screen tests they found a kind of raw, romantic power. Before I knew what was happening, I, myself, was in Gable's arms for *Honky Tonk.*"

That same year, 1941, *Photoplay* called her "the newest love goddess"—besting the sultry Hedy Lamarr.

"I wish I could tell you the secret of achieving romance on the screen," said Lana, at her plush penthouse in a tower apartment in L.A.'s Century City. "Chemistry is as close as I can get to describing it. Maybe I can tell you what doesn't work better than what does. I look at films now and I see people shoving their tongues down each other's throats and thrashing their nude bodies on top of each other. That is not it.

"We could do more with the quiver of a lip or the shrug of a shoulder than all the nude men and women today. It was titillation. It showed a look of innocence that we never see now."

"The Lana Turner love scenes sold the pictures," said Jack Cummings, a veteran producer at MGM. "We knew how to promote Lana's love scenes in a preview, and a sellout film would be created."

"It doesn't mean you have to have a hot love affair in bed with your leading man—offscreen," said Lana. "But it does mean that you have to blend when the cameras are rolling. You have to feel, within the characters, something so tender that each of you can tell if the slightest move of an eyelash is wrong."

Lana perfected the art of offscreen romance as well. When she was nineteen, and already making waves in New York café society, Louella Parsons told her daughter, Harriet, "Here is a girl who will make news as long as she lives."

Hedda Hopper and Sheilah Graham confidently predicted that the still teenaged Lana would marry studdish Hollywood attorney Gregson Bautzer. (Hedda was certain enough to predict the wedding date and the location.)

Louella read different tea leaves. Lana was more likely, she wrote, to marry "the snooty musician Artie Shaw." No sooner said than done. A midnight phone call from the beleaguered Strickling told her all she needed to know. "This is as much notice as I can give you, Louella. Lana and Artie are getting married in Vegas right now."

The columnist had Mildred Turner on the phone at an indecent hour the next day. "What happened?" she asked. "I thought you didn't like Artie Shaw."

"Well, I don't. And I'm not even sure Lana does. We're all waiting for an answer on that one." The answer failed to come until Lana shed the clarinet player two years later. "I actually had a date with Greg Bautzer the wedding night," Lana said. "He called up suddenly to say he couldn't keep it. Some kind of legal business had come up. I got mad, decided I'd go out anyway, and I thought of someone who would make Greg mad—and jealous. So I called Artie.

"About midnight Artie said it would be nice if we got married. I looked at him and said, 'I think it would be nice, too.'"

Legally, Lana's marriage lasted two years; realistically, less than five months. This first of Lana's seven marriages would set the pattern for the rest, each dissolving in apathy after an indecently short time.

Her seventh marriage, to a nightclub hypnotist, Ronald Dante, marked the low point. Gossip columnists always speculated on the reasons why Lana had such disastrous luck with men. And the circumstances under which this final marriage crumbled only added proof to the theories.

Lana, Dr. Dante (as he called himself), and the star's personal manager, Taylor Pero, flew to San Francisco, where Lana appeared at a film tribute.

"When it was over, Lana wanted to go out on the town," said Pero. "We ordered a limo and hit several spots. When the limo brought us back to the San Francisco hotel, Dante said he had an errand to run and that he would join us for drinks in a couple of minutes."

Dr. Dante never showed up. As the hours passed, Lana became more and more distraught, and finally decided to fly home with Pero.

"When we opened the door we could tell that Dante had already been there," said Pero. "His clothes were missing, leaving hastily emptied closets."

Pero says Lana walked from room to room, sobbing and grasping at her breast. "I followed her to the bedroom suite where she finally collapsed onto the floor. I leaned over her, calling her name over and over again," said Pero. "Nothing worked. Then I remembered that Lana had given Dante a check for thirty thousand dollars earlier that day, ostensibly to be used to form a business. I said, 'Lana, didn't you give him a check for thirty thousand?' Her eyes sprung open. And she yelled, 'Get my business manager on the phone.'"

The hard core of toughness within the wilting, romantic woman operated all through Lana's headline-making life. She put this ability to good use during the tabloid age, with its indecent brand of journalism that relied on long-range lenses and private detectives. The difference between Lana and others of her generation—stars who became victims of the tabloids—seems to have been humor. Lana could laugh at herself as well as the tabloids.

At breakfast one morning recently, Lana was presented with the latest copy of a tabloid showing her on the cover with a suspiciously pretty young man. "LANA'S NEW LOVE," screamed the headline.

'It doesn't bother me that I look like death warmed over," she said to Pero. "It doesn't bother me that they've added several years to my age. What ticks the hell out of me is that they have me passionately in love with one of the most flamingly fag queens in Beverly Hills."

Lana also has refused to change her life-style to accommodate the "standards" of papers like the *Enquirer* or the *National Star.* She's simply perfected her own brand of guerilla warfare.

Her royal progress as a queen of the cinema has been preserved—down to her bizarre habit of refusing to walk in and out of any airport. Since the mid-sixties a wheelchair has fetched Lana from curb to ramp, and not all the machinations of the *Enquirer* or the *Star* have resulted in a photo of the odd event.

There have been near misses. The closest call came on a rainy day in Maryland, where Lana had just closed her SRO play, *Forty Carats.* In a mink coat, shaded glasses, and wheelchair, she was being swept through a New England airport when Taylor Pero saw a well-armed *Enquirer* photographer at four o'clock. He yanked the coat from her shoulders, tossed it across the front of her, and began wildly spinning the wheelchair through the lobby. With Lana's personal hairdresser and a makeup man running interference, Taylor propelled her through the swinging doors leading to a loading deck.

Lana glared at him. "This had better be good."

They laughed their way into the first-class section, settled in, and Lana leaned over to whisper, "The laugh's on them this time."

The moment was shattered by the unmistakable whine of a motor-driven camera. You guessed it. The *National Enquirer* had taken both first-class seats opposite Lana and Taylor Pero.

Lana merely winked and raised her champagne glass. "Cheers!" she said.

9

Three's Company

DEBBIE—EDDIE, EDDIE—LIZ, DEBBIE—

There stood little Debbie Reynolds with a diaper pinned over her demure dress. She was cuddling a baby with one arm and drying her eyes with the other. The only thing missing were the tears.

But some of the reporters who surrounded her cried, and that was what counted. Holding Todd Fisher, her second child by teen idol Eddie Fisher, Debbie was haltingly announcing their separation.

"It seems unbelievable to say that you can live happily with a man and not know that he doesn't love you," said Debbie with a dramatic sigh. The handkerchief dabbed at her eyes. "But as God is my witness, that is the truth."

It was a public relations coup of the first magnitude. America's favorite Girl Scout, the movies' adorable dancing chipmunk, had been jilted by Little Boy Blue. Eddie and Debbie, Debbie and Eddie—the fan magazines had been chirping about Hollywood's most perfect love affair for more than three years. He was the "Coca-Cola kid," the golden-voiced holder of fifteen million-selling records in a row. She was "Tammy the goat girl," this country's fantasy of sweetness and light. Debbie had worn a ponytail so long that her hair was almost congealed. Her Peter Pan dresses would have looked underage on a college freshman. And Eddie's dimples must have chafed from wear.

"These two adorable kids are the best thing to happen to Hollywood since Mary Pickford," said Hedda Hopper. "They're like mom and apple pie—something we haven't seen here in a long time." Aunt Hedda, as she once asked Debbie to call her, wrote those words just five months before the maudlin separation. It apparently never occurred to her that Eddie was thirty, Debbie was twenty-six, and the scarlet woman who tore them apart from each other was twenty-five.

Debbie never mentioned the scarlet woman, of course. Her homey, intimate press conference was too well designed for that. She merely widened her eyes to intimate the hurt she really didn't feel. And the members of the press didn't bother Debbie with ungallant questions about her former MGM buddy, Elizabeth Taylor. There was really no need. The image of the lady who was soon to glide on sails of infamy down the Nile was the unspoken presence behind Debbie's mock tears.

Liz was in Palm Springs, still wearing black in mourning for Mike Todd, who had been killed in a plane crash. And Eddie was at the home of friends. The date was September 8, 1958. Within days of this press conference, which unleashed a public fury around the world, Debbie Reynolds and Elizabeth Taylor, two of the last MGM Girls, were cast in the offscreen roles that haunt them today. The press, fans, and women's clubs who reacted so violently to this Hollywood home-wrecking had no idea that they were manipulated by a public relations stunt engineered by publicists at MGM and Debbie's own PR people. These men calculated (and it was no gamble) that the studio, Debbie, and even Liz would reap enormous financial rewards from this bit of chicanery. It was an MGM publicist, in fact, who pinned the diaper on Debbie's shoulder, cautioning her to hug the child as if for dear life. The studio was willing to bet that Liz, who laughed right out loud when she saw Debbie on television, would keep her silence.

One of MGM's great spoiled brats, Taylor had perfected her own brand of snotty public arrogance that was rivaled only by Garbo's. When a pack of reporters confronted her at the Los Angeles International Airport for reaction to Debbie's outburst, Liz pulled up the collar of her mink coat and lowered her eyes. "Oh, come on, Liz, give us just one word," said one television hustler. Liz turned on him and said, icily, "Hello." Yep, MGM could count on Liz. If she said anything at all, it would be in anger. And that would be so much the better.

Nobody bothered about Eddie much. It took all his energy to hold onto his career as the two angry stars waged battle all around him.

As the story developed, some truths seemed obvious. Liz and Eddie *appeared* to be in love. Debbie *was* losing her husband. And five months did seem, to some, to be an indecently short time for Elizabeth Taylor to wear sackcloth for the love of her life, Michael Todd. (His plane had crashed in March; the Liz–Eddie fires hit first flame in August.) There the resemblance to truth ended.

This absurd chapter of MGM's history officially began on Labor Day weekend 1958. Eddie and Liz just happened to be in New York City, both without a previous engagement, on Labor Day evening.

Eddie called Liz. "What about dinner?" She said she'd think about it, calling back in half an hour to accept.

"I was lonely that weekend," Liz said in an interview. "Eddie was there. He had been one of Mike's best friends and had idolized Mike to the point of making himself over in his image. Now I knew Eddie was not very happy. And I knew he loved to talk about Mike almost as much as I did. So we went out in public together several times—after that all hell broke loose. The press and the public—the whole world in fact—was convinced that I was breaking up a perfectly happy home."

Liz has always had a charming way of minimizing the public hurricanes that have raged around her. Perhaps this is because she is always operating from the comparative calm of the eye of the storm.

Actually, she and Eddie made such a public progress through the holiday-crowded watering holes of New York that Madame Pompadour might have blanched at their audacity. Only Liz and Eddie know precisely what happened that first night. They have wisely chosen to remain silent. The gossip columnists, however, fashioned a version that could be put, unchanged, into a romantic novel.

Supposedly they sat in a darkened corner with long faces and talked about Mike Todd. They told Mike's jokes, pointed out gifts each had received from the great man, and shared misty eyes along with an evening full of strong cocktails. The legend has it that Eddie made the first move. He looked deep into Elizabeth's eyes, then allowed an arm to drift over her shoulder. Still the grieving widow, Liz is depicted as recoiling with a shudder. Eddie moved still closer. If you believe some reports of the fated evening, they must have been well nigh on each other's laps. Eddie then grabbed her hand: "You lost a husband and I lost the best friend a man ever had." There was a flood of tears.

Right there in that restaurant, they say, Liz took out the charred, partly melted wedding ring Mike Todd was wearing when he died. She did everything but beat her breasts: "I shall never love anyone so much again. Mike was the greatest love I shall ever know."

"Oh, Liz, I know that, Liz. I know that." Eddie's voice was supposedly a sobbing whisper.

And, oh my gosh, they were the last couple in the restaurant.

Waiters buzzed noisily around the most famous widow in the world and the skinny little singer on her arm. "Eddie," she said—and remember all this is right out of the gossip columns—"it's time to go home."

Eddie looked at his watch—the macho band given him by Mike Todd two years earlier. "Say, Liz, can you believe it's one-thirty?"

As they came out of the restaurant into a balmy New York night, photographers snapped their picture. This photo is as close as the world will ever come to proof of the gentle rendezvous that began the torrid love affair. All it shows is two weary stars looking both sheepish and shell-shocked.

"It's such a warm night," said Eddie. "Game to walk over to your hotel?"

"Why, how lovely, Eddie!"

Eddie Fisher grabbed her tenderly. Liz almost danced. Within moments Eddie's "Coke Time" voice was crooning "The Way You Look Tonight."

Can you just imagine it?

"Lovely. Never, Never Change."

"Keep that Breathless Glow."

It must have seemed as if *The Sound of Music* had moved right out onto that sidewalk. Somehow, still a'singin' and dancin', they managed to reach her hotel without slamming into a street light. The heavens parted. The angels sighed. A great American love affair had been born.

Those who believed this account, printed at various times by almost every gossip columnist in Hollywood, were playing right into the hands of the MGM publicity men.

The truth was actually more interesting. Elizabeth Taylor, for the first time in her twenty-two-year career, was unprotected and alone. Since she first walked onto the MGM lot with her mother, Liz had been surrounded by an oriental court of family, husbands, studio functionaries, maids, hairdressers, and constant companions, such as fellow child star Roddy McDowell. Mike Todd, for better or worse, had cleared Elizabeth's life of this flotsam and jetsam, hoping, perhaps, to make her stand on her own two feet. But he had died before he could finish the process.

Ruth Waterbury, the intrepid editorial consultant and columnist for *Photoplay* magazine during those years, believes that the fateful New York trip was the first time Liz had ever been alone. "It must have been frightening for her to suddenly face that fact," the columnist said. "This may have made her turn, against her own better judgment, to Eddie Fisher, a person as equally troubled as she."

Whatever the case, Liz was back on the phone to Eddie at 6 A.M. the next morning.

There are different versions of what happened next. Had Eddie forgotten about Debbie waiting to pick him up at the Los Angeles airport? Or did he remember and decide, then and there, to end their relationship without so much as a phone call? Eddie Fisher has never addressed that question. But everyone agrees that he asked Liz to accompany him to Grossinger's, the poshest watering hole in New York State. To quote Ruth Waterbury, "There may have been more *public* places to go on a Labor Day weekend, but I can't think of one."

Grossinger's had great sentimental importance to Eddie. His first success had been there, in the early fifties, when fans began packing the lounge in record numbers. Even worse, it was at Grossinger's, in an orgy of pink and white, that Debbie and Eddie had exchanged marriage vows with a few hundred of their closest friends and the press looking on.

Liz was stylish in widow's black, and Eddie was hidden behind dark glasses when their limo pulled up to the front steps of the resort. Naturally, they both unwisely made reservations under their real names. There was a buzzing mob crowded onto the porch. They stormed the car, grabbing at Liz as she stepped out. People climbed up on chairs and children were hoisted on their parents' shoulders to catch a glimpse of Mrs. Mike Todd (this was the way the world still viewed her).

The weekend was a nightmare. When Liz tried to swim in Grossinger's pool, it suddenly swarmed with bathers. She screamed out to Eddie that she felt as if she were going to drown, and he pulled her from the pool. The bridal walk, under a bower of summer trees, sprouted fifteen hundred gawkers when Liz, Eddie, and friends tried to take a stroll. Liz ran back to the hotel in tears.

They returned to the city early. Newspapers already on the street printed only hints about their trip. And the few columnists who did take notice mentioned the problems Elizabeth Taylor was beginning to experience in her restless search for privacy.

"They won't leave this heartbroken girl alone," said Hedda Hopper. "It's like a scene from a bad old Hollywood movie come true."

"Give her a break," said Walter Winchell.

The day after Liz and Eddie returned to New York City, Debbie was waiting for Eddie at the Los Angeles airport. Several members of the press followed her there and noticed her disappointment. This was Eddie Fisher's first public relations disaster. Since he and Liz had been to dinner and then to a show in Harlem with actress Eva Marie Saint and Debbie's publicist, Rick Ingersoll, it seems inconceivable that Eddie forgot to call Debbie about his change in plans. He must have decided at the last minute to remain with Liz. Still, Debbie said nothing. She told one reporter that she must have misunderstood. Eddie would be coming on a later flight, she said. Later Eddie finally called Debbie, saying he would be home in several days.

On September 9, the first of a thousand headlines finally showed up in the New York *Daily News:* "EDDIE FISHER ROMANCE WITH LIZ TAYLOR DENIED." On the advice of MGM, Debbie had reacted angrily to a routine call from a wire service reporter. "I've never heard of such a thing," she said when asked about Eddie's dalliance with Liz. "I am so shocked that such stories would be printed that I won't even dignify them with a comment." Naturally, there was no word from the dalliants.

To Louella Parsons, Debbie said, "Eddie and Liz are good friends. He was Mike Todd's best friend. I think these stories are disgusting."

And Liz told Winchell in New York: "You know I'm a friend of Eddie's. Everybody knows that. We can't help what people say." It's interesting to note that she used the pronoun "we."

Reporters began making regular trips to the house Debbie and Eddie shared in Beverly Hills. It paid off. Neighbors heard the echoes of a whopping fight between America's most darling couple. At one point Debbie yelled, "What's the matter with you anyway?"

"DEBBIE AND EDDIE FEUD; LIZ RETURNS," said a headline in the *Los Angeles Herald* the next day.

On September 11, Liz called Hedda Hopper. Hedda, who had been the first reporter to interview Liz when she was a child star on the set of *Lassie Come Home,* offered her auntly shoulder.

Liz later said that Hedda betrayed her confidence. "It was like calling up a best friend and having them use your words against you," she said. If Liz believed this she was more naive than the rawest starlet in town. Nobody confided anything to Hedda or Louella that she or he didn't want the entire world to know—the very next day! More likely, Liz, determined to continue the relationship with Eddie, felt that Hedda would present her side.

In any case, she blurted out Eddie's version of the marital rift between him and Debbie. "Hedda, you know I don't go about breaking up marriages. Besides you can't break up a happy marriage. Debbie's and Eddie's never has been."

Hedda asked her about her grief over Mike Todd's death. "Mike's dead, and I'm alive," she said.

The gossip columnist crucified her before thirty-five million readers: "Well, Liz, you'll probably hate me for the rest of your life for this. But I can't help it. I'm afraid you've lost all control over reason. Remember the nights you used to call me at two and three in the morning when you were having a nightmare? You had to talk to somebody, and I let you talk your heart out. What you've just said to me bears not the slightest resemblance to that girl. Where, oh where, has she gone?"

Within two days of this national story, accountants at MGM reported a box office rush at theaters playing current Elizabeth Taylor and Debbie Reynolds films. The worse Liz appeared publicly, the better the fans liked it. The more heroic little Debbie seemed, the bigger the ticket sales. It helped, of course, that the studio had already cast Liz as the scarlet woman and Debbie as the girl next door.

There was no going back.

It was several days later that Debbie made her pitiful appearance on the lawn of her home. Never, before or since, has the media been so abused by a handful of publicists. Everyone took the bait, from *The New York Times* to the lurid tabloids of London. Even when Debbie lashed out with fury, reporters slanted the stories in her favor. Today her remarks don't seem so cute. "First of all, Miss Taylor and I were never friends. Oh sure, we went a lot of places together, Mike and Liz, Eddie and I. But she and I were never close friends. Miss Taylor had—has—few female friends. It's also not true that Eddie and I were dreamy together. When he wasn't working, I used to get home from the studio in the afternoon and find the front room full of his friends in their undershirts, all eating pastrami sandwiches, playing cards and listening to records."

Finally, a bit of truth had come out. But nobody noticed.

Debbie and Eddie had been having major trouble for more than a year. Their friends expected a quick separation and then divorce. There's no doubt that the marriage would have dissolved on its own. The only effect of the Liz–Eddie dalliance was to create a hurricane of publicity. "It didn't seem to matter much that home-loving Debbie and fun-loving Eddie had been squabbling for more than a year," said *Life* magazine. "But then such reality was not in demand."

At the press conference, MGM press agents passed out coffee, hamburgers, club sandwiches, and ice cream to the reporters from a regular shuttle connection with the studio commissary. "I am still in love with my husband. I hope this separation will iron out the difficulties and we can get together and be happy," Debbie told the well-fed journalists, who also received the latest stills of Debbie in pigtails. "I am deeply, deeply shocked over what has happened. We were never happier than we have been in the last year. While Eddie was in New York he called me every day. Eddie's a great guy. Do not blame him for what has happened."

Debbie now admits that MGM provided a script for this press conference and for those she would subsequently conduct. Actually, Debbie and Eddie had been seeing a marriage counselor for months. He had made very little progress, and Debbie had told friends she would soon file for divorce.

The Reynolds–Fisher marriage had been born in the MGM publicity department. In 1954 MGM realized that Debbie Reynolds' career hadn't taken off as they had planned. After her socko starring role in *Singin' In the Rain,* they had tried her in musicals and teenage soap operas, with only middling results. Her career needed the oomph only romance could give it.

Some intrepid MGM flack decided that Eddie Fisher's opening in Los Angeles that year would give Debbie a chance to shine in the crooner's glory. The studio had already tried to pair her with teen idols Russ Tamblyn and Tab Hunter, with no result. Eddie was bigger game.

Debbie was dressed by the studio's wardrobe department in a high school prom dress and transported to the nightclub. They told her to look up in adulation at Eddie, adding that a sigh here and there certainly wouldn't hurt. Eddie's manager, Milt Blackstone, was in on the deal and agreed. He told the singer to address several songs directly to her. One of them was "Hold Me." It was all just too cute for words. At a party given for Eddie by Eddie Cantor, Debbie never left the singer's side. They coasted into the ideal fan magazine marriage.

Eddie's career was enhanced. The arrangement did little for Debbie's. The Hollywood musical cycle had run its course by 1958. The fortunes MGM had made on films like *Seven Brides for Seven Brothers, Good News,* and *Gigi* failed to continue during the final years of the fifties. Debbie was in trouble. After all, you could only carry a cute smile and the ability to do the Charleston so far. The Liz and Eddie scandal was made to order.

It was a different story with Elizabeth Taylor. She was already considered one of the ten greatest superstars in film history. She ranked number eight in the top box-office draws. And she made no bones about her desire to be free from the confining limits of MGM. She slaved at the studio under the same sweatshop standards that had bugged Judy Garland. She had no choice of scripts and had to take any old thing MGM threw her way. And her pay was ridiculously low for the era. MGM paid her about $150,000 for *Cat On a Hot Tin Roof*, for which almost any other studio would have guaranteed her $500,000. By the time the scandal broke out, Twentieth Century-Fox had already tentatively agreed to the million dollars she would eventually earn for *Cleopatra*.

Liz had only one film left on her MGM contract, and she was ready to leave the cocoon. She was one of the few stars who never took the MGM hierarchy seriously. She couldn't be bullied, cajoled, or bought. She wasn't even intimidated by Louis B. Mayer.

She had come to Hollywood with her parents in 1938 to escape the Nazi blitz attacks on London. With her raven hair, violet eyes, and flawless complexion, her teachers at the exclusive Beverly Hills Hawthorne School signed a petition urging David O. Selznick to cast her as Scarlett O'Hara's daughter in *Gone With the Wind*. Selznick agreed to look at snapshots and told the Taylor's that he was willing to test Elizabeth. Howard Taylor, a staid art broker, objected. "I don't even want Elizabeth growing up in this sick city," he said at one point. "It will ruin her life." His wife, Sara, who was to be one of the least objectionable screen mothers in history, was determined to at least get her daughter a test.

Universal was the most receptive studio since it was looking at children to replace their money machine, teenage soprano Deanna Durbin. Truthfully, there was little excitement about Elizabeth's test. But she was pretty, so they cast her in *There's One Born Every Minute*. Less than three months later her contract was dropped.

She became an MGM star through one of those mistakes for which the studio was known. Howard Taylor served as an air raid warden with Metro executive Sam Marx, who continually described the trouble MGM was having trying to cast the young girl in *Lassie Come Home*. It seems Taylor's objections to a child star in the family had diminished. He offered up Liz, and she was put under long-term contract.

While still a teenager she was the first child actress to refuse Mayer a kiss on the cheek during his annual birthday celebration on the studio's largest sound stage. Mayer, fat and badger-like by that time, gave strict orders that every star on the lot be assembled for the unveiling of his birthday cake. He would listen tearfully as everyone sang "Happy Birthday." Then he made his annual speech. He would address the assemblage with, "You must think of me as your father. You must come to me, any of you, with any of your problems no matter how slight they may seem to you, because you are all my children."

Heaven help him or her who took the old man up on that promise.

The cutest couple in Hollywood, Debbie Reynolds and Eddie Fisher, on a date arranged by MGM, which also hustled them to the altar.

Debbie Reynolds with daughter Carrie on the set of MGM's *The Mating Game*. Trouble lay ahead for Debbie and Carrie's father, Eddie Fisher.

The tragic Pier Angeli, said to be the only true love of James Dean, visits pal Debbie Reynolds on location for MGM's gay collegiate comedy, *Affairs of Dobie Gillis*. The film also featured Bobby Van and Bob Fosse.

During the balmy days of Liz Taylor's tenure as MGM's most obedient
star, she posed with her closest friend, Montgomery Clift, for stills to
advertise *Raintree County*.

Honeymooners Liz and Eddie at St. Tropez on a quiet afternoon. But the scandal over Eddie's desertion of Debbie was still raging back in Hollywood.

Forgiveness at last. Two years after Hollywood ostracized Liz for stealing Eddie from Debbie, her peers gave her the Oscar for *Butterfield 8.* *Below:* The triumphant, forgiven Liz Taylor in her Academy Award-winning performance in *Who's Afraid of Virginia Woolf?*

But that's exactly what Sara Taylor did when she heard that Elizabeth was to be cast in a dancing and singing role in *Sally in Her Alley.*

MGM historian James Robert Parrish recalls the fireworks that ensued. "Mayer shouted, 'You're so goddamned stupid, Mrs. Taylor, you wouldn't know what day of the week it is. Don't meddle in my affairs. Don't tell me how to make motion pictures. I took you out of the gutter!'" (A strange thing to say to the wife of a well-to-do art broker.)

Parrish says that Elizabeth, then fourteen, jumped to her feet, yelling, "Don't you dare speak to my mother like that. You and your studio can both go to hell." She ran out of the office, down the studio's main street, and out the gate. Sara stayed behind to smooth the edges.

"I will never go into that man's office again," Liz told her father. "He's a thoroughly dreadful man." Luckily for Liz, Mayer's power dwindled horribly during the next several years, and she became an international superstar. She never had to confront "Rumplestiltskin," as she called him, again.

Her standoff with Mayer gave Liz an edge over other stars of her generation who had always cowed in fear before his will. While the careers of Lana Turner, Ava Gardner, Greer Garson, and Jane Powell were consigned to increasingly dismal productions, Liz fought each step of the way for better scripts. When George Stevens at Warners expressed an interest in casting her as Rock Hudson's wife in *Giant,* the actress argued all the way to the front office in New York to gain permission. Onscreen in *Giant,* she was the only member of the cast to measure up to James Dean's portrayal of Jett Rink.

Back at MGM, Dore Schary ordered the studio to purchase Tennessee Williams' *Cat on a Hot Tin Roof* for her and offered a new studio contract with the most lucrative terms any actress had been offered since Greta Garbo.

Then the scandal hit.

Less than a month after Debbie's press conference, *Cat on a Hot Tin Roof* was taking in half a million dollars a week—pretty big stuff in 1958. Its business had been only fair to middling until the journalistic dam burst. To make certain they were reading the situation correctly, the studio took a national audience survey. "People are coming to see Elizabeth Taylor," Howard Strickling reported to New York. "And women are making up sixty-five percent of that audience. It's incredible." She became the second biggest box office star in the country within eight weeks as MGM rolled out a selection of her forty-five films to cash in on the trend. (Rock Hudson was number one.)

This didn't make it any less unpleasant in the eye of the hurricane. Liz was at the Beverly Hills Hotel, Eddie was with friends, and both of them were Hollywood outcasts. Louella and Hedda made certain that Debbie was everywhere. And where Debbie was, Liz wasn't. People who had been a regular part of her set when she was married to Michael Wilding gave intimate parties without her.

"One time I telephoned someone and asked if I could drive out to his house," said Liz. "It was near the beach, and I felt so absolutely trapped in the Beverly Hills Hotel. He said something like, 'Oh, I'm terribly sorry, darling, we're going out to the beach with the children, but we'll be back around seven. I'll call you.' Of course, he never called."

The press turned nasty. A cartoon in *The New Yorker* depicted a drunk who, coming home late, explains to his wife, "I just got to worrying about Debbie and Eddie." "HOW CAN SHE BEHAVE THIS WAY?" demanded a four-column headline in the *London Daily Herald*. "FATAL LIZ," said a banner head in the tabloidish *London Daily Sketch*. In less than six months Elizabeth Taylor's picture (often opposite Debbie's) appeared on the cover of sixty-five fan magazines and Sunday newspaper supplements.

Debbie was spending an average of ten hours a week in the MGM still photography labs just to keep the media supplied with wholesome photos. And the money kept rolling in.

If there was a casualty from the collapse of this hyped-up marriage, it was Eddie Fisher. Up until the scandal, Eddie Fisher was on top of the world. He earned as much as $500,000 for one recording session. His show, "Coke Time," established the popular format for TV musical shows, and he had become one of a new wave of singers to pack the largest rooms in Las Vegas without expensive frills or backing. Eddie was also a big spender. He had gone through the fortune he'd made and was living off the royalties of old hit records. When he was playing at the gambling city's tables one night, Debbie came up to him and blurted out, "Eddie, you've lost enough tonight to put our children through college."

After Debbie's press conference, Eddie found that Coca-Cola, NBC, and RCA-Victor Records were suddenly cool to him. He decided to hold a press conference of his own. "Debbie and I tried very hard to make our marriage work," he told the press. "We have been having problems for some time. Debbie especially has done everything possible to make our marriage work. I alone accept full responsibility for its failure. But I have to say that our marriage would have come to an end even if I had never known Elizabeth Taylor."

Debbie's lawyer replied in an equally public statement. "There is nothing magnanimous about Eddie assuming the blame for this tragedy. That's exactly where the responsibility rests. So far as I personally am concerned, his attempt to relieve Miss Reynolds of the responsibility falls completely on deaf ears."

If Eddie had lost his grip on a career, Liz lost a massive part of her identity, which, whether she liked it or not, had been tightly bound to the studio apron strings. The studio had designed her clothes, picked out her dates, helped finance her homes, and even planned her first wedding, to Nicky Hilton, the hotel heir. Since Liz was making *Father of the Bride* at that time, MGM even provided the wedding dress and catered the reception. Jane Powell, the blond soprano, was tabbed by MGM as Elizabeth's maid of honor, as Liz would serve as Jane's.

"I didn't really know Liz," said Jane. "We saw each other on the lot and may have eaten lunch together once or twice. But that's all there was to it. They had kept us so busy that we had no friends. So MGM supplied the bridesmaids."

While the studio may have killed the marriage to Nicky Hilton (it only lasted two months), it had done a fabulous job of turning out a bride. *Father of the Bride* became one of MGM's most successful films of the fifties.

Whatever succor Liz had received from the studio ended when she married Eddie. The relations between MGM and its most popular star turned hostile and remained that way.

Eddie Fisher temporarily filled the void. "Through all those months of grief for Mike, I felt that I had loved and that there would never be anything like that again in my life," Liz said. "Eddie, who loved Mike, too, was the one man who could understand that my heart would always belong to the memory of Mike. And Eddie, somehow, made Mike seem more alive.

"At the same time, I felt cold and trapped by circumstances— without any of my own resources to find a way out. Maybe with Eddie I was trying to see if I was alive or dead. Also, for some idiotic reason, I thought Eddie needed me, and I should make somebody happy. Anyway, we got married.

"It was clearly a mistake. We both, I think, tried very hard, but the marriage was untenable—for both of us. To describe the indignities we inflicted on each other—and so many others—would be too private to go into. It was just a dreadful mistake."

In scores of interviews since the furor, Liz has seemed to apologize to Debbie for the public nature of the indiscretion. At least Debbie saw it that way. "People say 'write a book,'" Debbie said. "I say 'What for? Liz already wrote it.'"

After MGM lashed back at Liz through its support of Debbie, she showed little willingness to continue her contract. In fact, Liz said savagely several times that she would never sign another long-term contract.

Then the studio, in a blatant attempt to cash in on Elizabeth's new image, cast her as a glorified call girl in John O'Hara's *Butterfield 8*. (It was to be her last MGM film and they knew it.) She told wire service reporters, "It's a terribly mean thing they are trying to do to me. I refused to do the picture for two reasons. First, it's the most pornographic script I've ever read. Secondly, I don't think the studio is treating me fairly. They have the power to keep me off the screen for two years if I don't agree to do *Butterfield 8*. Even if they cleaned up the script, the main character is still a sick nymphomaniac."

Liz haggled over the script for more than six months, whittling away at the more objectionable scenes. Finally, to get free of her pact, she agreed to do it—providing they gave Eddie Fisher a part. (Eddie had spent more than a year without a singing engagement by this time.)

A day later Liz caved in to the MGM demands. Eddie was offered a two-week engagement at the Desert Inn. There were strong rumors that Elizabeth had promised to be ringside each night—which resulted in the job offer. Whatever the story, she was there every night. At exactly 11:48, two minutes before showtime, she would enter the lounge and sit at a tiny table up front. Eddie introduced her to the audience, and sang one or two songs directly to her. The audiences were ecstatic. It was more of a burlesque act than anything else. But how long could Liz afford to follow Eddie around the country as part of the supporting cast?

She flew to New York several days after Eddie's engagement to begin work on *Butterfield 8*. The weeks flew by. It was an easy shoot.

Her seventeen years as an MGM Girl were over. There wasn't even a telegram of goodbye, just a lawyer's note confirming that her years of servitude had ended. Months before she had confronted MGM production chief Sol Siegal, saying, "Is this any way to end a seventeen-year relationship?" Siegal looked out from behind an enormous desk and answered, "Fortunatley or unfortunately, Miss Taylor, sentiment went out of this business long ago."

"I don't know what I expected," Liz said later. "Garbo, Joan Crawford, and Norma Shearer all had to slink out the studio gate with their tails between their legs. Why did I think it would be any different for me?"

Butterfield 8 was released in 1958 to tumultuous reception. In New York City fans lined up before 7 A.M. for the noon show. Somehow, MGM talked Liz into doing promotion for the film. She had only seen parts of it. "And that made me run to the theater bathroom and puke," she said. "I'm not kidding, that's how bad I felt about it."

At least she was free to make *Cleopatra*, where an offscreen affair would break up still another home (Richard Burton's) and make her more famous than Garbo, Harlow, or any other of her MGM predecessors.

In February of 1960 Liz was nominated for an Oscar in the best actress category for the fourth year in a row. (Her previous nominations had been for *Raintree County*, *Cat on a Hot Tin Roof*, and *Suddenly Last Summer*.) MGM budgeted $500,000 in advertising funds to get Liz an Oscar in her final Metro film. It seemed that *Butterfield 8* refused to go away. "I don't understand it," she told a London reporter the day nominations were announced. "This one, I didn't deserve."

Although filming had started on *Cleopatra*, the film had been shut down after a series of accidents, not the least of them the realization on the part of Twentieth Century-Fox executives that Elizabeth's salary would amount to over $1 million.

Liz, who looked as strong as an ox onscreen, had been prone to illness since she was a child. Two days after she arrived on the set in August 1960, an early cold spell hit England. Liz was in bed with a high temperature the next day. Not since the heralds had appeared on the steps of Parliament to announce the progressive, final illness of Napoleon Bonaparte, had a city and its newspapers been so concerned with the minute details of a celebrity's health. Liz's temperature was up to 102; she was asthmatic; her breathing was better; it was worse.

In all, she was absent from the set forty days during the months of September and October, costing Fox $2 million with little to show for it. A series of physicians examined her with varying results. Queen Elizabeth lent her personal doctor. He put Liz in the hospital and discovered that her system was poisoned by an abscessed tooth. It was pulled, and Liz continued her royal residence on the top floor of the Dorchester Hotel.

On November 14 she was rushed through the streets in an ambulance suffering from meningitis, a spinal cord or brain irritation. Spiros Skouras, head of Twentieth Century-Fox, received a call from the president of Lloyd's of London. "Mr. Skouras, I've talked to the Queen's physician, and it's his opinion that Liz may not be able to work regularly on *Cleopatra* for some time. I would like to suggest that Marilyn Monroe, Kim Novak, or Shirley MacLaine play the role. We must protest the delay." (He hinted that Lloyd's would cancel their insurance.)

Cleopatra was already costing Fox more than $40,000 a day, but, by the end of January 1961, producer Walter Wanger had only ten minutes of usable film. Days later, Rouben Mamoulian (an old-style director whose career began in the era of the silents) was taken off the picture and replaced by Joseph Mankiewicz. Liz approved. Mankiewicz, however, said that Liz was fine but the script was dreadful. A rewrite was ordered; Elizabeth Taylor continued to receive her salary of about $2,000 a day.

Before the new screenwriters got paper into their typewriters, illness struck again—in deuces. Eddie had an appendectomy and Liz came down with the Asian flu. Although she had around-the-clock nurses and an oxygen tent, nobody realized how ill Liz was. A nurse on the graveyard shift began checking the actress every five minutes when she noticed the star was having trouble breathing. "All of a sudden her face turned blue," the nurse said later. "At first I couldn't reach a doctor and felt hysterical. Nobody told me she was in critical condition."

"But we can't find the hotel doctor," the night clerk told the special-duty nurse. Then he remembered that Dr. J. Middleton Price, a noted British anesthesiologist, was in the hotel.

"There had been a sudden collapse," the doctor said. "Miss Taylor was unconscious and gasping for breath."

Dr. Price found that Elizabeth's breathing passage was almost closed from inflammation. He took a plastic bag from his satchel and pushed it into her mouth and into the trachea. He then used a tiny oxygen bag to push air directly into her lungs.

The desk clerk had promised a journalist friend that he would call him in case of any change in the star's condition. He made good, and a bulletin reached the Associated Press wire in America. Ironically, it was just two days before the final Oscar ballots were to be mailed. Headlines in Los Angeles said, "LIZ DYING."

By then Dr. Price had moved the actress to a London hospital. He chose London Clinic, the private hospital where she had been treated the previous October. Eventually, doctors put her on an electronically operated iron lung that actually "breathed" for a patient. It seemed to give Liz more strength. But doctors were still giving her only a 50–50 chance to live.

With seven doctors at her side, it was learned that she had pneumonia and anemia. A rare drug, staphylococcal bacteriophage-lysate, was hand-carried to London by Eddie's agent, Milt Blackstone, and administered.

Nurses described her as the "most lifeless" patient they had ever seen. "I could feel myself dying," Liz said later. "I could see a small dot of light far off in the distance. And that was closing up. I remember using all my strength to open up that light again."

One of the nurses, Catherine Morgan, described it: "I've been around patients for seventeen years, and during that time I've seen some who died in several days, several hours, several minutes. But in comparison to Miss Taylor, they all looked in bonny health. I still get goose pimples when I think of it."

Liz said the experience was not peaceful but "horrifying."

"There's a saying that when you're drowning, you see your whole life come before you. It wasn't that way with me. Even though I was suffocating, I dimly knew that I had had some kind of operation. I couldn't make a noise with my throat.

"I knew I was dying, there's no doubt about that. When I would come out of unconsciousness, the only question I wanted to ask was whether or not I was dying and when I would die. I couldn't make myself hear. It seemed to me, though, that I was screaming. I was frightened. I was angry. I was fierce. I didn't want to die."

Liz said she "died" four times. "You feel yourself going, falling into a horrible black pit. You hear a screaming jet noise. Your skin is pulling off. But even when I was unconscious, I had my fists clenched. The doctor told me later that the reason I'm alive is because I fought so hard to live."

The day after the special drugs were administered, Liz Taylor was out of danger. Without knowing it she had regained the affection of her peers. As she lingered near death, fellow Academy of Motion Picture Arts and Sciences' members had chosen her as best actress for *Butterfield 8*.

It was her final moment as an MGM Girl.

10

No Sorrow Now

THE RETURN OF CONNIE FRANCIS

MGM's veteran sound engineer Jesse Kaye was mumbling to himself as he plowed through a floor-to-ceiling case of the studio's hit albums— 1947–1979. Almost angrily, he pulled out successive piles of records and let them slide across his desk. "Look at this," he said. "This girl was the most popular vocalist in the world for ten years. Then she vanished.

"I wrote her. The letters came back. I asked mutual friends They hadn't heard from her either."

The face on the extravagant spill of albums was unmistakable, having melded into the teenage consciousness for eight years—Connie Francis, one of the later MGM Girls and a massive moneymaker for the studio in the fifties and sixties.

For a decade she was a Metro dynamo whose yearly record sales equaled the profits of many pictures. (The studio earned $3 million from "Who's Sorry Now.") "She was everywhere. Then nowhere," said Kaye.

Several months later Jesse Kaye received a memo from Polydor Records (now owner of the MGM catalogue) that it was "re-releasing part of the Connie Francis catalogue to honor her return to show business." A week later she was booked on the Golden Globes Show (annual awards given by Hollywood's foreign press).

Connie Francis walked briskly onto the rehearsal stage for the

Golden Globe Awards with a bundle of sheet music under her arm. The conductor and members of the orchestra almost bowed to her. It was a historic occasion and everybody knew it. Not only was Connie singing all five nominated songs—the first to do so since Judy Garland's tour de force in the '50s—but she was making a comeback, after almost ten years of silence, and she was doing it before a worldwide television audience of a hundred million people.

Some Hollywood old-timers viewed the rehearsal with considerable amusement. This was not the Connie Francis they had known two decades ago, a sweet, timid girl who sang what was put before her. The new Connie Francis chaffed at some of the unwieldy songs nominated in 1982. For instance, as she picked up the sheets for "Butterfly," a contrived melody written for the Pia Zadora film of the same name, she turned toward the musicians and asked, "I'd like to know whose relative wrote this thing." And the theme from *Arthur,* written by Burt Bacharach and three others, had her laughing in amusement. "Catch this lyric: 'When you get caught between the moon and New York City.' What's that supposed to mean?"

The night of the telecast she glided onto the stage in an electric blue gown and gave those same songs her all, proving to the world, but mostly to Hollywood, that she had come back from the hell of a rape and the subsequent loss of her voice to a self-assuredness she never possessed when she was known as "one-take Connie," the third best-selling vocalist in the history of recording, ranking behind only Elvis Presley and the Beatles.

Connie's nightmare had begun in the early morning hours of November 9, 1974, at Westbury, Long Island, where she had just made a triumphant comeback after a three-year, self-imposed absence, at the Westbury Music Fair. Exhausted but exhilarated by her reception, she fell easily into a deep sleep in her room at a nearby Howard Johnson's Motel.

About an hour later she bolted awake to find a man with a knife at the foot of her bed. She could see only his silhouette against the dim lights of the parking lot as he moved closer and closer. Finally, he dived onto the bed and held the knife against her throat, whispering, "Kiss me, or I'll kill you."

He raped her and left her bound to a desk chair and buried under a mattress and one of her suitcases. Connie remembers it as an eternity, but it took her less than half an hour to work her way across the room, slip her hands free, and telephone her secretary (in the next room) for help. The secretary gathered Connie in her arms, got her dressed, and took her, in shock, to a hospital.

When she walked out that motel door it was her first step into the darkness of a crippling depression—the first of a series of calamities that would make her life resemble a classic Greek tragedy.

The next blow came when she sued Howard Johnson's, Inc., for negligence in a trial that deteriorated into a smear campaign of Connie's private life, particularly her relations with her three husbands. She demanded $5 million but settled out of court for $1.5 million to keep some semblance of privacy.

"They had microfilm that would have turned my life inside out," she said. "You hear nasty rumors, but you have no idea how bad innocent things can look if they are taken out of context in a public courtroom."

Then the combined strain from the rape, the trial, and her own depression destroyed her third marriage. Joseph Garzilli, who had supported her during the trial, decided "he didn't want to be married to me anymore." (The divorce became final in 1977.)

Less than a year later her father found out he had stomach cancer, which required immediate surgery and left him hovering near death for months. As if all this wasn't more than enough for anyone to bear, her younger brother, George Franconero, an attorney Connie had helped through school, was shot to death, execution-style, in front of his New Jersey home less than a month after he was convicted of bank fraud.

"That was it!" she said. "My brother's death in 1978 was really a turning point for me. I had to head out of my own morbid depression. I could no longer afford the luxury of a nervous breakdown. My parents needed me."

The day her brother died Connie began making the first of her now daily lists. "Pick up flowers. Call mother. Buy coffin," were her first three entries.

As she climbed out of her cocoon of neurosis she was finally able to look back at the hell she'd been in—a state of fear so powerful that she couldn't even bring herself to say the word "rape" until a year ago.

"I didn't have a nervous breakdown after the rape. Not right after it. My nervous breakdown came as a delayed reaction. At first I was too afraid.

"I would watch the television and believe my face was there on the screen, or I would look at the handle on a door, and it wouldn't look straight."

Even when she started to slip into deep depression Connie tried to hide it from anybody who tried to help. "Italian people don't like things like this. I was so ashamed of it that I almost blew the Howard Johnson's trial. The defense people had some microfilm which graphically depicted my private life. This to me was such an infringement, such a contrast to my 'apple pie' image that I was ready to walk right out of that courtroom."

After the out-of-court settlement, Connie put her life on hold and retired to her bed and her thoughts. She would stay in bed for weeks at a time, and she was terrified of going anywhere alone. She couldn't even read a newspaper or watch a newscast. Years were erased from her life, which drifted by like a shadow play.

"I remember hoping that I would wake up with cancer or some other fatal disease. It was just too painful to suffer anymore."

No trace of a smile crossed her face for three years. "This was a terrible shock to my friends and family. I'd always been the life of everybody's party. My aunt Marie said I had kept her laughing for years."

Her depression deepened, but it was hard for others to see. "It was a slow buildup, beginning, I now believe, long before the rape. It was caused by external pressures building up over a very long period of time. You either recover from this or you commit yourself to an institution."

The roots of her unhappiness could be found in the nonstop career she had begun twenty years earlier when she was thirteen. Born Concetta Rosemaria Franconero, she sang her first notes at the age of four with a performance of "O Sole Mio" as part of a recital by the students at Miss Masciola's Music School in New York City. In her teens she performed on weekends and during summer vacations in an upward spiral that earned her a Metro-Goldwyn-Mayer recording contract when she was seventeen.

"She was the sweetest girl I ever worked with," said Jesse Kaye, the artistic director of MGM Records. "Her voice was clear as a bell, and she had none of the temperament so common to other stars. She never developed a head—even after her incredible success."

The studio picked her songs for the first two years, and she recorded ten straight flops. With her contract set to terminate after two more singles, Connie's dad, George Franconero, studied a song catalogue, determined to find a song that would carry her and her voice to fame. He suggested "Who's Sorry Now," a song that had been written early in the century for New York singing star Mrs. Carter DeHaven.

"Connie, you can sing it with a slight rock 'n' roll beat," he told her. "The kids may like it, and the adults will remember it as an old favorite."

"Are you kidding?" she answered. Still, she reluctantly followed his advice.

Ironically, MGM already owned current rights to the song, having

The early Connie Francis, whose albums often earned MGM $500,000
a week during her peak years.

Connie Francis as she looks today.

purchased it for the film *Three Little Words*. Released in November 1957, "Who's Sorry Now" sold a million records in the first fifteen days of release. And it soared to number one in Great Britain, the United States, Australia, and France—the only record to do so until the Beatles appeared on the scene.

Her next twelve songs were all number-one hits, and she charted the punishing course she would follow until the Westbury incident. She was the queen of the record industry from 1957 to 1967, eventually selling 90 million single records and releasing seven million-selling albums, second only to Elvis.

She was rushed into five movies (almost all forgettable), made a record twenty-two appearances on "The Ed Sullivan Show," was the first pop singer since Judy Garland to open at New York's Copacabana, and sailed into Las Vegas at a weekly salary equaled only by Marlene Dietrich's.

"As an actress I was the worst. I was a joke. Each of those films was as bad as the other," she said, laughing at herself. "No, I take that back. Each film got progressively worse."

She paid for the success, however. She never had a private moment to herself for almost fifteen years. "She seemed to have unlimited energy," said Kaye, her MGM mentor. "Looking back on it, we worked her too hard. But then, we worked everybody too hard."

But even her dreadful films, such as *Where the Boys Are* and *When the Boys Meet the Girls*, made tidy profits, good actress or not. The hangover from her acting stint suddenly appeared recently when a top executive at Universal, which has bought the rights to her upcoming autobiography, asked if she'd be interested in playing herself. Connie laughed right out loud. "Quite frankly, I wouldn't be able to even play myself convincingly," she said. "And I wouldn't want to."

She was amazingly sheltered during her travel through the show-business fast lane. "Until Westbury I lived a charmed life. I was never exploited. I had a very traditional upbringing and a mother and father who loved me. I didn't go to clubs after the show. And I didn't drink or party. I'd go back to my room with my aunt or my mother and play Scrabble.

"I thought sex was a store on Fifth Avenue, and I was a virgin until the day I first married at the age of twenty-five."

Perhaps this cloistered existence drained her marriages of any vitality they might have had. Her first, in 1964, to a Las Vegas hotel publicist, lasted four and a half months. The second, to a Vegas hairdresser, also failed to make it through the first year. "Don't ever go to Vegas for a husband," she now says, bitingly.

Hindsight, of course, is just that, and it was only from her sick bed that she was able to look back and see the cracks appearing in the fragile armor that she had built up around her life.

At her lowest point, she was taking an incredible number of antibiotics (following the assault) and other drugs, and she had the feeling that her mind was slipping slowly away from her. "I knew that both my body and my mind were falling apart."

Still, Connie's family didn't want to confront her with the full reality of her mental deterioration. This was when her closest friends, Lou and Charlotte Sukoss, took over. "They came to see me, and Charlotte sat on the edge of the bed. 'Connie, we are your best friends. You need professional help.' They eased me into it." Lou and Charlotte told her over and over, "You're going to get well again. Not tomorrow or next week. But you are going to get well."

She looked out at them through the haze and didn't believe in their promise. "I wasn't sure that I wasn't making all this up," she said. "An hour after someone came to see me I couldn't remember what they had said."

Connie says she must have seemed pretty hopeless at times. "I had no sense of taste and no real perception of touch. My skin felt like sandpaper, and I reached to touch those who came to visit to assure myself that they were actually there."

She remembers waking up one morning and hearing what she thought was applause—for her. "It was really a big truck out in the street, but I thought for a moment that I was onstage."

Lou and Charlotte told her in the simplest of terms that she no longer had a choice. She needed psychiatric help or else.

"The thought of a psychiatrist was so alien to me. Charlotte explained that she and Lou, probably the happiest couple I have known, had been in psychiatric analysis for years. Then I could accept it.

"I called them the day I wanted to take a bottle of pills. I had them in my hand but thought perhaps I should call Charlotte first. They were there within an hour."

During the first part of her crisis, Connie was still trying to fulfill club dates, however marginally. One night as she walked toward the stage she began to wilt and had to grab the piano to hold herself up. "My agent, not realizing how far gone I was, kept insisting that I could do it. I was a walking bottle of pills. It was really a bottle of pills out there performing. I had a twenty-four-hour psychiatrist."

Her friends stayed by her side, almost literally, for five years—until the death of her brother shocked her the rest of the way out of her depression.

"As far as I was concerned my career was over," she said. "I had resigned myself to the reality that my career would simply fade away with no fuss and no publicity." But her voice returned almost as suddenly as it had disappeared. "I decided that my career was important to me and that I wanted it back. I figured that the best place to do it was at the scene of the crime, Westbury. If I could do it at Westbury, I could do it anywhere."

On November 12, 1981, she did just that. Sleek and dressed in daring gowns the old Connie Francis would never have worn, she brought the house down at Westbury. She swept onstage singing the Gloria Gaynor disco hit "I Will Survive" and was greeted by a standing ovation.

She forgot the words to some songs, her voice wavered in quality, and her poise slipped a bit here and there. But nobody cared. She was held over by the opening night audience until she finally ran out of encore arrangements. "Forgetting the words to a song would have been a catastrophe for me before," she said. "But I didn't care. I was so happy to be back. I knew I had missed performing, but I didn't realize how much until that night."

To celebrate her return she has signed for a new album. "But I'm still not in top form. And I don't want to record until I am. I recorded several albums when I was at my worst. If I didn't get it right they simply used equipment to even it out. I don't like that. Today an orangutan could make an album, and they would simply touch it up with the equipment."

MGM has also announced plans to reissue four of her albums with new lyric sheets and updated sound—the first time vintage Connie has been available since 1966. A check of rare record stores in Los Angeles and New York shows that copies of some of her albums (in mint condition) are selling for prices that range from $50 to $125 each.

One other good thing has come out of the ordeal—her son, Joey, now seven. Shortly before her tragic Westbury appearance in 1974 she received a letter from a woman with a six-month-old baby in her home that was available for adoption. Connie was ecstatic. But her lawyer was wary of the idea, so she decided to go see the woman herself after the Westbury engagement. She put the woman's address and telephone number in the pocket of her mink coat—which was stolen by the rapist as he ran from her room.

"I was crushed," she said. "I couldn't remember the woman's name." Her lawyer had been so opposed that she was certain he had destroyed the information she had given him over the phone. But one month after the rape her husband came home with the baby wrapped in a blanket with a big red Christmas bow. Her lawyer had had the information after all. "He was meant to be my baby. I know I couldn't have gotten through the years without him."

It was a miracle, she said. It was the luck on the other side of the disaster.

BOOK FOUR

The Survivors

Survivability MGM style! Mickey Rooney and Ann Miller at the New
York opening of *Sugar Babies,* 1980.

They Built 'Em Right

ANN MILLER, DEBBIE REYNOLDS, AND THE OTHERS . . .

On August 17, 1953, MGM staged the last of its splashy movie premieres for the opening of *The Bandwagon*. Dancer Ann Miller, wrapped in ermine, arrived on the arm of hotel millionaire Conrad Hilton. Debbie Reynolds was on the arm of sigh guy Tab Hunter, leading a parade of stars that included Lana Turner, Ava Gardner, Norma Shearer, Maureen O'Hara, and two hundred others with names well known in any corner of the globe.

Five months later the show business newspaper *Variety* proclaimed the "worst crisis of the Talkie era." Crowds at the Technicolor musicals and all-star films had slumped to their lowest point since 1919. The big studios began unloading contract players as if they had caught the plague. Hardest hit was MGM, which had a talent payroll of more than $1 million a week. Scores of stars of the Golden Age drifted into personal and financial obscurity and ruin. Still others fled to Spain and Italy, where they made cheap exploitation films.

But the MGM Girls, with only a few exceptions, climbed up from the wreckage of the Cinemascope sound stages to become more successful than ever—some of them drawing salaries today that top those of the movie executives who kicked them off the lot. They are starring, not in Hollywood, but in middle America, in regional theaters whose patrons pay handsomely for a sight of the old glamour, for a whiff of the sweet perfume that made the old Hollywood so magical.

Only a few miles from the skeleton that was once the Metro-Gold-wyn-Mayer backlot, Debbie Reynolds slipped out of her own giant rehearsal studio as dawn cracked the fog in the San Fernando Valley of Los Angeles. She had been sealed in a private world of mirrors, dancers, and disco music for eighteen hours. Her dancing shoes were scuffed along the sides. Her Tammy-colored hair was bunched inside an outsized scarf. Her shoulders slumped, but her grin was infectious as she gave a whoop and packed up to take her new act to Las Vegas. The road was paved with platinum; only hours earlier, the Hughes-Summa Corporation announced it would pay Debbie "more than $2 million for twelve weeks of shows."

In another part of town, a mile above the creeping Pacific mist, on the rarified rim of a Beverly Hills hilltop, Cyd Charisse tied her long brunette hair into a scarf, sipped coffee out of a Sevres porcelain cup, and slipped into her car for the drive to the city below. For at least two hours and probably three, she pushed herself through a tortuous series of classical ballet lessons—a routine she hadn't varied a fraction since 1946, when she went before the cameras in *The Ziegfeld Follies.*

This Monday was a bit different for Cyd, however: she carried under her arm the playbook for a new role in *Affairs of State,* a sophisticated comedy. Her casting by the directors of Scottsdale, Arizona's elegant Windmill Playhouse was further evidence of her growing bankability as a dramatic actress—a subtle victory for a star once called "Miss Frozen Voice" by a New York critic.

Two thousand miles across America, in Lexingtonville, Indiana, Ann Miller had already been up for hours. With a clipboard under one arm and a private secretary by her side, America's most tireless tap dancer was in the home stretch of a publicity blitz to sell her roadshow, *Cactus Flower,* a play that was well into a seventy-week run in middle America. She chatted with five disc jockeys, two newspaper reporters, and a pair of TV talk show hosts before 11 A.M. She changed at least three times—from a star's ransom of clothes, wigs, and jewels packed in thirty suitcases. She then plowed on to meet two mayors and a baseball pitcher.

Ann long ago became her own carnival barker and front man—with increasingly lucrative results, including a weekly paycheck that has risen from $5,000 to around $10,000 in just two years. "If I don't do it, honey, nobody will. Those old days when Hollywood sent out a big entourage are long gone." She chatted for a moment with a TV newsman and then ran off to a chartered plane that carried her to a talk show two states away.

Much further east, in New York City, Jane Powell, still sunshine blonde and petite, worked before a blinding bank of lights and two Technicolor cameras on the ground floor of New York's Museum of Modern Art. Makeup artists, a hairdresser, and a costumer buzzed around her—just like in the old days at MGM. Only this time, Jane was selling savings plans instead of songs. She was in her seventh year as New York's "Dry Dock Savings Girl"—a media job that brought thousands a year into her own California bank accounts and that she sandwiched in between musical comedy and symphony dates that kept her busy an average of forty weeks a year.

These stories are typical. In 1969, Lana Turner, who had never stepped onto a live theater stage, launched a tour of the play *Forty Carats* that brought in SRO crowds in twenty-two states. Liz Taylor did much the same thing, on a larger scale, with *The Little Foxes* in 1981. And little needs to be said about the way Lucille Ball and Ann Southern conquered television.

In the last nine years, productions starring the MGM Girls have grossed an incredible $300 million, more than all their pictures.

"We have literally built an entire industry around these girls out here on the road," said Ben Segal, whose Oakdale Musical Theater in Connecticut has featured Jane Powell and Debbie Reynolds every summer since 1969. "When we put together deals out there on the Coast, we just pray that we can get Miller, Reynolds, or Powell, because the word has gotten around that they can really deliver. They are this generation's Ethel Merman and Mary Martin. We build whole seasons around them."

All this has translated into cash.

"MGM, by default, left us an incredible legacy of well-trained, well-oiled talent," said Bob Young of the Indianapolis Starlight Theaters. "It's lucky for the road that Hollywood closed down those big productions."

Back in 1955, however, when their wide-screen, stereophonic world fell around them, the future seemed to promise little more than a theater exit sign.

"MGM kicked us out; that's the politest way to put it," said Debbie. "But Mayer was already gone, and he was the only one in the front office who believed in our pictures. He wasn't all that nice, but he did know how to make movies. I was all set to do a big, big musical called *Peg o' My Heart*. The songs were even set. Then I never heard of it again, and I was offscreen for three years until Howard Hughes took a chance on me for *Susan Slept Here*."

The economic deluge that caught the MGM Girls may not even have been all that noticeable on old Sound Stage Seven, where most of the big productions were filmed, but it was a harsh fact of life out in America. In 1949 there were almost 19,000 movie theaters. By 1955 there were only 14,500. Ninety million Americans went to the movies in 1947; only 45 million in 1955. And, most important, MGM profits had dropped from almost $20 million in 1947 to a dismal $5 million in 1955.

"It hit all at once," said Ann Miller. "And who was I to scream? After all, the big ones were cut—Lana, Ava, Judy. Even Gable! Compared to those stars, Ann Miller was a small fish.

"We are truly survivors," she continued. "Some survived and some fell flat on their faces. I think it had a lot to do with which of us actually grew up in the Hollywood grind. Hell, I started when I was thirteen; Janie started at eleven; Debbie at fifteen, and Cyd when she was seventeen. When it fell apart, I looked up and said to myself, 'Sister, there's no quitting now—just keep on dancing.' And, honey, I decided right then not to look back. I never have—not even when everybody gets so excited about all those old movies that show up on television like measles."

Of them all, Debbie has proven to be the toughest, especially in Las Vegas, where only guts translate into cash.

At her most recent show, one stout lady with blue-rinse hair punched another with a Dacron-covered elbow. "Here she comes . . . she's gonna come out this way. Gimme that book," the lady said. "I missed getting her autograph twenty years ago in Hollywood, and I'm not going to miss it this time."

There was a flash of red sequins, a toss of ash-blonde hair, and Debbie, the eternal "Tammy" of the movies' gilded era, popped out of a well-guarded door at one of the entertainment world's prestige show spots, the Desert Inn. A muscular chorus boy tried to ease her through the surging crowd. But she planted her short legs and said through her teeth, "I've always got time for this. It'll only be when they don't come that I'll worry."

Three teenagers in jeans pressed toward her—much too young to have seen *Singin' in the Rain*, except on late-night TV. "Would you sign this program?" asked the youngest, blondest of the girls.

"Sure, sure," said Debbie.

Then the girl stuttered for a minute. "And, uh, would you, uh . . . would you sign it, 'Carrie Fisher's mother?'"

Debbie's blushing-bride smile didn't change a fraction. "Sure, I'm glad to. And I am glad to," she said to a reporter, narrowing her eyes to a squint. "Very glad to."

If this changing of the guard (from Debbie to her daughter, Carrie, the famed Princess Leia of *Star Wars*) bothered Debbie Reynolds, she didn't let it show. And she never has.

Louis B. Mayer said of her in 1950, "She just smiles that impish smile, but you know those wheels are turning, scheming, pushing her forward to the next step. She's the last person we'll ever have to worry about."

Debbie signed the last of the autographs and disappeared with a full-fledged Hollywood entourage of chorus boys, choreographer, maid, and secretary. The limousine door closed on the last of MGM's contract stars, the last starlet to get the "full build-up" from Leo the Lion.

She was called the movies' most bankable teenager. But now she is dangerously close to fifty, with a rowdy style and sense of humor that has rid her, finally, of the pinafores and cutesy bangs that were fashioned for her as a studio star. Whether she consciously realizes it or not, her position as a sort of missing link between the last of the old Hollywood stars and the first of the new has become a dominant theme in her life. With one hand and at least one foot dancing to the latest punk rock beat, Debbie is dragging the fossils of the sound stage era into the eighties with her. She has even built her own studio.

"I was spoiled, you know. We had the best . . . so it made me awful tired of rehearsing my act in the filthy back room of some dance studio or upstairs in the American Legion Hall. So I built this."

Debbie ran her hand across the facade of what used to be the North Hollywood Post Office. Where ugly government-issue lamps used to stand, she put up a staircase from the MGM prop department. It sweeps up from the street toward a pair of garish, golden Ibis birds—the same birds Liz Taylor hugged during her entrance scene in *Cleopatra*.

Never mind that the birds might be grim reminders of a time when Liz was hardly the friend she has since become. "I'm part of the old Hollywood, Liz is part of the old Hollywood. They're part of the old Hollywood . . . let's just leave it at that, shall we?"

Inside a set of double doors (also from MGM) and down a hall displaying two hundred movie posters, past a room full of costumes that once draped the svelte figures of Garbo, Harlow, and Shearer, Debbie built Hollywood's first complete rehearsal studio.

Once inside, Debbie goes to work. It's slightly after 2 A.M. when she sends her dancers home. "Here I am," she says, sinking like a wilted Barbie doll onto the gilt steps. "Here I am—the pampered star. I can't let down for a second—haven't been able to since *Two Weeks With Love* in 1950. I had to go out and pound the doors to get a job.

More romping in the teenage star stable. Jane Powell, Vic Damone, and Debbie in the convertible Mickey Rooney had driven in the *Andy Hardy* movies. *Below:* Ann Miller doing *Something for the Boys* in the waning years of World War II. Louis B. Mayer was courting her at this time.

Born to dance! Ann rehearses a production number on an MGM sound stage. She had to give up her relationship before Metro took her seriously (1938).

Considered one of the world's most beautiful women, Ann Miller was out on the town with steady beau, hotel magnate Conrad Hilton. "He just liked to dance, and that's all there was to it," Ann said.

Thirteen-year-old Jane Powell was brought up by Mayer as the world's most darling soprano. MGM, refusing to let her grow up, crippled her later career. *Below:* Jane Powell, Debbie Reynolds, and Ann Miller are serenaded by Tony Martin, Vic Damone, and Russ Tamblyn in the last of the truly big budget musicals, *Hit the Deck.* Filmed on California's coast and partly on an aircraft carrier, the film cost about $1.2 million. In today's inflated economy the same film would cost an estimated $30 million. The services of Powell, Reynolds, and Miller today, would cost a combined $25,000 per week.

Somewhere under the silly clothes and newspapers is the beautiful Cyd
Charisse, slaving for the MGM publicity grind.

Cyd Charisse, seemingly able to stop the clock, in a publicity photo taken in 1979, twenty-five years after she debuted at Metro.

"When I first came to Vegas in 1959, they asked, 'What can you do, kid?' I learned right then that in this business it's not just what you've done. It's what you can do. And whether you can prove it or not.

"That's what I'm doing in this hall—proving it. You think I like dancing to punk music? I don't. I want to tap. But this year, they aren't paying for tap . . . they don't want to see tap. So I'm doing punk."

She ran an arm around the neck of an ibis, looked up toward a press camera with her luminous eyes set in an ageless face that still looks like it was drawn by Norman Rockwell for a *Saturday Evening Post* cover— the same face that was called by the MGM publicists the "cutest face in the movies."

"Cute! Cute! God, will they ever stop calling me cute?" she asked. "How would you like to be forty-nine and still be called 'cute'? When will it stop? When I'm ninety-three? I guess when I make my entrance in a wheelchair—and I will if I have to—then they'll stop calling me cute and start taking me seriously.

"And the name—Debbie. That just makes it worse. I don't think I'm really a 'Debbie'? Do you? I really wanted to remain Mary Frances Reynolds—Mary Frances Reynolds from Burbank."

That is the gospel truth.

Debbie hadn't planned to be anything but Mary Frances Reynolds, a gym teacher, when she bounded out onto the stage in a talent contest at Burbank High School in the spring of 1948.

"My mom made me go. I had entered the 'Miss Burbank' contest on a lark to get a blouse and a scarf. Mom made me go through with it. I had a rip in my swimsuit and no shoes for the talent portion. But by some peculiar quirk—I won.

"Two talent scouts were there. I got signed. And you know the rest."

Burbank High School's auditorium is only four miles straight east from her new studio in the San Fernando Valley, but the distance in time, life-style, and philosophy that separates Mary Frances Reynolds from Debbie Reynolds is a cultural and economic chasm.

"She was just darling when she first came to MGM," said Ann Miller, who was already making $5,000 a week when Debbie's mother drove her daughter through the MGM gates in Culver City. "She really did expect to go back to school and become a gym teacher. I think she expected it right up until the time she struck it big in *Singin' In the Rain*. But all the rest of us knew different."

Kay Thompson, Broadway actress and arranger, watched Debbie on a rehearsal stage and told Gene Kelly, "This girl's gonna be big, and she's gonna stay around—look how much she sweats."

Debbie wondered at it. "I didn't dance. I didn't sing. I wasn't pretty. And I sure couldn't act. When Gene asked for me [for *Singin' In the Rain*] they locked me in a sound stage with the best teachers in the business, and I came out three months later completely different."

The film began a decade for Debbie that formed a complete Hollywood cycle: stardom *(Singin' in the Rain)* to fall *(Athena)*; a storybook marriage to Eddie Fisher followed by the scandal; most popular movie star in the world (1959); and down again (*The Unsinkable Molly Brown*, which she only got by taking a $30,000 salary cut); and then back up again (her multimillion-dollar contract with the Vegas hotels).

"Personally, I think she remained Mary Frances Reynolds at heart, a high school cheerleader in spite of it all," said a *Photoplay* editor who covered her for ten years. "Debbie was a creation like the other MGM stars, but her sense of humor made her stand out. She would be nuts like so many of the others if she hadn't become such a character."

There's a sense of that in Debbie. Occasionally she talks as though Debbie Reynolds were some perplexing third person—someone you talk at and about, but not to.

If Debbie was the creation and Mary Frances Reynolds the reality, there are still some unanswered questions. Was it Mary Frances or Debbie who spent a cool $1 million buying up and storing the golden trappings of MGM? "A lot of us went to the auction," said Ann Miller. "But it was Debbie who did something about it. She inherited the heart of that studio." Was it Mary Frances or Debbie who met the press wearing diaper pins when Liz and Eddie went public with their romance? And which one was it who vowed to pay off the $1.2 million in debts left behind by her last husband, Harry Karl?

"People keep wanting me to write a book. But it's already been written. Doris Day wrote the financial part, Joan Blondell wrote the marriage part; Mary Astor wrote the rest. It's been done. It's too late for me. I just look ahead. I have blinders about the past."

Ann Miller has also refused to concentrate on those dead, golden days.

At 8 A.M. on a recent morning Ann's black hair was already studio perfect. Her makeup was correct to the last eyelash, and the lines of her clothes could have been aligned by a surveying crew. She gave her palatial house a last glance, and then gathered a load of gifts in her arms before departing.

Ann Miller had flown into Los Angeles only hours before to the house in the hills she has dubbed "my own Tara"—the house she bought in 1939 after her first flush of movie success. She didn't have time for the house this trip because her long-overdue rest from the live theater (*Sugar Babies* on Broadway) was spent as close as possible to her ailing mother. That meant days at the hospital.

"Life out of a car," she described it. "I'll do it for as long as I have to." This dedication didn't surprise any of Ann's friends from the MGM days—the bond between the classy dancer and her mother was already a legend in the thirties.

"Now that was a partnership—Ann Miller and her mother, Clara," said Zelda Cini, Time-Life's major Hollywood correspondent in the heyday of the movies. "Clara was the original stage mother, and Ann was only about thirteen when it started, so a lot depended on Clara."

It was Clara who paid for Ann's dancing lessons (the first ones at age three) and sewed her costumes (even at RKO). It was Clara who groomed her until the calls finally came in—from RKO, then Columbia, and, finally, MGM.

So it's no surprise, either, that Clara's recent illness put added steam into Ann's revived stardom. "I called up my agent, Ben Pearson, and said, 'Look, I've got five thousand dollars monthly expenses at the house. My mother's sick. What kind of show can you get me that's good and that will hold up?' " First, Pearson launched *Cactus Flower* on a national tour that upped Ann's salary to a minimum of $5,000 a week. Harry Rigby's *Sugar Babies* followed on its heels.

Ann Miller was the last of the MGM Girls to leave the comfortable confines of Hollywood for the road—the last of them to break out of the celluloid-mold of typecasting and into live entertainment.

"We got the idea pretty quick that studios couldn't make those musicals anymore," said Ann. "We knew we couldn't sit around and maintain that *Sunset Boulevard* image forever."

Miss Cini, who covered the decline of MGM for a special *Life* magazine cover story, believes the secret of Ann Miller at fifty-seven lies with the image itself. "She literally froze that exuberant glamour girl character and brought it through twenty-five years into the eighties. This is a girl who came in at the very end of the glory era. But this is a girl who really had it. She didn't just talk about it. Conrad Hilton courted her. Harry Cohn wanted to divorce his wife and marry her; as did Louis B. Mayer. When Ann Miller showed up at a premiere, you knew somebody had arrived.

"I think she reminds audiences today of an age when you not only had to have talent to make it—you had to be glamorous as well."

A major assistant producer of "The Merv Griffin Show" agrees. "Ann Miller comes onto this show camera-ready; she's wearing a designer dress; her makeup is exquisite; her hair is perfect and she even smells nice. It's such a pleasure for us. You know what I mean—so many of the people come here in jeans with their hair flying all over. What's so special about that? You can get that at home."

Joan Crawford called Ann Miller "the last of the Hollywood glamour girls."

Ann herself believes that the carefully guarded image is behind the resurgence of her popularity in the eighties. "I had been working in Hollywood for ten years when I went to Metro," she said. "But it was still an eye opener to see Lana, Ava, Greer Garson, and Elizabeth Taylor. And Hedy Lamarr—my God, Hedy Lamarr. You knew those women were stars.

"People want to see a leading lady who is still glamorous and who can wear good clothes. And, buster, they'll pay for it."

Ann can still get into her costumes from 1954's *Kiss Me Kate*. "But I won't let myself sleep past eight A.M.—not as long as there's an interview to be given."

Of course there's been much public chuckling over Ann's persistence in preserving the image she had on the MGM sound stages—the jet black, overcoiffed hair that sometimes makes her look like the Flying Dutchman, the toothpaste smile, and the tailored flashy clothes.

Fashion guru Charles Blackwell kept her on his "Worst Dressed List" for five years in a row. "She looks like she was painted on an MGM backdrop," he once said.

Ann answered: "I can't imagine him saying that since I buy mostly his designs." And she does.

Then former MGM chum Polly Bergen said in her best-selling beauty book that "Ann sure has the makings. But I'd love to get my hands on that hair."

And Ann replied—by United Press wire: "Let her keep her hands on her own hair. My hair sells tickets. And, anyway, what's wrong with keeping a hairstyle that's thirty years old? It didn't hurt Marlene Dietrich."

Finally, Carol Burnett spoofed Ann as a ninety-year-old dancer in a skit called "That's Entertainment, Part 50." With her hair flying in the wind, Carol portrayed Ann as a doddering, aged tapster.

Ann fought back through the Reuters News Service: "I didn't notice her trying any of my complicated tap routines."

"Look," said Ann, "I didn't used to be so tough or so public. But the MGM hothouse flower I used to be couldn't survive out here. I can't afford a thousand dollar-a-week press agent so I do my own interviews. I hustle."

Ann spreads the glamour around gratis. With thirty trunks and a wig closet trooping behind her, the dancer shows off her figure and her $800,000 stage wardrobe in a fountain of glitter that literally touches every media outlet in whatever area she plays.

But to see her tap, you have to buy a ticket. "Heck, that's what folks are coming in to see. Why should I give that away?"

Ann calls tap her "gimmick." Others are far kinder. "I think she's the best," said Debbie. "And remember, I had to take dancing lessons with her every morning. There I was between Cyd Charisse and Ann Miller trying to learn to tap. It was so discouraging."

Ann has come to hate the constant revivals of the so-called Golden Age. "I go to these film festivals and to interviews in the basements of museums, and I'm flattered. I really am. But I'm not dead. I'm only fifty-seven. I want to scream: 'Hey, look what I'm doing now.'"

She actually did that on network television a few years ago during an "Ann Miller Retrospective." A TV reporter had just asked her about that era. "To hell with the Golden Age of Hollywood," she said. "I'm only interested in today—right now!"

Cyd Charisse, Ann Miller's dancing contemporary at MGM, has shown similar staying power and has remained one of the world's most beautiful women. Her house in Beverly Hills seems to tumble down a canyon plateau, hugging a huge swimming pool and garden reminiscent of the "movie star opulent" style that dominated the Hollywood of the twenties. But there is no orchestra playing a Cole Porter love song, no bank of turquoise lights to create an afternoon in Paris, no wind machine to ruffle her hair. For light there is only the uncompromising glare of the California sun—blasting through Beverly Hilltop windows to light a $5,000 sofa. But that's quite enough. Director Vincent Minnelli used to say that Cyd Charisse was the one movie star who didn't need any trappings.

She still doesn't.

She appears from the darkness of a marble hall—a cascade of brunette hair, the classic face that dominated a dozen MGM musicals. Like some smoky apparition from the Bijou or from the balcony of Peter Bogdanovich's *The Last Picture Show*, she still knows how to make an entrance. "How nice to see you," she says in her studio-sculptured accent and settles onto the couch—about halfway between the piano where her husband, Tony Martin, still works and a bank of photo tributes to her from every American president since Harry Truman.

The scene could have been lifted from one of Tom Tryon's gothic novels about Hollywood, featuring a movie queen from the fifties who commanded time to stop at twenty-five while her audiences aged to thirty, then forty, then fifty, and on toward sixty. But any resemblance between Cyd and a Tryon heroine ends quickly with the facade. Hollywood's most famous ballerina stepped out of the Cecil Beaton sets forever and won a battle for survival in the clawing, grappling worlds of Las Vegas, dinner theater, and television.

During the first six months of a recent year, Cyd played eleven club dates, starred in three "stock" plays, packed them in at the retirement hillock, Sun City, and taped appearances on three television series.

"If you're going to be in the business, you have to *be* in the business," Cyd said. "You can't just drift in and out at your own pleasure because people forget—and you forget. If I have any secret at all, it's just that I have kept going."

Cyd and her husband, one of the five best-selling ballad singers of all time, put together their first act in 1958 when the ruins of the musical era were still piling up around them. "We've been on the road ever since," she said. "We're in Beverly Hills less than four months out of the year."

But unlike some of the other MGM Girls who pine for the stay-at-home comfort of movie-making, she likes it that way. "I know that one-week stands and the ceaseless moving from city to city wear a lot of people down. I like it that way."

Her eternal staying power came home to Cyd Charisse in 1980 when a special air courier arrived from Paris and heaved a huge parcel onto her marble doorstep. Inside she found ten copies of a new Paris best seller called *The Art of Cyd Charisse.* She opened one of the copies on a coffee table. "Isn't this incredible? I was so highly touched by this book. You know, a career can slip by so quickly, and you never put it in perspective. Now, here it is all back again. There are things in this book that I had forgotten and many stills I never saw before. I guess this means I'm a legend."

Cyd wonders about the ingredients that blend into a legendary ambiance. "I don't know what it is that makes a movie or a performer survive the erosion of time. For instance, when Robert Taylor and I made *Party Girl* in 1958, nobody was particularly excited about it, particularly the studio. Now it's considered by thousands to be a classic. There are even *Party Girl* cults. What happens in between? Survival is the real mystery of films."

Half a world away, the forty-dollar book on the Charisse legend had already sold its way through three printings, making it the most successful cinema book on the Continent.

If there is any drawback to the celluloid nature of her legend, she believes it is the ability of film to freeze a star in time, allowing fans to project forward and backward at whim. The Technicolor images of Cyd follow her from decade to decade, from city to city like a shimmering "Picture of Dorian Gray" that never ages, while its subject grows inevitably older. (Cyd is fifty-eight now.)

"Those were wonderful years, but dancing in the live theater is so different. In some ways it's more exciting. But Fred and I would rehearse six weeks for just one minute on the screen. That could never be done now.

"I owe a lot to MGM. When you started an MGM film, the publicity department geared up and people suddenly knew about you all over the world. They made sure they knew your name in Hong Kong, in Sydney, in Calcutta. The name value is what we all trade upon now. I'm very grateful.

"It wasn't easy at first, before I was a star. At first there were the years when they would truck you into the photo studio to take those pictures for the fan magazines. They always had me with ears as the Easter bunny . . . really dreadful stuff.

"Later on, I think it was the dancing that really mattered. This is still true."

Every day of every week, Cyd dances as much as she did at MGM. "It's something you can't stop . . . not for a minute. Or it just fades away."

The Cyd Charisse image is fragile, seemingly spiritual. But there's iron inside.

The same is true of one of the movies' eternal teenage sopranos, Jane Powell. But her survival is even more impressive—since her career was blown apart after her starring role in *Seven Brides for Seven Brothers.*

Jane, too, lives in a movie-star house, just over the hill from Cyd Charisse and Ann Miller. And the MGM set designers couldn't have done it any better. Her house in the canyon is just the sort of place Mayer loved to see her in. The front is all sunshine yellow and in back, beyond the shimmering glass windows, is the requisite Esther Williams swimming pool. The living room is two tap steps down, with acres of beige carpet. Setting it off is the sombrero Jane wore in *Holiday in Mexico*. It is exactly the sort of room in which she pined over Bob Stack in *A Date With Judy*, the kind she brought Vic Damone home to in *Hit the Deck*.

The sun of an early California summer has turned the garden outside the windows into a rainbow that would make a Cinemascope cameraman sigh—purples to set off a Carmen Miranda hat and azalea hedges perfect for hiding a teenage Elizabeth Taylor. Then she trips down the stairs and it is no longer a dream from the forties.

"Have some coffee," she says over a suntanned shoulder. "Don't mind the dogs. They'll love you." Then she disappears into the kitchen.

Jane Powell at fifty-two is a cool, chic denial of her own movie past. Whatever ghosts there are of Metro's haunting, teenage soprano have been exorcised by four marriages, a career that stopped mid-note, and then the slow, grueling rise back up to her current status as queen of the roadshow musicals.

"I really am amazed that I'm still working," she says, draping a Raquel Welch frame over the arm of a chair. "A career was a very fleeting thing in those days. I really didn't think I'd be working this long. One day my business manager called up and said, 'How much longer are you going to be doing this?' And I said, 'I shouldn't be doing this now.'

"It wasn't all that hard when the movie musicals stopped. I simply started all over again . . . and again . . . and again." Her words tumble out in the same soft soprano that crooned "Too Late Now," but it's easy to see the tough woman behind it.

Her assessment of her career is fairly modest for a woman who has survived twenty-four years on the road—years in which her weekly fee boomed from around $10,000 to as high as $25,000. Her production of *South Pacific* now holds the all-time surburban roadshow record, taking in a whopping $310,000 for one week in Washington, D.C., and $295,000 for a single week in Toronto.

"I just kept singing and training," she says.

There was, of course, more to the secret than that. Part of the answer can be found in a cozy office on another rimtop in Pacific Palisades. From there, behind a window where he can almost see the house he shared with Jane for ten years, Jane's ex-husband and manager, Jim Fitzgerald, manages her career.

"It was a case of taking a proven talent—a girl who could sing, dance, and act—and guiding it into newer fields," Fitzgerald says. He met Jane when she signed into a show he produced for the Seattle World's Fair.

"There was instant rapport," says Fitzgerald, a tall, handsome tennis player and entrepreneur. "The marriage lasted ten years; the business partnership will go on, I guess, until we both quit."

Jane Powell had been missing from the screen for four years when she signed on with Fitzgerald for his Seattle show. It had been seven years since she walked out on MGM when the studio wouldn't let her out of the teenage prison to play sultry Ruth Etting in *Love Me or Leave Me.*

"I was twenty-seven years old, had two children, and was still considered the baby of the MGM lot." Jane had just finished one of the classic movie musicals of all time, *Seven Brides for Seven Brothers,* but Metro shoved her right back into the teenage mold for a tawdry little musical about the health food industry called *Athena,* featuring Steve Reeves.

"So it was over."

Except for the shouting. The Jane Powell teenage image created by the formidable MGM publicity department kept getting the headlines: when she married dashing ice skater Geary Steffan, then divorced him; when she romanced then-married car executive Pat Nerney and divorced him; and when she romanced, publicly, Gene Nelson, her co-star in *Three Sailors and a Girl.*

"All the fuss about my domestic troubles seems so ridiculous now, doesn't it?" Jane said. "But that was then . . . and it was a sign of the times to make scandals out of a basically simple private life. You know, Liz Taylor was one of my bridesmaids and I was one of hers, and everyone thought it was just dandy. The truth was, we didn't *know* anybody else."

Now you'd call that hype.

That hype and Jane's silvery voice, however, carried her from the death throes of MGM to the opening salvo of the television spectacular era. In the two years after she left MGM she made *Meet Me in St. Louis* and more than twenty other prime-time shows that almost always ranked in the top ten.

"She knew what she wanted to do," says Fitzgerald. "If you ask me, I think she always knew what she wanted . . . right from the time she had her first radio show at seven, back in Portland.

"When I took over her career, we set certain standards and kept to them. Jane had this second sense about what it would take to remain a star. I remember her telling me: 'I don't want to do any junk.' And she hasn't."

"We turned down hundreds of offers—a lot of them involving big money. Jane would play a symphony date for five thousand dollars and turn down a bad show that paid twenty thousand dollars."

It finally translated into hard cash. She now commands the nation's top roadshow salary of $25,000 a week—five times her top weekly paycheck at MGM.

Jane is wistful about only one thing: she would have preferred to go right on working in Hollywood. "I went out on the road because that's where the work was. But I find it lonely. Living out of a suitcase gets hard when you wake up to it day after day."

There are some—particularly master musical director Vincent Minnelli—who feel Jane Powell was slighted by MGM. "She was the girl with the most unfulfilled promise," Minnelli said. "Some of the films she made showed what she was able to do. But they didn't believe it."

Perhaps the final insult from MGM came in 1974, when the studio released the highly successful retrospective of the movie musical era, *That's Entertainment*. In the final print of both parts one and two, Jane Powell is the only major star of the era not given at least a single-number showcase. Her only singing bit included two choruses of "It's A Most Unusual Day." And during that, the camera remained mostly on Liz Taylor.

"MGM seemed to have a painfully short memory," she says.

But the fans didn't—five thousand letters poured into the Metro lot in complaint. And there's reason for this. Jane Powell has one of the strongest fan clubs still remaining from the era of the great movie musicals. Run by a well-organized legal clerk, Ron Parker of Oak Park, Illinois, the Jane Powell Fan Club has at least two thousand paying members, publishes a "Jane Powell Newspaper," and often attends Jane Powell appearances en masse. Parker's basement in suburban Oak Park is literally a Jane Powell museum, with six hundred fan magazines, three thousand stills, rare MGM color negatives that were never published, every version of her recordings, wigs, and props.

The Parker–Powell relationship started nearly eighteen years ago when he wrote her, saying she had helped him through some rough times with her "up" image. "There are places in England where they show Jane Powell movies every four or five weeks," Parker said. "And in Australia and New Zealand, fans react to the old films as if they were just now being released."

It's an ironic fact that the history of such musical stars has been kept solely by dedicated fans like Parker. The MGM library of stills was demolished in the late sixties and the Academy of Motion Picture Arts and Sciences files have been raided over the years.

Still, the images are fading in the darkness, much as the legends of MGM's silent stars have dimmed. Which of them will still be stars in the year 2000?

Bibliography

Primary Sources

The original transcripts from the Johnny Stompanato, Lana Turner, Cheryl Crane inquest—655 pages.

The police reports and Los Angeles County Coroner's records on the Paul Bern suicide. 50 pages.

The coroner's reports, district attorney rulings, and papers left by Mrs. Nellie Ince pertaining to the death of Thomas Ince on William Randolph Hearst's yacht.

Twenty original memos, letters, and correspondence in the Judy Garland–*Annie Get Your Gun* incidents.

Contract cancellation documents and cost overruns in the Mae Murray–Erich Von Stroheim conflict.

Newspaper and Magazine Sources

Five hundred clippings from the *Los Angeles Times* library detailing the Johnny Stompanato murder from its inception through the trial.

Three hundred news and magazine articles on twenty of the MGM Girls dealt with in this book, including some stories never printed but willed to the Academy of Motion Picture Arts and Sciences.

★   279

Constance McCormick's star biography albums (most of them more than a hundred pages long) obtained through special permission of the University of Southern California Film Collection.

Books

Agee, James. *Agee on Film:* McDowell Obolensky, 1958.

Ardmore, Jane. *The Self-Enchanted, Mae Murray: Image of an Era.* New York: McGraw-Hill, 1959.

Astor, Mary. *My Story.* Garden City, New York: Doubleday, 1959.

Austin, John. *Hollywood's Unsolved Mysteries.* New York: Ace Book Corp., 1970.

Bainbridge, John. *Garbo.* Garden City, N.Y. Doubleday, 1955.

Behlmer, Rudy, ed. *Memo from David O. Selznick.* New York: Viking Press, 1972.

Bernard, Matt. *Mario Lanza.* New York: McFadden Books, 1971.

Blesh, Rudi. *Keaton.* New York: Macmillan, 1966.

Brownlow, Kevin. *Hollywood: The Pioneers.* New York: Alfred A. Knopf, 1979.

Carpozi, George, Jr. *Clark Gable.* New York: Pyramid Books, 1961.

Charisse, Cyd, and Martin, Tony. *The Two of Us.* New York: Mason/-Charter, 1976.

Corless, Richard. *Greta Garbo.* New York: Pyramid Publications, 1974.

Cottrell, John, and Caskin, Frances. *Richard Burton, Very Close Up.* Englewood Cliffs, N.J.: Prentice-Hall.

Crawford, Christina, *Mommie Dearest.* New York: Berkley Press, 1978.

Crowther, Bosley. *Hollywood Rajah, the Life and Times of Louis B. Mayer.* New York: Henry Holt, 1960.

Davies, Marion. *The Times We Had.* New York: Bobbs-Merrill Co., 1975.

Dietz, Howard. *Dancing in the Dark.* New York: Quadrangle, 1974.

Eames, John Douglas. *The MGM Story.* New York: Crown, 1976.

Finch, Christopher. *Rainbow.* New York: Grosset and Dunlap, 1976.

Fordin, Hugh. *The World of Entertainment.* Garden City, N.Y.: Doubleday, 1975.

Fowler, Gene. *Good Night Sweet Prince*. New York: Viking Press, 1943.

Frank, Gerold. *Judy*. New York: Harper and Row, 1975.

———. *Zsa-Zsa*. Los Angeles: Crest Giant, 1965.

Goodrich, Diane, and Rich, Sharon. *Farewell to Dreams*. Los Angeles: Jeanette MacDonald, Nelson Eddy Friendship Club, 1979.

Guiles, Fred Lawrence. *Marion Davies*. New York: McGraw-Hill, 1972.

———. *Tyrone Power*. New York: Berkley Press, 1980.

Harris, Radie. *Radie's World*. New York: G. P. Putnam's Sons, 1978.

Higham, Charles, and Greenberg, Joel. *The Celluloid Muse*. New York: Signet Books, 1969.

Hopper, Hedda. *From Under My Hat*. Garden City, N.Y.: Doubleday, 1952.

———. *The Whole Truth and Nothing But*. Garden City, N.Y.: Doubleday, 1963.

Kohner, Fredric. *The Magician of Sunset Blvd*. Los Angeles: Morgan Press, 1977.

Lambert, Gavin. *On Cukor*. Los Angeles: Capricorn Books, 1973.

Likeness, George. *The Oscar People*. Mendota, Ill.: Wayside Press, 1965.

Mank, Chaw, and Steiger, Brad. *Garbo*. New York: Merit Books, 1965.

Marion, Frances. *Off With Their Heads*. New York: Macmillan, 1972.

Marx, Samuel. *Mayer and Thalberg, the Make Believe Saints*. New York: Random House, 1975.

Maxwell, Elsa. *R.S.V.P.—The Story of Elsa Maxwell*. Boston: Little, Brown, 1954.

Miller, Ann, and Browning, Norma Lee. *Miller's High Life*. Garden City, N.Y.: Doubleday, 1972.

Minnelli, Vincente, and Arce, Hector. *I Remember It Well*. Garden City, N.Y.: Doubleday, 1974.

Nuetzel, Charles. *Hollywood Mysteries*. Reseda, Calif.: Powell Fact, 1969.

Parish, James Robert. *The Jeannette MacDonald Story*. New York: Mason/Charter, 1976.

*———. *The MGM Stock Company*. New Rochelle, N.Y.; Arlington House, 1973. (This book deserves extra note since there is no other studio

reference work like it. It makes it possible to see all the ingredients that went into MGM's success.)

Platt, Frank C. *Great Stars of Hollywood's Golden Age.* New York: Signet Books, 1966.

Parsons, Louella O. *The Gay Illiterate.* Garden City, N.Y.: Doubleday, 1944.

Romero, Jerry. *Sinatra's Women.* New York: Manos Books, 1976.

Rooney, Mickey. *I.E. An Autobiography.* New York: Bantam, 1963.

Russell, Rosalind, and Chase, Chris. *Life Is a Banquet.* New York: Random House, 1977.

Schary, Dore. *Heyday.* Boston: Little, Brown, 1979.

Shaw, Arnold. *Sinatra.* New York: Pocket Books, 1968.

Steiger, Brad. *Judy Garland.* New York: Ace Books, 1969.

Swanberg, W. A. *Citizen Hearst.* New York: Scribners, 1969.

Taylor, Elizabeth. *Elizabeth Taylor—Her Own Story.* New York: Avon Books, 1965.

Thomas, Bob. *Thalberg, Life and Legend.* Garden City, N.Y.: Doubleday, 1969.

Waterbury, Ruth. *Elizabeth Taylor.* New York: Popular Library, 1964.

Wright, Jacqueline. *The Life and Loves of Lana Turner.* New York: Wisdom House, 1960.

Special Treatise

Summer, Rev. Robert L. *Hollywood Cesspool.* Memphis: Sword of the Lord Publishers, 1955. This vicious little book scared Hollywood to death in the fifties because of its accounts of sexual activity, boozing, and divorce. MGM was a special target.

Index

★ 283